CIVIL DISOBEDIENCE AND MORAL LAW

IN NINETEENTH-CENTURY AMERICAN PHILOSOPHY

CIVIL DISOBEDIENCE

AND MORAL LAW

IN NINETEENTH-CENTURY

AMERICAN PHILOSOPHY

BY EDWARD H. MADDEN

UNIVERSITY OF WASHINGTON PRESS

SEATTLE AND LONDON

Copyright © 1968 by the University of Washington Press

Washington Paperback edition, 1970

Library of Congress Catalog Card Number 68–11043

SBN 295–95070–6

Printed in the United States of America

FOR MARIAN, KERRY, AND DENNIS

CONTENTS

CIVIL DISOBEDIENCE AND MORAL LAW

IN NINETEENTH-CENTURY AMERICAN PHILOSOPHY

day, most notably the slavery controversy. Far from being prototypes of staid conservatism, as members of the orthodoxy are usually pictured, these men contributed fundamental insights to the nineteenth-century liberal view of reform. And far from being gray and uninteresting as persons, they are all fascinating in one way or another and, in the case of Mahan, even exciting. Mahan had a volatile character, and there was much infighting among the Oberlin "perfectionists" during his presidency.[1]

The background of Academic Orthodoxy is important for understanding all the members of this group and for putting the word "orthodoxy" into its proper perspective. Toward the end of the eighteenth century Christianity was at its lowest ebb in the history of the American settlements. Moral repugnance against Calvinistic theology had in large part made the American counterpart of the Enlightenment possible. But natural theology soon proved as unpalatable as Calvinism, and at the turn of the century a new brand of evangelical, pietistic, free-will Christianity began to flourish and attract converts by droves.[2] It was the great day of evangelists like Charles Grandison Finney, who went to Oberlin College as professor of theology and later became its second president. These were the days of Bible, tract, Sunday school, and missionary societies. Moreover, revivals and assorted "societies" were by no means confined to the Methodists and Baptists and other denominations that appealed to the common uneducated man, but extended to most Plan of Union Congregational-Presbyterian churches. Eventually the Plan of Union was dissolved, and the Congregational churches were almost always non-Calvinistic. Even where Calvinism remained in some of the Presbyterian churches it was often watered down. Princeton Theological Seminary remained the bastion of strict Calvinism, and within its precincts Charles Hodge, professor of Oriental and Biblical literature, charted counterattacks against Finney, Beecher, and the whole tribe of New Light ministers. He finally had to enlist the services of the Reverend Albert Baldwin Dod of the Princeton Mathematics Department.[3]

Many new colleges were founded in the first forty years of the century to meet the surging demand for ministers. These new colleges, like most of those already founded, produced young ministers of the non-Calvinistic, free-will mold that had become standard in almost all of the Protestant denominations. It was in these colleges that the "academic orthodoxy" held sway—a misnomer in one sense, we can now see, since most members of this group really represented the liberal thrust of Protestant Christianity (if one ignores, as we are doing for the moment, Unitarianism). The members of the "orthodoxy" generally exhibited the syndrome of minister-philosopher-college president.[4] In addition to Wayland, Mahan, Finney, and Fairchild, the following names, at the least, would have to be included in any representative roster: Jeremiah Day (Yale), Henry P. Tappan (New York University), Laurens Perseus Hickok (Union), Thomas C. Upham (Bowdoin), Noah Porter (Yale), Francis Bowen (Harvard), James McCosh (Princeton), Mark Hopkins (Williams), Andrew Preston Peabody (Harvard), Tayler Lewis (New York University), and Leicester A. Sawyer (Central College, Ohio).

Philosophically the members of the "orthodoxy" generally were followers of the Scottish realists, particularly of Thomas Reid and Dugald Stewart. The reasons for this allegiance are not difficult to discover. Scottish realism appealed to the no-nonsense common-sense orientation of American thought in general and because it was wholly consistent with (although, of course, not specifically required by) non-Calvinistic, free-will Protestant theology. The good minister-philosopher-presidents turned out an incredible number of texts on metaphysics, ethics, political philosophy, and psychology influenced strongly by Reid, Stewart, and various faculty psychologists.[5] (However, the Scottish influence, while strong, was not universal. By the 1840's and 1850's the influence of German philosophy was quite evident in academia, and even as early as the 1830's the work of Mahan was much influenced by Immanuel Kant and Victor Cousin.) However, although there were exceptions to this rule, metaphysics was not the forte of this group of philosophers; their ability lay rather in the direction of moral philosophy. These men wrote numerous books on the problem of determinism and free will, most of which were devoted to showing the errors of Jonathan Edwards and to developing some sort of faculty psychology that seemed to insure freedom of will and choice.[6] They also wrote voluminously about the nature of moral law, some supporting various versions of utilitarianism and others defending vigorously some intuitive system like that of Bishop Butler. The disagreement was quite spirited and shows that the views of the orthodoxy were not by any means monolithic. Some first-rate work was accomplished both in ethical theory and in what these philosophers called "practical ethics." [7] Practical ethics usually turned out to be discussions about the nature of government, reform, and the nature and extent of civil obedience.

In the following five chapters of this book the theories of moral law and the reform commitments of Wayland, Mahan, and Fairchild will be considered in detail. Wayland and Mahan, as we shall see, defend an intuitionist viewpoint, while Fairchild defends a "benevolence" version of utilitarianism. Their arguments and counterarguments are quite sophisticated and worth close attention. Their reform views will be considered carefully, as well as the practical ways in which they implemented these views in the tumultuous affairs of the young republic. Wayland, after agonizing struggle, embraced the principle of civil disobedience; Mahan propounded and vigorously followed such a view from the start; while Fairchild, though he advocated it, applied it scarcely at all. The biographical details of their adventures, both intellectual and actual, are themselves fascinating, exhibiting as they do much turmoil and self-growth.

II

The background required for understanding transcendentalism is also religious and theological in nature. Transcendentalism cannot be understood without knowledge of nineteenth-century American Unitarianism, and that, in turn, can be understood only as another revolt against Calvinism.[8] The Unitarians objected to Calvinism on moral as well as speculative grounds. Man in some cases is morally responsible; hence he must, in some sense, be free. On speculative grounds, of course, they rejected the trinitarian concept; Jesus Christ is not part of the Deity. However, it is important to keep nineteenth-century

American Unitarianism distinct from contemporary American Unitarianism. The former was still earnestly Christian. Its adherents believed in the "divinity" of Christ, even though rejecting the "deity" of Christ; they firmly believed in the Bible as divine revelation; and they stressed the importance of miracles as indications both of God's existence and of God's power. These Unitarian views captured the majority of Congregational pulpits in the Boston-Cambridge area, as well as the Harvard community where Andrews Norton, as Dexter Professor of Biblical Literature, was extremely influential.

While he had participated effectively in the Unitarian critique of Calvinism, Norton became, in turn, with his stress on the authenticity of the Scriptures and the importance of miracles, the center of a new Unitarian orthodoxy. It was this orthodoxy against which the transcendentalists, themselves mainly Unitarian ministers in the beginning, revolted.[9] George Ripley launched the attack by criticizing the crude sensory theory of knowledge that made miracles so important as religious evidence and by stressing that the true source of religious knowledge is intuitive. Ralph Waldo Emerson generalized this criticism to include all the "second-handedness" of Unitarianism, its exaggeration of the *person* of Jesus as well as its insistence on external revelation, all of which misses the point that Jesus beautifully represents that fragment of the divine which is to be found in every man to some extent.

Norton was shocked by both Ripley and Emerson and predicted that worse heresy was certain to follow. From his standpoint he was right, since Theodore Parker soon appeared proclaiming that the only valid part of Christianity is the claim that one should love God and man with all his heart—what Parker called the truth of Absolute Religion. Such a claim would constitute true religion, Parker stressed, even had Jesus never lived and proclaimed it. This view was too much even for the more liberal Unitarians like James Walker, Chandler Robbins, and A. P. Peabody, who had in some ways defended Ripley and Emerson. They suggested that it is somewhat pointless to call yourself a Christian when your views have no essential connection with the historical facts of the life and death of Jesus Christ.

In addition to Ripley, Emerson, and Parker, there were numerous other critics of the New Orthodoxy. Indeed a critical attitude toward Unitarianism is the criterion which some scholars use to define the transcendental movement. If such a criterion is used the following names might be included in the "movement": Ripley, Emerson, Parker, Frederic Henry Hedge, James Freeman Clarke, Orestes Brownson, W. H. Channing, and, perhaps, Convers Francis, William H. Furness, Charles Brooks, Christopher Cranch, John Dwight, Sylvester Judd, Samuel Osgood, Caleb Stetson, Jones Very, and Cyrus Bartol. However, if sharing some specific positive doctrine becomes the criterion of transcendentalism, then smaller and different lists will be produced depending upon which positive doctrine is chosen.

If to elements of German romanticism via Coleridge are added elements of Neoplatonism and Eastern religious thought, among others, then Parker, for example, is clearly eliminated. But if the elements are German romanticism, a distinction between Reason and Understanding, a basic optimism about human nature, and a general commitment to intuitionism as a theory of knowledge, then the list, which would seem to me a reasonable one, would include the names of Emerson, Ripley, Parker, and Thoreau, among others of the older group, and George William Curtis and James Bradley Thayer among the younger transcendentalists. It is this group in which we are primarily interested and which we will consider in detail in chapters 7, 8, and 9. We will carefully analyze the metaphysical and ethical thought of Emerson and, in a lesser degree, that of Ripley, Parker, Thoreau, and Thayer. All of these thinkers were implicitly antiutilitarian in their moral philosophy, but Thayer was explicitly and articulately so. While he showed much respect for J. S. Mill and avoided the trivial criticisms of utility made by people like Thomas Carlyle and others, he nevertheless offered trenchant criticisms of Mill's discussion "Of What Sort of Proof the Principle of Utility is Susceptible"—the famous chapter iv of *Utilitarianism*.

On the theory of conscience and moral reform from the

standpoint of transcendentalism, we will be particularly interested in the work of George William Curtis, the most level-
headed of the abolitionists, more effective in long-run results
even than Theodore Parker.[10] Some of Curtis' abolition activity,
as we shall see, contains high drama. Emerson and Curtis make
an interesting contrast, the former being, so to speak, the de-
tached "theoretician" of the movement and the latter being
primarily a "practical transcendentalist." Curtis admired Emerson immensely, and his thought was dominated in early years by
the Sage of Concord. But in the end he became his own man and
contributed what was authentically his to the transcendentalist
movement.

It is interesting to note several similarities between the academic orthodoxy and transcendentalists, since it seems unlikely
at first that they would have any similarities at all. The free-will,
trinitarian professors depended upon their own versions of the
inner-light theory in rejecting Calvinism just as the transcendentalists depended upon theirs in rejecting Unitarianism. The Old
School Calvinists "clung to the ideal of an organic Christian
society guided by the spiritual leadership of the clergy; the New
School stood for the individualistic view of society in which each
citizen made his own peace with God and went his own way in
life." [11] And the strength of the inner-light claims varied similarly within the two movements. Mahan and Finney were the
radical advocates of inner light among the free-will professors,
just as Parker and Thoreau were among the transcendentalists.
Just as the Oberlin "perfectionists" were a bit too much of a
good thing for other New School critics of Calvinism like Asahel
Nettleton and Lyman Beecher, so were Parker and Thoreau a
bit too much of a good thing for Emerson. Moreover, the
free-will trinitarians and the transcendentalists shared the same
sort of egalitarian, optimistic, and reformist attitude toward life.
They were likely to be political liberals. The Old School Calvinists were the reluctant democrats, pessimistic about the nature
of man and cool toward reform. They were usually among the
well-to-do and inclined toward political conservatism. In a qual-
ified way the same can be said about the Unitarians. In any case,

it was trinitarian Oberlin and the transcendentalists, not Calvinist Princeton or Unitarian Harvard, that spearheaded the abolitionist movement and many other reform measures. Calvinists and Unitarians always appeared to be extremely obedient. It was Mahan, Finney, the reluctant Wayland, Emerson, Parker, Thoreau, and Curtis who preached the doctrine of the Higher Law.

III

As we have seen, philosophy in nineteenth-century America was dominated by religious concerns and most frequently pursued in religious precincts. However, the appearance of Darwin's epochal work *On the Origin of Species* in 1859 effectively changed the philosophical atmosphere.[12] A scientific frame of mind came to dominate almost all of American philosophical thought after 1860. For a while, to be sure, the controversy was now between scientific claims in biology and certain aspects of revealed Christianity, but soon the notions of evolution, natural selection, and survival of the fittest entered into and eventually dominated the whole of American thought. The influence of Darwinism specifically in philosophy, however, was quite diverse. All the philosophers were influenced, but the influence produced radically different results. John Fiske and E. L. Youmans followed the lead of Herbert Spencer in England. All three generalized what for Darwin was a biological hypothesis about the origin of species into a speculative "Law of Evolution" which supposedly applied to all physical, biological, and social systems whatever. The nebular hypothesis in astronomy, for example, was favored by Spencer over competing hypotheses because it seemed to be another example of his Law of Evolution. Spencer became in a real sense America's philosopher. He was avidly read by farmers, mechanics, and industrialists alike. His notion of the survival of the fittest seemed to these people the perfect philosophical justification of laissez-faire politics and atomistic individualism.

The influence of Darwin on Chauncey Wright, mathematician and philosopher of Cambridge, Massachusetts, was also very great but produced completely opposite results, as we shall see in chapters 10 and 11.[13] From 1860 until his death in 1875, Wright was a constant critic of Spencer's evolutionary cosmology, insisting that the latter had a superficial understanding of both the content of the sciences and the logical form of explanation in any science. The so-called Law of Evolution, Wright felt, was simply an abstract summary of certain facts and so quite unlike a real scientific law or theory which contains theoretical terms and hence requires deductive elaboration and testing. Scientific laws are not simply summaries of observations but are leading principles or working hypotheses. They are finders, not merely summaries, of truth. Later pragmatic philosophers like Charles Sanders Peirce, William James, and John Dewey generalized Wright's analysis of scientific principles to include all empirical sentences whatever, including the ordinary ones which contain no theoretical terms, and hence parlayed Wright's view of scientific explanation into pragmatic "theories" of mind, meaning, and truth. There is little doubt that Wright would not have wholly approved of such extrapolations.

Wright also rejected Spencer's optimism and social philosophy, to say nothing of the extreme forms of social Darwinism. He saw no "progress" in America's manifest destiny and jingoism. He was even less sanguine than J. S. Mill about what positive results can be achieved by legislation and rational planning. His pessimism about the chances of progress ran very deep, as did that of his friend Charles Eliot Norton, but it never led to Burkean conservatism. There was much that could be done, he felt, to alleviate the miseries and evils that beset mankind. The same things do not make all people happy, but in general the same things make them miserable and full of despair.

Wright's character and thought keenly influenced the attitudes and ways of thinking of his friend Charles Eliot Norton, art critic and founder of the Fine Arts Department at Harvard University (chapters 12 and 13).[14] Like Wright, Norton became an agnostic, skeptic, and utilitarian, quite a strange destiny for the son of the Unitarian stalwart Andrews Norton. This comes as a surprise also to many modern writers who know Norton only as the Dante scholar, art critic, and friend of Carlyle, Emerson, Ruskin, Longfellow, and Lowell. It is true that Norton had some doubts about the value put upon art by the utilitarians, but his worry was assuaged by a letter from Chauncey Wright and by J. S. Mill's St. Andrew's Address, in which Mill stressed the importance of esthetic education for the creation of "whole men."

Norton, like Wright, was far from optimistic about the nature of man and the prospects of progress. There is some small progress, he believed, but at an unbelievably terrible cost in suffering. One comes to expect less of men, he consoled himself, when he learns to think of him as just above the apes instead of just below the angels. That is the real message of Darwinism. This pessimism led several modern scholars to classify Norton erroneously as a Burkean conservative.[15] It should be clear from the reference to apes and angels that Norton was no Burkean! As we shall see, Norton followed Wright in giving a negative cast to Millian liberalism and hence produced a new sort of ideology that is only now coming into its own on the contemporary scene. In his own day Norton was the severest and most outspoken critic of America's manifest destiny and jingoism. He spoke out against the Spanish-American War to his students and reaped a whirlwind of abuse from those who fed on the doctrine of fitness and survival. Some people concluded that the ferocity of the response indicated how badly America needed Old Norton in the latter part of the century.

IV

There are two important pervasive themes that give unity to this book in spite of the authentic uniqueness of each of the philosophers considered. One theme is the conflict between intuitionistic and utilitarian interpretations of what constitutes moral law, and the other is the conflict between different attitudes toward reform in general and abolitionism in particular. Wayland, Mahan, and the transcendentalists are critics of utilitarianism, while Fairchild, Wright, and Norton defend various forms of this position. Wayland, in spite of his intuitionism, even incorporates elements of William Paley's brand of utility into his own system; Mahan is ruthlessly consistent in rejecting all forms of "calculational ethics"; and Thayer, among the transcendentalists, is the most effective critic of J. S. Mill. Fairchild espouses a "benevolence" form of utilitarianism and is quite critical of the versions of utility offered by Paley, Taylor, and Metcalf. Wright and Norton defend the classical views of Bentham and J. S. Mill and usually follow the latter when he departs from Bentham. So it can be seen that the concepts of utility defended and criticized vary a great deal in content. The persistent way in which some form of this doctrine is always on the scene suggests that it, along with Calvinism, the free-will issue, and Darwinism, is one of the ties that binds together the otherwise divergent discussions in nineteenth-century American philosophy.

All of the philosophers considered in this book believed in the desirability of some sort of reform, and all were antislavery advocates. And yet within this framework of agreement there are numerous crucial and fundamental differences of opinion that quite cut across the "movement" lines. The crush of political events beginning with the Mexican War carried Wayland from an extremely conservative view of reform to an eventual defense of civil disobedience.[16] Mahan justified civil disobedience from the beginning at Oberlin, where the whole community systematically practiced it most successfully. Oberlin became one of the safest and most populated stops on the Underground Railroad. It had the enviable record of never losing a slave to the federal authorities, not even in the famous Wellington Rescue Case. Fairchild was a fascinating hybrid. He was part of Oberlin and so, of course, believed in the Higher Law, and he formulated a fine defense of civil disobedience in his *Moral Science*. And yet in his later years he was not above justifying American jingoism and pursuit of manifest destiny—a clear sign that even Oberlin was at last on its way to conformity.[17]

Parker held the most extreme views of reform and abolitionism; he considered "gradualism" of any sort immoral and never ruled out the need of force. He rode through the streets of Boston and Brookline with the escaped slave Ellen Craft beside him and a hatchet in his hand.[18]

Curtis was more moderate in his views of reform and abolition: his civil disobedience never bordered on insurrection, and he tried to achieve results through established political channels. When such channels were no longer plausible avenues of redress, he helped create new ones. He admired the tradition of the Liberal and Free-Soil parties and was an influential member of the Republican party from the beginning. Curtis was here following the Oberlin tradition of political dissent. He denounced his good friend Nathaniel Hawthorne's views on the slavery issue, and this famous rebuke, as we shall see, still makes fascinating reading and merits careful attention.[19]

Wright and Norton were impressed with the complexity of life and the frequent unpredictability of the future and so doubted that rational planning for the general happiness is always or even generally useful. Since the best-laid plans tend to have unexpected consequences, we should rely on instinct and moral rules in achieving utilitarian goals. Given these views, they were not enthusiastic reformers. Yet they thought that while reform was not likely to bring about Utopia, it could help much in relieving the evils and misery of life. Slavery and woman's suffrage, they thought, were prime examples of the sorts of evil that could be successfully combated.

Shy as a hermit crab, Wright did not contribute anything significant to either reform movement. Temperamentally incapable of civil disobedience or political action had he ever even seriously considered them, he offered a helping hand to many people, but he always operated in a personal way. Norton was much more effective on a larger scale, although, for health reasons, he was also unable to fill any dramatic role in reform movements. During the Civil War Norton played an important part in the formation of public opinion in the North as editor of the New England Loyal Publication Society. Broadsides were distributed twice each week to loyal newspaper editors who, by reprinting them, made Norton's efforts available to a million readers.[20] Both Norton and Wright admired their friend George

Curtis' reform activity both before and after the war, and Norton and Curtis became America's most outspoken critics of America's abandonment of principle after the war.

The different views of reform advocated by our authors, the ways in which they were implemented, and the different results attendant upon them, it should be clear, constitute parables for our own times. Examining the parables in detail, as we shall do, should prove instructive.

2

I

B O T H "academic orthodoxy" and "transcendentalism" are extremely loose classifications. Individuals collected together under these rubrics share a few general characteristics but disagree on a number of quite fundamental issues. This type of warning has been emphasized for transcendentalism[1] but has not been sufficiently stressed for academic orthodoxy. After 1825 the professors of philosophy in American colleges shared these general characteristics: they were all Christian apologists, mainly adherents of faculty psychology, and adherents of some form of Scottish realism. Furthermore these men often did not argue philosophy but simply "exhibited and illustrated truth." These generalizations are true, but they would be misleading unless certain qualifications were immediately added. The majority of professors were apologists for Arian views of Christianity, but there were still many defenders of Calvinism.[2] The Arians were certain to be adherents of faculty psychology, but not the Calvinists. Generally the Arian, faculty-psychology type was a straightforward adherent of some version of Scottish

16

realism but not always—certainly not by the 1850's, when German philosophy became influential in American thinking. But even as early as the 1820's and 1830's some of the orthodoxy like Asa Mahan already exhibited the influence of Kant and Cousin.[3] Some members of the orthodoxy were also more than willing to criticize other views and defend their own positions dialectically. Francis Wayland and Mahan were ardent critics of utilitarianism, while Mahan, Finney, Fairchild, Hodge, and Dod criticized each other's views quite substantially and sharply.[4]

Wayland was theologically Arian, a faculty psychologist, and a defender of common-sense realism. While he wrote on all these topics he contributed little of permanent value to these discussions. His real interest was in moral philosophy, and his most successful books are *Elements of Moral Science, Limitations of Human Responsibility,* and the strictly ethical parts of *University Sermons.*

The *Elements,* unlike *Limitations* and *University Sermons,* was essentially a textbook. It was clearly and carefully written and proved to be extremely successful. Two hundred thousand copies were sold during the sixty years it was marketed. Being a textbook, *Elements* was not, of course, as original as the other two books. Several writers in England labeled it a rehash of British intuitionism, though it was stoutly praised there also. The Reverend Dr. Hoby of Birmingham wrote that the condescension of some of his countrymen toward the *Elements* was completely unjustified.[5] And on his visit to Europe in 1841 Wayland was received at Oxford, Cambridge, Glasgow, and Edinburgh "with marked attention" and was "extended all courtesy" by philosophers of the rank, no less, of Sir William Hamilton.[6] The correct estimate of Wayland's *Moral Science,* I suspect, is this: it does depend much on the work of Bishop Butler—indeed Wayland says so in his Preface—but it also contains many original points and exhibits a New World look at the issues that interested the intuitionists, thereby providing, so to speak, a parallax of these problems. I shall consider *Elements* in the present chapter and *Limitations* and parts of *University Sermons* in the next.

II

The success of Wayland's *Elements* can be explained in part by its antiutilitarian tone and array of arguments against the view that duty consists in producing the greatest amount of happiness. Wayland launches into his attack early in the book and produces a convincing case against utility and yet eventually and quietly brings elements of Paley's view back into his own system. He was far from confused, however, as we shall see. He knew precisely what he was doing, since he brought Paley back on his own terms.

Wayland's arguments against utilitarianism differ somewhat from edition to edition of the *Elements,* although essentially he uses the same general type of attack.[7] Sometimes he criticizes utilitarians as if they were trying to define the concept of "right" as "conducive to greatest happiness," while most of the time he criticizes them for trying to derive judgments of specific duties from judgments of what is likely to lead to greatest happiness. (1) The two concepts of right and general happiness, Wayland wrote, are utterly different in meaning, as we can verify simply by examining our consciousness.[8] They are as distinct in consciousness as beauty and utility or any other dissimilar ideas. (2) The lack of connection between the concepts of right and general happiness is manifest in many other ways. Children and heathens, for example, are perfectly aware of the differences between right and wrong without being capable of comprehending the notion of the greatest amount of happiness.[9] (3) The Bible nowhere asserts that the production of the greatest amount of happiness is necessary to the existence of moral obligation.[10] The view there is quite different. God's will is mandatory and independent of the consideration of consequences or any deliberations whatever. (4) We are usually ignorant of what will happen in the future; hence any moral judgment based on the consideration of likely future consequences is doomed to fail. A utilitarian, of course, has an easy answer. In spite of such difficulties we manage quite well in ordinary practical decisions. Why not also in ethics? But Wayland detects a more fundamental difficulty. Every act has infinite consequences. Where, short of infinity, can the utilitarian draw the line and make his judgment? [11] (5) Were we to determine the moral character of an act by calculating the amount of happiness it would produce, we would destroy all moral distinctions. Crimes, for example, sometimes have the happiest result—indeed, given this moral view, "we must award to the treachery of Judas the praise of the greatest virtue." [12] This criticism, again, is easily countered by the utilitarian. He simply distinguishes between the rightness of an act and the moral worth of the agent. A saint by accident can produce terrible consequences, and a knave by accident can produce good ones. The saint is morally worthy, nevertheless, even though he committed a wrong act, because he generally does the right thing. The knave is morally unworthy even though he did the right thing, because he generally does wrong. If the utilitarian were willing to ignore the theological presuppositions of Wayland's example, he could answer it simply. Judas was morally unworthy even though he did the right thing. Wayland has no adequate reply to this point.

Wayland attacks the utilitarian position because, he thinks, it is wholly incompatible with the data of moral experiences. [13] If we attend to our moral judgments we can see that they are unique and unanalyzable. Moral judgments are direct, not discursive. We do not give reasons why keeping a promise is right; we simply "see" that it is so. Moreover, the notion of right cannot be defined by any other notions. It is just as basic and indefinable as words that refer to natural properties like "red," "sour," and "to the right of." You cannot explain to a person who has been blind from birth what "red" means by giving a definition of it. He has to experience something in order to know to what the word refers. Similarly, you cannot explain to someone what "right" means by giving a definition of it; you have to have a moral experience, via a moral sense, to know to what the word refers.

Wayland's most cogent criticism of utilitarianism involves a further excursion into his own intuitionistic viewpoint. [14] The nature of duty, he thought, depends upon the special relationships that exist between man and man and between man and God. Consider the virtue of gratitude. One is obliged to return a favor to a specific person because that person has helped him. Gratitude depends upon this special relation. You repay kindness to just that person because of that special relationship. On the utilitarian view which requires the indiscriminate production of general happiness, however, it seems impossible to do justice to the notion of gratitude. It is man's duty to produce the greatest amount of good for everyone concerned, not simply or primarily for those who have a special relation to the agent. Or take the virtue of filial obedience. If a child obeys his parents because this will lead to over-all happiness, he may have acted in some sense morally but he has not exhibited filial obedience. Filial obedience depends upon acting obediently because of the special child-parent relationship and for no other reason. Again, it is difficult to see how the utilitarian can explain the existence of this virtue as distinct from all other virtues.

Wayland's attack on utility comes early in all editions of the *Elements*. Many chapters intervene between it and his discussion of natural religion. One assumes that he has finished entirely with the principle of utility, but such is not the case. In the chapter on natural religion, while he never refers explicitly to utilitarian views, it becomes quite clear that he is trying to introduce some teleological element into his own system.[15]

At the beginning of his chapter on natural religion Wayland assumes that a universal First Cause exists and that the intentions of the Creator are benevolent. The Creator clearly intends for human beings to do those things which have pleasant consequences and avoid the things which have unpleasant ones, both for ourselves and for others. Thus we know it is God's will for men to avoid drunkenness since the unhappy consequences of it are open to the most casual inspection. The same is true for revenge, the unhappy consequence of which was never more clearly seen than in the extinction of those Indian tribes that practiced it as a duty. And so on for case after case. It becomes clear, of course, that Wayland is embracing some sort of teleological, even utilitarian, criterion within a theological context. He is apparently trying to enfold this criterion within his own system so that it is subordinate to his overarching deontological commitments. He is perfectly clear and explicit about this maneuver, for he writes:

We ask in order to determine what is our duty, What would be the result if this or that action were universally practiced among men? Or, how would it affect the happiness of individuals and of the whole? By the answer to these questions, we ascertain what is the will of God in respect to that action or that course of action. When once the will of God is ascertained, conscience, as we have shown, teaches us that we are under the highest obligation to obey it. Thus from the consideration of the greatest amount of happiness, we arrive at the knowledge of our duty, not directly, but indirectly. The feeling of moral obligation does not arise from the *simple fact that such a course of conduct will or will not produce the greatest amount of happiness;* but from the fact that *this tendency shows us what is the will of our Creator;* and we are, by the principles of our nature, under the highest possible obligation to obey that will [italics in original].[16]

The first point to note is that Wayland's appeal to what would happen if this or that action were "universally practiced" is precisely the view presented by Paley in Book II of his *Moral and Political Philosophy.* Paley explicates this view by saying that the reason for prohibiting and punishing an action is that it would produce dire consequences if everyone did it. Wayland's use of Paley, even indirectly, is surprising when one considers how carefully he dissociated himself from Paley in the Preface to the *Elements.* Other intuitionists in America, particularly Asa Mahan, were far more consistent than Wayland in rejecting any concession to Paley's view of utility, or any other. According to Mahan, "if an action be not evil in itself, its indefinite multiplication would not be an evil." [17] And, if it is a good of indefinite value, "its indefinite multiplication cannot give us a definite result; since it is the multiplication of an unknown quantity." [18]

The second point to note is that Wayland, in essence, ascribes a utilitarian view to God even though he avoids ascribing it to man. The reason that God wills an act is because of its good consequences, while the reason that man should will the same act is because God wills it. From Mahan's point of view, which was also intuitionistic, Wayland commits two errors simultaneously. For Mahan there can be no double standard in morality. Since we are reasonable beings made in God's image, we must suppose our reason in moral judgments to be identical with God's.[19] Moreover, we would not be acting morally if we did an act simply because God did it; we must do it for the same reason. Finally, according to Mahan, the notion that we should do an act simply because God does it runs into the following difficulty. The willing of x by God does not establish that x ought to be willed. If God's will determined what was right, then we could never sensibly say that God's will was right in some independent sense of "right." But that God is good in some independent sense of "good," and that he always acts rightly in some independent sense of "right," Mahan believed, is the very cornerstone of Christianity.[20]

III

There are a number of systematic issues of interest in the *Elements,* but I shall, at present, limit myself to a consideration of three of them: (1) the relativistic attack on conscience theory; (2) the claim that one is responsible for acting with perfect virtue; and (3) the nature of the relationship between the concepts of right and wrong, on the one hand, and ought and ought not, on the other.

1. Wayland presents the relativistic attack on conscience theory in the following way.[21] Since the dictates of conscience in different contexts contradict each other, conscience is not a trustworthy guide to duty. What some nations consider right, like dueling, infanticide, parricide, other nations consider wrong—and the same can be said about *every* moral judgment. Wayland replies by first agreeing that there is moral diversity. There is no doubt, for example, that people in different cultures treat their parents quite differently. In most countries children help their parents live as long as possible, but in certain Indian tribes they execute them when they reach the age of forty-five. But behind this surface relativism, Wayland insists, there is a nonrelative, benevolent, and moral intention. The Indian youth in his own way is taking the most benevolent care of his parents. He is trying to promote their welfare because they all share the

religious belief that a person goes through all eternity in the physical and mental state he had at the moment of death; hence it is a child's moral duty not to permit his parents to become old and senile. Wayland makes this point in the following general way:

. . . we have said that we discover the moral quality of actions in the *intention. Now it is not the fact* that this difference exists, as stated in the objection, if the *intention* of actions be considered. Where was it not considered right to *intend* the happiness of parents? Where was it not considered wrong to *intend* their misery? Where was it ever considered right to intend to requite kindness by injury? and where was it ever considered wrong to intend to requite kindness with still greater kindness? In regard to the *manner* in which these intentions *may be fulfilled* there may be a difference; but as to the moral quality of these *intentions themselves,* as well as many others, there is a very universal agreement among men.[22]

Moreover, Wayland continues, the criticism of relativism is really self-destructive because it admits that everywhere men make moral distinctions but affirms that in different cultures they refer the moral quality to different actions.

And still more, it will be seen on examination that in these very cases in which wrong actions are practised [i.e., parricide, etc.], they are justified on the ground . . . of some view of the relations between the parties which, if true, would render them innocent.[23]

Finally, Wayland wrote, savages never violate every moral commitment of a civilized society; hence such relativity proves not the absence of conscience but the presence of a defective or imperfect one.

Wayland's arguments, I submit, are subtle and interesting ones, but their importance cannot be appreciated unless it is clear that they have significance far beyond the context of criticism in which Wayland used them. Wayland was explicitly meeting a criticism of conscience theory—namely, that the relativity of moral judgments shows that there are no "universal deliverances of conscience." But some sociologists long after Wayland wrote were to use the same sorts of arguments not simply to prove the conscience theory inadequate but to prove that objective, universal moral judgments, however conceived or justified, are groundless. Indeed, sociological relativism around the end of the nineteenth century had become, along with the determinism issue, the major root of ethical skepticism.

Wayland's answers to the relativism of the dictates of conscience are applicable in every case to the more serious problem of sociological-ethical relativism; and they form, in my opinion, at least a part of the correct answer to this sort of ethical skepticism. However, to avoid misunderstanding, I qualify this claim by saying that they form part of a correct answer if they are dissociated from certain extraneous and accidental features. Wayland's main point about the difference between intentions and the manner in which they are fulfilled is independent of the framework of his own conscience theory. The utilitarian, for example, could adopt Wayland's point quite readily. The intention of the Indian who slays his parents is morally good and hence qualifies him as a morally praiseworthy agent, although he in fact out of ignorance produces a wrong act in terms of consequences.

2. Wayland defends the view that one is responsible for acting with perfect virtue. He does it so plausibly that one almost neglects the obvious deficiency of the claim. According to Wayland, if a man, as the result of his own previous decisions, debases his conscience, he is still responsible at any subsequent time for doing what his conscience would have required if unimpaired.

That this is the fact is, I think, evident from obvious considerations: It is well known that the repetition of wickedness produces great stupidity of conscience, or, as it is frequently termed, hardness of heart. But no one ever considers this stupidity as in any manner an excuse. It is, on the contrary, always held to be an aggravation of crime. Thus we term a man who has become so accustomed to crime that he will commit murder without feeling and without regret, a *remorseless* murderer, a *cold-blooded* assassin; and everyone knows by these epithets we mean to designate a special and additional element of guiltiness. This I take to be the universal sentiment of man.[24]

If man is not responsible for perfect virtue, Wayland says, but is only responsible in terms of his "present light," the following paradox occurs. Assume that one person has scrupulously done right and thereby increased his capacity for virtue while another man has done wrong willingly and thereby decreased his capacity for virtue. When both subsequently act according to the dictates of their respective consciences they act quite differently but, on the view of "present light," would be equally innocent. To avoid this paradox Wayland insists that man is responsible for acting with perfect virtue.[25]

Wayland's conclusion, however, clearly leads to equally paradoxical results. It requires that a person be responsible at any given time for doing a certain act even though, in fact, for whatever cause, he is incapable of doing it. Wayland himself in other contexts, particularly when he was attacking Calvinism, was quick to insist "that ought implies can." The interesting point, then, is to discover why in this context he lost sight of this notion. And the explanation is not long in appearing. The point of Wayland's claim that the demand for perfect virtue is legitimate, it turns out, is to show the necesssity of the new dispensation of love in the New Testament.[26] Jesus forgives men their sins even though they are guilty, undeserving, and condemned as far as the moral law is concerned. Unfortunately for Wayland this way out is not open to him. He cannot insist that "ought implies can" when he attacks Calvinism and then insist that the demand for perfect virtue is legitimate in order to provide moral evidence for the need of a new revelation. Wayland, in fact, is unaware that his own argument in ethics is dangerously isomorphic with the classical Calvinistic view in theology.

3. For Wayland the relationship between the concepts of right and ought is exceedingly intimate. He suggests that statements using either concept reciprocally imply each other.[27] Conscience not only discloses what is right but also imparts a corresponding feeling of obligation. When we intuit that an act is right we also have the coincident feeling that it is our duty to do it. And when we know that an act is our duty we know also, of necessity, that it is right. The implication of this view, explicitly held by some contemporary moral philosophers, is this: it is our duty to do only what is right, and whatever is right is our duty to do.

I think that Wayland and the modern theorists who hold this

view are wrong. I would agree that one ought always to do what is right, but it is not equally clear to me that whatever is right ought to be done. Consider the following moral view: "A voluntary action is right, whenever and only when no other action possible to the agent under the circumstances would have caused more good; in all other cases it is wrong." [28] Notice that such a view does *not* say that an act is right only if it produces *more* good than any possible alternative act. On this latter view it would follow that two acts could never produce equal goods and hence be equally right. The first view is much closer to ordinary thought: we frequently suggest in everyday moral discourse that, while a man acted rightly in one way, yet he would have been acting equally rightly if he had acted in some other way. On this first view, then, it is claimed that two alternative acts may produce equal amounts of good and hence be equally right. From such a view it follows that, while one ought always to do what is right, this does not necessarily mean that whatever is right one is obliged to do. If two acts are equally right I am not obliged to do either one of them specifically. In short, according to this view the implication goes from "ought" to "right" but not necessarily from "right" to "ought."

One might argue that, since the moral view I have sketched was not, in fact, Wayland's, it does not follow that the breakdown of the "right"-"ought" implication in this system shows that it breaks down in Wayland's system. But this is not a telling defense. If we can successfully construct *any* system in which the implication breaks down, then it follows that one cannot simply assume that the relationship holds in any system—it must be proved to hold within the system in which it allegedly does. But Wayland offered no such proof: he simply assumed it as self-evident that if an act is right then one ought to do it. And this assumption does seem plausible until one sees that in some systems it breaks down.

IV

Although Wayland was essentially an intuitionist and moral sense advocate, he believed that natural and revealed religion added moral wisdom unavailable elsewhere. We have seen previously the way he thought natural religion added to our stock of moral wisdom—namely, by contemplating consequences. The Bible, he felt, also supplements conscience theory in several ways.[29] It supplements our moral knowledge by telling us to love our enemies, to love God above all else, and to worship God in certain morally acceptable ways. Moreover, the Scriptures provide additional and stronger motives for doing our duty; whatever may be the source of our knowledge of duty, God assures us that the wicked shall ultimately be punished and the virtuous shall be rewarded with eternal happiness.

Unfortunately Wayland loses far more than he gains by this last maneuver. No doubt the fear of eternal damnation for doing wrong and the hope of eternal happiness for doing right are powerful motives for eschewing the former and striving to do the latter; but insofar as one is motivated to do his duty by fear of punishment if he does not do it and a hope of reward if he does do it, then clearly he is not yet acting morally and does not deserve the benefit for which he strives.

While Wayland was wholly convinced that the New Testament contains priceless moral wisdom, he was a bit uneasy about some of the Old Testament.[30] He was familiar with the eighteenth-century deists' critique of the Old Testament as a source of moral wisdom. Thomas Paine had characterized this part of the Bible as a succession of nasty and vulgar stories unfit for the eyes of a child!

> Whenever we read the obscene stories, the voluptuous debaucheries, the cruel and torturous executions, the unrelenting vindictiveness, with which more than half the Bible is filled, it would be more consistent that we called it the word of a demon than the word of God. It is a history of wickedness that has served to corrupt and brutalize mankind; and, for my part, I sincerely detest it, as I detest everything that is cruel.[31]

Criticisms were not always so blunt as Paine's, but they were frequently made, and Wayland felt called upon to state a principle of selection that could winnow from all that is written in the Bible just those parts of it that constitute moral law. Nothing in the Bible is morally binding, Wayland says, unless the performance of an act is signified as the will of God and it is clear that we are among the number commanded to do the act. This principle excludes as morally binding anything in the Scriptures that is merely history, and also excludes commands with purely local importance or significance:

Such was the command to Abraham to offer up his son; to Moses to stand before Pharaoh; to Samuel to anoint Saul and David; and a thousand others. Here, evidently, the Divine direction was exclusively intended for the individual to whom it was given. No one can pretend that he is commanded to offer up his son because Abraham was so commanded.[32]

But Wayland had missed Paine's central point. To Paine, and to other critics of historical Christianity, it seems weirdly immoral for God to command *anyone* to offer up his son. One hardly eases the immorality of the command by pointing out that the command was not universal. Yet Wayland's principle is not without some merit. If one already believes in a Christian God and is unwilling to believe that anything He commands can be immoral, he still needs a criterion for sifting out what in the Bible is obligatory and what is not. Wayland provides in greater detail than I have indicated just such a criterion.[33]

Wayland takes a parting shot at the Deistic critics of Christianity. The Deists argued against revealed Christianity because it depends upon a written language rather than upon the universal language of reason and nature.[34] The Deists proved that God exists by the design in the universe, not by depending upon what some scribes have recorded. Think of the chance of errors in translation, communication, interpretation, and so on, in the recorded revelations of historical religions. Think of the way the supposed divine word was edited—by a vote of the Church fathers. No, the Deists argued, these features of Holy Writ belie a divine origin.

Wayland, however, thought he knew why there had to be a written revelation.[35] In the first place, facts can be made known only through language. The existence of immortality, the doctrine of the resurrection, and the notion of a remedial dispensation are all facts, and they could be made known to man in no other way than by language. One could inspect the order of the natural world to his heart's content and find no hint of these truths. Moreover, not everyone is clever enough to read the messages of God written in the natural world; most people need to be told about God in a straightforward fashion. According to Wayland,

. . . God has seen fit to *reveal* His will to us by language. Here the truth is spread before us without the necessity of induction from a long and previous train of reasoning. This knowledge of the will of God, thus obtained, renders man responsible for the additional light thus communicated.[36]

To an impartial judge, Wayland's remarks probably do not seem to constitute a crashing refutation of the Deist's criticisms. They do not even touch the Deist's point about errors, origins, and so on. But they do constitute nevertheless an interesting countercritique of the Deist's claim that the word of God can be wholly read in the works of nature and reason. It is a pity that Wayland did not develop these views in more detail, although to him, no doubt, it was not a pity. Anyone who needed a defense of Christianity spelled out in detail, he felt, was probably hopelessly lost anyway.[37]

3

THE ISSUE OF CIVIL DISOBEDIENCE

FRANCIS WAYLAND opposed slavery and abolitionism alike. He believed slavery to be a monstrous moral wrong and unequivocally condemned it in his *Elements of Moral Science*.[1] Such a condemnation in 1835 was hardly fashionable; the ministers and merchants of the North seemed to have entered a conspiracy of silence on the subject. On the other hand, Wayland was extremely cautious and conservative in his views about the extent of man's responsibility in getting rid of this evil. This conservative strand of his early thought occurred most strikingly in his *Limitations of Human Responsibility*,[2] a book that cost him many friends in his own country and in England.

Wayland's conversion to a more militant view of man's responsibility for evil began in the early 1840's. It appeared dimly in his contribution to *Domestic Slavery Considered as a Scriptural Institution* but showed up more clearly in parts of his *University Sermons* and in the final revision of his *Moral Science*. His later correspondence and public actions reflected even more dramatically his change of heart. Wayland's "conversion" is historically interesting for he was representative of much Northern moderate antislavery thought. His shift is philosophically important, too, for the issues of individual responsibility, reform, and the limits of civil obedience are always with us, and each generation must examine for itself all of the possible positions.

I

In *Elements* Wayland argued that economics, morality, and religion all join together in repudiating slavery.[3] Economics denounces it because it is wasteful, while morality rejects it because it leads to the degradation of both master and slave. The Scriptures reject slavery as incompatible with the principles of behavior laid down by God, most notably the Golden Rule and the injunction to "love thy neighbor as thyself." To be sure, the Gospel never explicitly forbids slavery, but it is enough, Wayland said, that God prescribes moral principles that are incompatible with the practice of slavery. In this way He rules out slavery just as effectively as if He had forbidden it explicitly. Perhaps God chose this indirect way of condemning slavery because a direct indictment of it might have caused civil unrest.

If God condemns slavery, what then, Wayland asked, are the duties of masters and slaves in nineteenth-century America? The slave masters in the South say that immediate emancipation would be disastrous for the slaves themselves—they are not ready for self-government. That may or may not be true, Wayland said—he is not competent to judge—but, supposing it is, then it is the duty of the master to work strenuously to remove the impediments to emancipation and to continue to hold the slave in temporary bondage as an obligation to him, not a right over him. The duty of a slave is correlative: to obey and to submit, even to a cruel master, as a duty to God, not as an obligation to the master.

Convinced that he had shown slavery to be morally wrong, Wayland proceeded to this further question: how far does a citizen's duty extend in trying to get rid of this evil? He answered that question in ultraconservative fashion in his *Limi-*

tations of Human Responsibility.[4] Our duties, he said, concern us either as citizens of the United States or simply as human beings under God.

1. As citizens of the United States we have no power whatever to try to abolish slavery in the Southern States. Whatever legal power we have is conferred upon us by the Constitution. Since the power of abolition is not conferred upon us by the Constitution, it does not exist. Moreover, the Constitution expressly says that those powers not named are not granted. Since the power to abolish slavery is not named, it is, by this article, expressly withheld. Any power that has not been submitted to the nation at large remains in the power of the individual states, "and the citizens of the United States have no more to do with it, than they have with the affairs of Iceland." [5]

Since as citizens of the United States we have no power over slavery we, of course, have no responsibility for it. "The guilt, if guilt exists, will not rest upon us as citizens of the United States. . . . Whether slavery be bad or good, we wash our hands of it, inasmuch as it is a matter which the providence of God has never placed within our jurisdiction." [6]

2. As human beings under God we have our limited duty. We must make known the truth as we see it—declaring to all who will hear that slavery is morally and religiously wrong, thereby hoping to change the hearts of those who think otherwise. We have no right, however, to force our views upon those who will not listen. "They have as good a right to their ears, as we have to our tongues." [7] If they will not listen, we have no further responsibility. But, Wayland said again and again, people *will* listen to moral arguments. Right carries a natural force to conquer wrong. Moral exhortation is God's way and will carry the day. Southerners, in fact, were willing to listen before the abolitionists began their shrill name-calling and illegal acts. The abolitionists have made no headway whatever. They have raised a violent agitation without offering any definite means of legally accomplishing their object. They have embittered the feelings of the South. They have riveted the bonds of the slaves in the very states where they had been about to fall off.

Wayland characterized the abolitionist as a moral fanatic:

one who believes that it is his duty not simply to do what is within his power to eliminate slavery—that is, moral exhortation—but actually to remove the evil. It is this belief that makes him heedless of the disastrous consequences of his actions for law and order. In general, Wayland said, it is the belief that they are morally responsible for the actual removal of an evil which leads people to accept the notion that the end justifies any means.[8] They regard the removal of some evil as such an important end that they come to regard any means, no matter how evil it may be, as a legitimate course of action. The Inquisition is a perfect example of this fanaticism in the past, just as abolitionism is a perfect example of it in the present. Moreover, the action perpetrated by such fanatics is peculiarly fierce and effective, he said, because, being a moral disease, abolitionism has the whole force of diseased conscience behind it.

In addition, Wayland felt that abolition societies, like all reform groups, really worked against their own causes. The essence of a reform society is that the members are pledged to some truth, to the achievement of some goal. But outsiders always believe that people who take pledges are prejudiced and hence listen less to them than if they were not members of such a society. Moreover, Wayland felt that such groups tend to become entities in themselves, with the result that societies and associations "will perpetrate acts, at which every member of the association would individually revolt." [9]

Finally, Wayland was convinced that abolition reform movements had put the cart before the horse: you cannot change society without fundamentally changing the nature of the men in it. Political agitation and social manipulation can attain nothing significant; the only effective reform is regeneration of the individual heart and soul.[10] Thus morally exhorting the slaveowner, not threatening him, is our duty. Right and justice have a natural power over wrong and evil. The regeneration would occur if only reckless abolitionists kept still.

II

We can all agree that Wayland's views were hardly inspirational. His views, no doubt, would have been cold comfort to a sorrowing Negro Rachel who had pondered for forty years the fate of a child taken from her bosom, or small consolation to Anthony Burns as he was marched back to slavery by the Massachusetts militia. Theodore Parker and George William Curtis thundered back counterarguments against the kind of view expounded by Wayland and repeated by countless other "moderate" and "sensible" men.[11] The counterarguments came better from men like them, as far as Wayland was concerned, because these men, unlike William Lloyd Garrison and Wendell Phillips, cherished the Constitution and the Union as much as he.

According to Parker and Curtis, there is something too neat and comfortable about the view that since we can do nothing legally to abolish slavery we need only speak against it, provided some will listen, in order to meet our responsibilities in this case. This argument is terribly weak. It would be like arguing in this fashion: Mr. White murdered Mr. Black, but I have no responsibility for this death because I morally exhorted Mr. White not to draw his gun and begged him not to shoot. Moreover, they thought, the man who advances Wayland's argument is a practical atheist—that is, one who believes in the existence of God but is unwilling to follow his commands. The law of God says that men are morally equal; certain aspects of civil law in the United States either deny this or prevent its recognition. At this point it is the duty of an honest man to follow God's law, the Higher Law, and defy certain aspects of the civil law.[12] Not to do so is to be a practical atheist.

One need not fear, Parker and Curtis continued, that civil disobedience will lead to anarchy or will undermine the benefits of civilized society and stable government. They were willing, for the sake of stability, to countenance many questionable laws, but they insisted that some laws are so stridently immoral that they must be openly disavowed and disobeyed. Moreover, the person who is willing to break a law in extreme cases is the very person who can be counted upon to be the strongest upholder of law in general and unlikely to break it for selfish reasons. Finally, they launched this counterattack: you cannot trust any person who would obey any law whatever just because it is a law. Such men would never have thrown the tea into Boston harbor; and this country, whose Constitution some people love so falsely, would never have seen the light of day.[13]

Curtis, in particular, saw the errors in Wayland's line of argument against the abolitionists. The abolitionist is not a moral fanatic who would justify the use of immoral means to abolish slavery. To be sure, some particular abolitionist may have a "diseased" conscience and be like the worst elements of the Inquisition. But the problem of the diseased conscience is a general one, and anyone, on either side of any issue, may have one. The only way to decide the health or sickness of any conscience is to put the goals and methods in the context of motives and previous performance. When this is done the majority of the abolitionists appear in much better light than most of their opponents.[14]

On the other hand, Curtis always emphasized that the abolitionist is morally sincere and will not shrink from attempts to abolish slavery because the results would be extremely painful for all concerned.[15] Curtis grew weary of hearing the argument that abolitionists were troublemakers, likely to cause disastrous consequences, but he never failed to reply patiently with one of his Mr. White and Mr. Black parables. Mr. White points a pistol at Mr. Black, but a hand-wringing group of spectators tells the abolitionist, "Don't interfere or he might shoot all of us!" The slave states depended precisely on this moral cowardice of the "moderate" people both North and South. Most often the best way to avoid real trouble in the last place is to take a strong moral stand in the first place. When will people realize that it is compromise on moral principle in the first place that produces catastrophic consequences in the end? But say that the worst comes and we must fight for freedom. Then, no doubt, we are all, one way or another, responsible for the terrible havoc. But the abolitionist, at least, has this ground for belief in moral progress: the agony would be more justly distributed than before.[16] At least some people would no longer batten on their brothers' blood.

Curtis denied that abolitionist societies really work against the success of their own cause. Wayland may have been right in saying that associations are never the best means of gaining converts. But the crucial point he missed with amazing innocence—namely, that associations are the best way to exert the power of the already converted. A person like Wayland misses the point that any joint action has far greater political efficacy than individual effort. Curtis never tired of making this point in his many antislavery lectures. "In human society, while the individual conscience is the steam or motive power, political methods are the engine and the wheels by which progress is effected and secured." [17]

Finally, it is unlikely, Curtis thought, that abolitionists "had rivetted the bonds of slavery when they were about to fall off." Arguments like Wayland's tend to credit moral suasion with too much causal power. It was not the abolitionist, in fact, that fastened the loosening ties of slavery but rather the increased price of cotton. And the abolitionists had much less influence in bringing about an antislavery view in the North than the actions of the South itself.[18] The acts of the slave party in Congress and in Kansas, not the words of Wendell Phillips, carried the day for the abolitionists in the North. As Curtis saw it, that was the pity and the tragedy. Would moral considerations ever make any difference?

III

Wayland began to shift his views sometime in the early 1840's, a shift first noticed by one of Wayland's Boston friends, Charles Sumner, later the ardent antislavery senator from Massachusetts.[19] Wayland's conversion to a more militant view about man's responsibility for removing evil is a parable for our times, because it came about not by the light of reason or the prick of conscience but by the crush of events. He never quite arrived at views like those of Parker and Curtis, but he came close, in the end, to views like Curtis'. But he was driven to them; he did not go to meet them. He represented perfectly what Curtis had in mind as the pity and the tragedy of the good people in both the North and the South.

From the first, Wayland considered the annexation of Texas a mad scheme. He rejected the notion of America's manifest destiny and saw in this scheme, worst of all, a means of increasing and extending the power of slavery. The Mexican War itself he regarded simply as national wickedness. According to his sons, "he never ceased, in public and in private, to urge the cessation of a wicked invasion, and to pray for those whom we were, by cruel hands, reducing to widowhood and orphanage."[20]

Wayland's disgust with the Mexican War led him, in 1847, to preach three sermons on "The Duty of Obedience to the Civil Magistrate," later published in *University Sermons*. In these three sermons he explicitly confirmed the shift in his views already noticed by Sumner years before. The tone is remarkably more liberal than that of *Limitations*. Of course, he devoted most of the first sermon to extolling the virtues of society and the values of stable government, and to censuring those who try to escape their responsibilities as citizens. Yet it is not difficult to find in the second sermon passages that sound precisely like those of Parker, Curtis, Emerson, and Thoreau. There could hardly be a better statement of the higher law doctrine and the notion of passive resistance than this:

The magistrate may not only do wrong himself, but he may command me to do wrong. How shall I regard this command? I will regard it as I do any other command to do wrong,—I will not obey it. I will look the magistracy calmly and respectfully in the face, and declare to it that in this matter I owe it no allegiance. I will have nothing to do with its wrong-doing. I will separate myself, as far as possible, from the act and its consequences, whether they be prosperous or adverse. It is wickedness; it has the curse of God inwrought into it, and I will have nothing to do with it. . . . The magistracy may punish me; I cannot help that. I will not resist, but I will not do wrong, nor will I be a party to wrong, let the magistracy or aught else command me.[21]

It turns out that Wayland loved the Declaration of Independence as much as the Constitution. The "natural law" of the Declaration, he thought, is after all as important as civil law, if not more so:

I have said that the great end for which civil society is established, and the magistracy appointed, is, to secure to man the enjoyment of those rights with which he was endowed by his Creator. If Society or the magistracy interfere with these rights, it is tyranny. If its acts transcend the limits of the authority committed to it, it is guilty of usurpation. In neither of these cases does the gospel of Jesus Christ command us to render to it obedience.[22]

It is not difficult to find many other passages to the same effect: "If it be said that in perpetrating wrong they only obey the commands of their government, I reply, they are moral and accountable men, and have no right to obey a wicked command," [23] and so forth.

It would be incorrect, however, to think that Wayland had become a transcendentalist and abolitionist—far from it. He did not, in fact, advocate civil disobedience. Civil disobedience, and even revolution, is permissible, he felt, only if the government in question had ceased any effort to ensure the natural rights of man. Such a magistracy would be "nothing but *power without authority;* and we are justified in setting it aside, and constructing a *government* in its place." [24] The United States government—while morally wrong in permitting slavery and pursuing the Mexican War—had hardly reached this state; hence it is our duty to fight its iniquities with only "innocent," or constitutional, means. But one must nevertheless fight hard. Wayland had certainly given up his simple doctrine that one must speak the truth as he saw it. One must not simply talk; he must also act vigorously through existing political channels and help create new ones. Wayland had begun finally to recognize the importance of political action, and he started acting accordingly.

The election of 1848 showed the need for a new political party, and Wayland wanted to be a part of it. In 1848 the Democrats nominated Lewis Cass of Michigan and made no reference in their platform to the status of slavery in the new territory taken from Mexico. The Whigs nominated Zachary Taylor and had no platform at all! All of this was too much for the antislavery men in both parties. The Van Buren Democrats, who had fought the annexation of Texas, and the Abolitionists met in Buffalo on August 9, 1848, and nominated Martin Van Buren and Charles Francis Adams to head their ticket. They adopted a strong antislavery platform and were dubbed the Free-Soil party.

Wayland supported the Buffalo candidates and rejoiced in

their relative show of strength.[25] They held the balance of power in many states and had thirteen members in the House of Representatives. The Free-Soil party lost ground, however, and later was replaced by the Republican party, in which Wayland was an eager participant from its beginning. He voted for Fremont in 1856 and was not discouraged at his defeat:

Well, the election is over, and I am satisfied. We have at last a North. It is an expression of decidedly changed public opinion. We have now a basis of operations, and have only to be united, to keep alive the moral sentiment of the people, to diffuse light, and to gain the next tier of states, and the result is sure. . . . Now I think the chances of freedom are good. God prosper the right! [26]

Wayland was thoroughly shocked by the Fugitive Slave Law of 1850, and this shock drove him into an even more militant position. Under this law, anyone accused of being a fugitive slave was denied the right of trial by jury, could not testify in his own behalf at his "hearing," and could be turned over to a supposed master on nothing more than the latter's affidavit. Moreover, the law applied to any slave who had fled from his master in the past; hence the free Negroes in the North shivered with fear from day to day. The act also stipulated that a commissioner should collect ten dollars if he decided in favor of the supposed master while he was to collect only five if he decided in favor of the slave. Such legislation as this was too much for Wayland; it went too far in subverting the natural rights of man. Wayland could no longer fight slavery only constitutionally and innocently; the time had come to break the law of his beloved country, quietly but nevertheless firmly. He fed, housed, and clothed a runaway slave.[27] And his indignation at the immorality of this law broke through the composure of one of his sermons.

Evidently his own soul was on fire with indignation against the enactment which hung over the head of every man in the North. There was no direct allusion to it. But breaking loose from the manuscript before him, pushing up his glasses on his forehead, as his wont was on occasion, he burst into extempore speech on the nature of human oppression, its injustice, and its intolerable evils. His whole frame seemed to dilate, the deepsunken eyes flashed from under the shaggy, overhanging brow, his voice trembled, and the sentences charged with the intensest feeling . . . fell like bolts upon the audience.[28]

Wayland, of course, was still no Theodore Parker and never would be—we must make no mistake about that. Wayland would help a fugitive slave escape, but he was not about to storm a jail or courthouse to set one free. The case of Anthony Burns shows the difference clearly.

In 1854 a federal marshal seized Anthony Burns on the streets of Boston as a fugitive slave. Commissioner Edward Loring was ready to send Burns south, but Parker, Thomas Wentworth Higginson, and the other abolitionists had different thoughts. They rushed the courthouse in an effort to set the fugitive free; but everything went wrong with their plans, and their efforts came to naught. Eventually the Massachusetts militia marched Burns back to slavery. Feeling was running high, and Wayland worried about the violence of the abolitionists in the Burns case. He resorted to his law-and-order strain of thought:

Keep down your passions; pray for the country; try to look as patiently as possible upon wrong doers. . . . Write, publish, inform the people, direct the present feeling in proper channels. This is all I see at present. . . . It seems to me that the thing to be done is not to be committed to any rash or sudden measure, but to deepen, extend, and unite the anti-slavery feeling.[29]

Wayland, however, was completely aroused by the Kansas-Nebraska bill in 1854. From this bill emerged Douglas' doctrine of popular sovereignty—all the settlers of each new territory were to vote how they wanted to enter the Union, as free or slave. So it has come to this, Curtis lamented; we now vote on whether all people or only some have natural rights! Wayland was equally shocked. At a protest meeting in Providence he spoke out militantly:

I protest . . . against this bill in the first place, because it proposes to violate the great elementary law, on which not only government, but society itself is founded,—the principle that every man has a right to himself. Second, as an American citizen, I protest against this bill. Third, as a citizen of a free state, I protest against this bill. Fourth, I protest against it, as a Christian.[30]

And yet, somehow, Wayland always fell short of complete commitment. The abolitionists were raising money to help free settlers emigrate to Kansas; they felt it was the only way to save Kansas from the grip of slavery and border ruffians from Missouri. Would Wayland help simply by recommending the scheme? No, he replied, he had not thought the matter through and must refrain from taking so important a step. "It is very painful to advise a step which turns out badly." [31]

In the meantime Wayland fought the good fight as he thought best. He continued to support the Republican party and to write and speak. When Preston Brooks bludgeoned Senator Sumner in 1855, Wayland again spoke at the protest rally in Providence. It was entirely clear to him now: the slave states represented the real threat to law and order. Is this country to be governed by laws "forced upon us at the point of the bowie-knife, or under the muzzle of a revolver"? [32] The question is this: ". . . whether in fact we will be free and sovereign states, or the mere province of a section of this country, under the same constitution as slave-holders have ordained for their chattels, from whom we should differ only in complexion." [33] No longer was it a question only of black slavery but of white slavery also.

In 1859 Wayland's abhorrence of slavery reached a crescendo. He could not even bear to condemn John Brown's raid on Harper's Ferry absolutely. It was madness, no doubt, because it was hopelessly doomed to failure; yet he could not help admiring the "bravery, coolness, and evident sincerity of the old captain." The result of Brown's raids, he thought, would be to "raise the tone of antislavery feeling several degrees higher throughout the North." [34] Wayland here was highly representative of Northern antislavery sentiment. The antislavery people generally condemned Brown, but found him a wonderful rallying point. Even the Republican party branded Brown's raid "among the gravest of crimes"; yet within a short time Union soldiers were marching to the words: "John Brown's body lies a-mouldering in the grave, but his soul goes marching on."

Wayland formalized his stronger stand on slavery and war in the last edition of his *Elements of Moral Science,* a labor begun in 1859. The moral condemnation of slavery in the earlier editions seems perfunctory compared to the later version. It was not moral exhortation any longer; he was deeply angry. His language was far stronger. He wrote of the horrors of slave trade:

As many as survive the horrors of the passage are sold by the slave-dealer to the citizens of a Christian country, and all the right which he acquired over them by the burning of their village, and murdering their dearest relatives, is transferred to the purchaser.[35]

There are words like "concubines" and "licentiousness" that had not appeared before. He repeated all his old arguments but added a good many more. And he brought in all the points he had made against Fuller's claim that Christianity sanctioned slavery. To Dr. Potter he wrote: "I do not see how we can much longer join hands with a Christianity which advocates the buying and selling of Christians. . . . I do not see how Satan could enact more wickedness." [36]

In this last edition of *Moral Science* Wayland also attacked, for the first time, the Southern view of the Negro as degraded, stupid, and fit only for the simplest forms of labor. With beautiful directness Wayland replied: "If they are thus stupid and incapable of civilization, why, in all the slave states, is it made a crime to attempt to teach them the rudiments of education?" [37]

Wayland's most drastic shift, however, was on the moral question of war. In the early editions of the *Moral Science* he defended a thoroughly pacifistic position. He felt that war could not be morally justified under any conditions. But what if a nation is attacked, should it not defend itself? No, Wayland replied, "And if it be said, we shall then all be subjected and enslaved, I answer again, have wars prevented men from being subjected and enslaved?" [38] But in the last edition he abandoned this view. In extreme cases unjust invaders "must be repelled by force, just so far as it is necessary to resist their evil design." In this effort "the whole people may unite, and strive to the utmost to transmit unharmed to their children the legacy of liberty which they have received from their fathers." [39] And soon he saw that in order to have a legacy of liberty to transmit there must come a civil war. Should one give up the high hopes of liberty for all in order to avoid the holocaust? Wayland sadly replied that "the best place to meet a difficulty is just where God puts it. If we dodge it, it will come in a worse place." [40] Though the cost of war is always great, Wayland felt that this was a just war for the North to fight.

4

ASA MAHAN

A S A   M A H A N was the first president of Oberlin College (1835–50) and professor of moral philosophy—the usual pattern during those years of academic orthodoxy when Christianity in some form or other was purveyed in American colleges as *the* philosophy.[1] In some ways Mahan fits the stereotype of academic orthodoxy.[2] He did not always offer reasons for his conclusions. His books are littered with phrases like "it could not be otherwise," "no one, it is presumed, will deny that . . . ," "it is intuitively evident," "everyone cannot but know," and so on. And he frequently cited other philosophers, as well as the Scriptures, as authorities. He even cited lengthy passages from Jonathan Edwards whenever he could, although he differed with Edwards on almost every major point.

In more important ways Mahan does not fit the stereotype. He was unlike Francis Wayland and most of the other academic orthodoxy before 1850 because he had read, and been influenced by, German and French philosophers, as well as the Scottish realists. Mahan was particularly influenced by Kant and

44

Cousin. An astute contemporary reviewer remarked that Mahan, like Cousin, was an eclectic:

His eclecticism degenerates sometimes into the merely aggressive, and he delights occasionally in strange and incongruous combinations of Kant, Coleridge, Cousin and himself, but showing here and there great vigor and acuteness, and very considerable philosophical ability.[3]

The aggressiveness of Mahan also sets him apart from the rest of the orthodoxy. He was too fiery by temperament to pass up polemics and hence got to the heart of some basic philosophical problems. He attacked the Edwardsian doctrine of determinism and was led, by the vigor of his attack, into what many nineteenth-century Christians considered heresy.[4] He attacked utilitarianism in all its forms, including Paley's, in a far more consistent and thorough fashion than did Francis Wayland and the other followers of Scottish realism and English intuitionism. And first and foremost he vigorously attacked the moral philosophy of his colleague Charles Grandison Finney, famous evangelist, professor of theology, and president-to-be of Oberlin. The spiritedness of his criticisms frequently aroused the ire of his Oberlin colleagues but fortunately was accompanied by a "considerable philosophical ability" that merits close attention.

I

Mahan's critique of Edwards appears in his *Doctrine of the Will,* first published in 1844. According to Mahan:

Edwards stands convicted of a fundamental error in philosophy, an error which gives form and character to his whole work—the confounding of the Will with the Sensibility, and thus confounding the characteristics of the phenomena of the former faculty with those of the phenomena of the latter.[5]

The trouble is that the whole of Edwards' work "is constructed without an appeal to Consciousness, the only proper and authoritative tribunal of appeal in the case." [6] If we attend carefully to consciousness, Mahan said, we can distinguish volition from the strongest desire and hence must distinguish between the separate faculties of will as personal activity and sensation as mere passive impression. The latter does not "act"; it merely "suffers." The will is the moving force in life, and unless it can be shown that there is some necessary connection between will and sensation—which, in fact, cannot be done—then it follows that the will is free, that is, the source of "personal activity." Mahan's rejection of universal determinism, of course, entailed the rejection of the Calvinistic doctrine of election. He believed that man is responsible for his own sins and his own regeneration and that he is able to accept or reject the salvation of Jesus Christ. Mahan was, to say the least, a "New Light" theologian.

The strategy behind Mahan's attack on Edwards was far from novel. From 1824 to 1845 there were numerous criticisms of Edwards along the general lines of Mahan's argument.[7] The new faculty psychology was sweeping America, and Edwards was attacked from all sides for ignoring consciousness and confusing volition and sensation. Professor Henry Tappan of New York University, in particular, had written brilliantly along these lines. Mahan knew Tappan's work well, had a high opinion of it, and followed him closely on many points.[8] It was not the newness or uniqueness of Mahan's critique of Edwards that makes his *Doctrine of the Will* highly important. It is rather that this criticism was the springboard to Mahan's enormously controversial notion of perfectionism, which came to be called "the Oberlin heresy." [9]

Mahan's doctrine of Christian perfection was called by some the doctrine of sanctification or holiness. Although they might qualify the doctrine in one way or another, most of the Oberlin leaders, including Finney, defended it. In the third volume of his *Lectures on Systematic Theology* (1847) Finney devoted over two hundred and fifty pages to the notion of sanctification, but Mahan's *Christian Perfection* (1839) was the most influential presentation and defense of this ardently anti-Calvinistic doctrine. According to Mahan, it is not impossible for a person in this life to live sinlessly and to attain Christian perfection before death. Because this doctrine seemed extremely radical even to the New Light theologians, Mahan carefully pointed out that the concept of sanctification meant neither "the certainty of never sinning again" nor "emancipation from all temptation." Far from it.

What he did mean, he declared, was emancipation of the will from "the thralldom of Sin," "emancipation of the intelligence from the darkness and tendencies of sin and introduction into 'God's marvelous light,' " and a consequent change in the sensibility so that the balance of its tendencies shall always be in favor of holiness.[10]

In spite of Mahan's efforts to clarify and qualify, the doctrine of Christian perfection was misunderstood generally. Worst of all, it was confused with antinomian perfectionism of the sort espoused by John Humphrey Noyes, whose theology formed the basis for the sexual experiments of the Oneida Community. Professor Henry Cowles of Oberlin pointed out emphatically the opposite notions of perfection involved. According to Noyes, man can receive Christ in such a way that He shall act in him and displace his moral agency and personal responsibility so that he *cannot* sin. Such a belief, Cowles pointed out,[11] is entirely inconsistent with the Oberlin doctrine of human ability and responsibility. The various misunderstandings were gradually minimized, and the Oberlin doctrine of perfectionism seemed less like heresy as time passed. Moreover, the furor passed because Oberlin leaders ceased, after a bit, to press the doctrine. Their interest in the topic died because they were too deeply involved in their own practical problems and moral reforms to spend much time canvassing their souls for signs of sanctification.

Mahan's rejection of Edwardsian determinism and his concept of Christian perfection reflect on the theoretical level his practical concern for reform measures. Oberlin College was a leader in many nineteenth-century reform efforts: the antislavery movement, the peace movement, "physiological" or health reforms, moral reforms, and educational experiment. It is man's duty, Mahan urged, to try to create a perfectly ethical and righteous social order. Now if it is his duty so to strive, he must be able, in principle, to achieve the goal. "Ought" implies "can."[12] Hence Mahan was led to his theoretical view that man must be free and capable of sanctification.

Mahan was the theoretical and practical reform leader of Oberlin. Finney's notion of reform was to regenerate the souls of men so that all specific reforms would follow. Mahan was not so optimistic. Evil must be fought on all fronts. The strategy of the whole war is to find a middle way between the timid social measures of the Unitarians and the radical disuniting measures of Garrison. "Ingenuous liberality," he felt was the proper spirit of reform.[13] The reformer must never be dogmatic but should always hear all sides. Garrison and the Fosters came to Oberlin to be heard.[14] And the true reformer must be the *universal* reformer, "seeking the correction of all evils."

This practical belief, again, was the commitment which had to be accounted for on the theoretical level and which led Mahan to his attack on Edwards and the defense of sanctification. These practical and theoretical views of Mahan continued to be present in Oberlin thought and action long after Mahan had been lost to Oberlin. The legacy that he left to Oberlin was a mixed and fascinating one, a legacy not yet wholly understood.

II

Mahan's critique of utilitarianism occurs most prominently in his *Science of Moral Philosophy,* published in 1848.[15] He was one of the most consistent and relentless of the critics of utilitarianism among the academic orthodoxy—more so even than Wayland, who supposedly owed his popularity as a writer to his vigorous rejection of Paley as well as Bentham. To bring out the consistency and importance of Mahan's criticism, and to see why it is superior to Wayland's, requires, however, an awareness of an ambiguity in the concept of utility which has become apparent in recent discussions about moral obligation.[16]

The utilitarian view of obligation can be interpreted in two radically different ways. The claim that one ought to contribute to the general happiness may mean that "ought" is defined as "contributing to the general happiness." In this case the utilitarian claim is not itself a normative one but is a meta-ethical claim about the meaning of moral terms. On the other hand, the utilitarian claim may mean that acting for general happiness is one's final and basic obligation. In this case the claim is a normative one, a basic moral principle by virtue of which all specific obligations are decided and conflicts among specific obligations resolved. The two views, however, are not simply separate; they are incompatible. On the normative interpretation, to the question, "Ought I keep my promise?" it is meaningful to reply, "Yes, since keeping promises contributes to the general welfare." The claim that an act contributes to general welfare, in short, is a *reason* why one ought to do the thing in question. However, on the meta-ethical view, since *"x* contributes to general welfare" and *"x* ought to be done" are synonymous expressions, it is no longer possible to give the former as a reason why we ought to do any given act.

Mahan consistently interpreted utilitarianism as a normative claim and criticized it accordingly—never inadvertently including criticisms that would be relevant only to a meta-ethical claim. Mahan saw utility as the only significant alternative to the Kantian imperative, and he viewed both unequivocally as providing the test or criterion of a right act, or as the reason why an act is right.

The question as to the foundation of obligation resolves itself simply and exclusively into this one, namely, *what are the reasons in view of which such affirmations are made?* What are the *reasons* for which the intelligence affirms that the will ought to put forth certain intentions or choices, and ought not to put forth others? This one question being correctly answered, we have discovered the real and only foundation of moral obligation. No one, it is presumed, will deny that this is a distinct and correct statement of the question.[17]

Mahan's criticisms of normative utilitarianism all depend upon an appeal to consciousness—almost as if the decision were a matter of introspective fact—and hence reveal his dependence upon the same faculty psychology that he used in criticizing Edwards. To the question, "Why should we love God?" the "universal spontaneous response" and the "direct testimony of consciousness" would be that our character demands it and not that some good, either to God or to man, stems from it. "In this response Utilitarians as well as others would unite, when their theory is out of their minds."[18] Moreover, everyone is aware that he never goes through the calculations that utility entails in making moral judgments. And utility could not always provide the reason why doing an act is our duty because we learn the tendencies of action only over a period of time. What, then, would be the ground of obligation in the first place? "I cannot but regard the above argument as having all the force of absolute demonstration." [19]

Mahan concluded his criticism of utility with a kind of *ad hominem* argument. It is a fact, he said, that the more one frees himself of utilitarian tendencies the less likely he is to be casuistic and make exceptions. "The more perfectly the mind is emancipated from the doctrine of utility, and the more perfectly it is confirmed and established in the opposite doctrine, the more sacred in its estimation, does the idea of obligation become." [20]

Mahan's criticisms of utilitarianism make an interesting contrast with those of Francis Wayland. [21] Unlike Mahan, Wayland unwittingly mixed the two meanings of utilitarianism. Wayland insisted that obligation cannot be given a utilitarian interpretation because (1) the two concepts, if we examine our consciousness, are utterly different in meaning; (2) we do, in fact, reach moral judgments without calculating the likelihood of desirable consequences; (3) we are usually ignorant of the future, and hence any moral judgment based on likely future consequences is doomed to failure; and (4) teleological derivations of obligation tend to destroy all moral distinctions since crimes sometimes have the happiest results—indeed, given this moral view "we must award to the treachery of Judas the praises of the greatest virtue." [22]

If we examine carefully Wayland's four criticisms of utilitarianism, we see that (1) is a relevant criticism only if utility is interpreted as a meta-ethical claim while (2), (3), and (4) are relevant criticisms only if it is interpreted as a normative claim. Yet Wayland mistakenly offered these criticisms as if they were all relevant to utility as a meta-ethical view. He explicitly interpreted utility as a meta-ethical claim, although he did not, of course, use this term. He never distinguished between deriving the nature of one's duty by considering consequences, and defining "duty" as "conducive to good consequences."

This blur reflects an identical ambiguity in his own intuitionistic moral philosophy. He never distinguished between the intuitionist claim that at least one moral term must be undefined, and the claim that obligations are known intuitively and hence underived. In this Wayland reflected the general ambiguity in much of English and Scottish philosophy. Even the utilitarians failed to note the crucial difference. Certain utilitarians, quite unwittingly, tried to profit from the ambiguity, suggesting that "right" is synonymous with "conducive to good consequences," and yet using the latter as a reason why a certain act is our duty.

From these considerations it follows that Mahan's clarity on this point is quite remarkable. I am not suggesting that Mahan himself made the distinction we are discussing, but rather that he clearly and systematically discussed utility and his own concept of moral law as normative positions as if this were the only significant point at issue between them. Yet Mahan was steeped in the tradition of English and Scottish intuitionism as thoroughly as Wayland was. I can explain his greater clarity only by the fact that he was a careful student of both Kant and Cousin. Their principles of universality were so evidently criteria, tests, and reasons that utility, clearly the only alternative view, must also be interpreted as a criterion, test, or reason. The utilitarian is not defining words or concepts in opposition to the intuitionist claim that moral terms are basic and undefinable, but he is deriving specific duties in opposition to the intuitionist's claim that moral judgments are intuitively grounded.

Mahan and Wayland fully realized that the consideration of consequences cannot be ignored altogether and that some provision for their calculations must be provided for even in the formalist's scheme of morality. But Mahan never compromised his formalism in accommodating calculations of consequences, while Wayland, whose reputation was largely built on his supposed rejection of Paley's view and utility in general, made serious concessions to the principle of utility and, in fact, still reflected some of Paley's notions.[23] The consideration of consequences, according to Mahan, does not determine whether an act is right or wrong—the intrinsic nature of the act and the intention of the agent determine the moral character of any act. However, the intentions of an agent are not open to the inspection of other people. The only way we can judge the nature of the intentions of someone else is by inference from the tendencies of what he does to produce good or bad consequences.[24]

No doubt by accident a saint could produce evil consequences sometimes and a criminal good consequences sometimes, but the saint would become suspect if his actions rarely had beneficial results, and the sinner who usually acted beneficially would exemplify some sort of contradiction in terms. Even more strongly, Mahan urged that an agent is responsible for the consequences of his act and hence must consider what they are likely to be, insofar as they are necessary effects of right or wrong intentions.[25] Intending to produce benevolent results is no excuse for not attending carefully to the means for bringing about the intended results. The consideration of consequences in both of these senses, it should be clear, does not entail any concession on Mahan's part to Paley's views or to those of the classical utilitarians. However, the same cannot be said for Wayland.

Wayland, as we have seen, still retained elements of Paley's brand of utilitarianism even though he had supposedly rejected Paley.[26] Wayland tried to introduce these elements indirectly into his own system and hence avoid a clash with his own fundamental deontological commitment.[27] According to Wayland, we should act in the light of general happiness but not because it is intrinsically right. We should so act rather because God wishes it. Mahan saw clearly, however, that deontologists like Wayland and himself could not consort with utility in this fashion. Mahan pointed out that, "if an action be not evil in itself, its indefinite multiplication would not be an evil." [28] And, if a good be of an indefinite value, "its indefinite multiplication cannot give us a definite result; since it is the multiplication of an unknown quantity." [29] Moreover, Mahan continued, it is wrong to believe that "because God wished it" or "because God did it" are ever the reasons why an act is right.[30] God himself wishes something or does a certain act because it is right; the wish or act is never right simply because God wishes or does it. If God's will determined what was right, then we could never sensibly say that God's will was right. But not to be able to say

that God is good and that what he does is right would constitute
a kind of negative blasphemy. Mahan's student and later colleague at Oberlin, James H. Fairchild, heartily agreed with this
point.[31]

Not only was Mahan a more consistent critic of utilitarianism
than Wayland, he was in general the most relentless critic of it
among the academic orthodoxy. He criticized it not only in the
form advanced by Paley but also in the classical forms of
Bentham and, later, J. S. Mill. And, as we shall see, he interpreted the various versions of "benevolence" and "love of
being," advanced by Jonathan Edwards and by his Oberlin
colleagues Finney and Fairchild, as merely thinly disguised variations on the theme of utility and hence open to all of the
objections relevant to the more straightforward versions.

III

In his *Science of Moral Philosophy* Mahan devoted the most
space of all to an exposure of what he took to be the errors in
the moral philosophy of his influential colleague Charles Grandison Finney.[32] Finney was a famous evangelist but no great
theologian or philosopher. Taking his cue from obvious sources,
Finney had argued that the highest well-being of God and the
universe of sentient beings is the end at which ultimate prefer-
ences and intentions ought to terminate. In other words, the
well-being of God and the universe is the absolute and ultimate
good and should be chosen by all moral agents.[33]

Mahan showed great dialectical skill in arguing against Finney's version of the moral philosophy of Jonathan Edwards.
The essential strategy of Mahan's argument was to claim that
Finney's views were simply a variation of the principle of utility
and to press the attack from that vantage point.[34] Mahan realized that Finney's views were not identical with classical utilitarianism or with Paley's views, but he argued that, in the long
run, they all have a common core of meaning. They all insist
that only one thing is intrinsically valuable—be it pleasure,
happiness, or well-being for me, you, or everyone, including
God—and that all other acts and events in the world are valuable only insofar as they are conducive to achieving this end.

Various as they appear to be, all of Mahan's criticisms essentially focus on the same point, namely, that there are many basic obligations in life which cannot be reduced to one all-inclusive principle. Obligations, duties, and rights depend upon perceiving certain "fitting relationships." Even Finney realizes, Mahan said, that there is a fitting relationship between virtue and happiness. Not just anyone but only the virtuous person intrinsically deserves the good, or happiness. Yet Finney did not see that he could not hold this view consistently with the overarching principle that only happiness is intrinsically good.[35] There are many variations on this point.

Furthermore, Mahan argued, man's whole concept of God's justice and his moral nature depends upon this concept of a connection between virtue, evil, and their deserts. "All men do, as a matter of fact, reason from the *connection* between holiness and happiness, and sin and misery, under [God's] government, to the moral character of God. In the scriptures also, the same principle is continually appealed to." [36] And "these statements no one will call in question. . . ."

Mahan also used the same *ad hominem* type of argument against Finney's view that he had used against the utilitarians, namely, that a view which calculates duties necessarily tends to stunt the development of a well-proportioned moral character.[37] The point was not that Finney had a badly proportioned character, he said, but that he had a good one in spite of his theory, not as a consequence of it! And, as we might have expected from previous remarks, Finney's worst error, according to Mahan, was that he ignored the complete testimony of consciousness.[38] From the fact that we are directly aware of an obligation to promote the welfare of God and of being in general, Finney concluded, without justification, that we are aware only of this one obligation and, hence, that there is only one basis of obligation. No doubt we are directly aware of this obligation, Mahan said, but we are directly aware of many other obligations also which cannot be reduced introspectively or theoretically to this one obligation. Finney, he said, makes the simple error of deducing a general theory from a single fact. He has no feeling for the complexity of man's psychological make-up.

Mahan included numerous variations on all of these criticisms; his critique of Finney, in fact, became so disproportionately long compared to the other chapters in *The Science of Moral Philosophy* that it takes on something of the nature of a symptom of aggressiveness toward Finney. And there is a curious and suggestive remark in the Preface to the effect that he had not written under ideal circumstances. One suspects that all did not go well for Mahan at Oberlin, and this suspicion is quickly confirmed by even the most cursory reading of Fletcher's interesting *History of Oberlin College*.[39] Mahan apparently was high-handed in dealing with the faculty and expected them not to grumble if their salaries were not always met. He became entangled in a famous Oberlin church trial as counsel and witness. And he was too radical; he actually wanted to allow women to speak at commencement in front of men! The faculty had followed his leadership through all reform measures— abolition, moral reform, physiological reform, and so on—but women speaking in front of men was too much. The conservative John Morgan was representative of the faculty, and Mahan eventually resigned in 1850 after much cloak and dagger activity on all sides. (Amidst such turmoil it is little wonder that the Oberlin doctrine of sanctification quietly died.)

Though many explanations have been offered for the friction in Oberlin's early days, it is interesting that the most likely one is never mentioned. Mahan was the president of Oberlin, but the world-famous Finney, professor of theology, was the idol of all and in most ways dominated the scene. Mahan's education and scholarly abilities were far above Finney's, and he was more deeply committed to universal reform than Finney was. All of these factors, combined with his own fiery but fine moral sense, set the stage for Mahan's departure from Oberlin.

Throughout the conflict no one denied that Mahan was a great teacher and writer of philosophy. Upon Mahan's death many years later James Harris Fairchild, one of those who had opposed him, wrote: "His work here as a teacher can never be forgotten by his pupils, and the impulse which he gave to the study of philosophy in the College is not yet exhausted." [40] And Fletcher observed that "it is a tribute to Mahan that years after his departure 'metaphysical investigations' should still have been considered Oberlin's strongest point scholastically." [41] Mahan also left a strong reform tendency at Oberlin, although, it cannot be denied, a somewhat tamed one. When Mahan's fire was gone most of Oberlin's experiments and heresies were on their way to oblivion and Oberlin was on its way to conformity. The very name Oberlin was no longer a byword in the country and was seldom hissed at any more.

philosophy—the teleological and deontological—and might well be labeled "intentional utilitarianism."

Fairchild believed that only the well-being of sentient beings is intrinsically good and that all moral duty is concerned with the production of such good. This view sounds much like classical utilitarianism, but in fact it is crucially different. He claimed that it is not one's duty to produce what are objectively the best results but only to intend to produce the best results and to do what seems most likely to achieve this end. Fairchild's hybrid, as we shall see, not only forms a consistent system but is a really worthy competitor of Mahan's view of justice as fairness.

I

Fairchild's teleological view of moral judgment emerges early in his *Moral Science*.[5] He writes that duty and obligation depend upon the prior notion of good. He admits that there is a moral use of the word "good" which is exhibited in sentences like "John has a good character"; but he has in mind a nonmoral use of "good" exhibited in sentences like "John had a good time." The latter sense of the word he calls "natural good," and it is this sense of the word, he thinks, which is fundamental in all judgments of duty and obligation. Unless natural good is the point of man's duty, the claim that one ought to do so-and-so makes no sense. Nothing would be wrong with lying, stealing, or deceit if no one were ever hurt by such acts. In a universe without sentient beings who feel pain and enjoy happiness there would be no point whatever in making moral judgments. But since there are sentient beings who feel pain and happiness it is man's duty, Fairchild avers, to promote their well-being or happiness in a perfectly disinterested manner—that is, it is one's duty to promote not simply one's own well-being or the well-being of loved ones but to promote the well-being of all.

Fairchild usually used the word "well-being" as his basic value term upon which all judgments of duty are based, but he was not averse to using the word "happiness" if that word is taken to mean the whole range of man's satisfactions and not simply the lowly sensuous forms of pleasure. It is only fair to add, however, that Fairchild did not rail against the "beastly

pleasures" in principle as many Victorian moralists did. He was critical of them only insofar as they were incompatible with the realization of man's whole range of satisfactions and incompatible with his disinterested love of well-being in general.

At this point Fairchild's principle of benevolence might well seem indistinguishable from the classical principle of utility, but there are several crucial differences.

1. While Fairchild and J. S. Mill were both utilitarians in the sense that they teleologically derived all specific duties from considerations of well-being or happiness, they nevertheless differed in the sorts of reasons they gave for accepting the principle. Fairchild simply claimed that one directly apprehends through his conscience that benevolence is his basic duty.[6] Mill, being in the British empirical tradition, had no such avenue of justification open to him. Yet he wanted to give some reason why utility is acceptable as a basic principle. He did not think the principle could be proved in any logical sense; hence he put the word "proof" within quotation marks when he asked the question, "Of what sort of 'proof' is the principle of utility susceptible?"[7] He did offer psychological facts which, he thought, made it reasonable to accept the principle even though it could not be proved in any logical sense or justified in any metaphysical sense.

2. There is an even more fundamental difference between Fairchild and Mill, and the elucidation of this difference helps not only to produce a more exact picture of Fairchild's particular brand of utilitarianism but also to point up its importance. For Mill the rightness or wrongness of an act depended wholly upon its consequences. Thus when a person intending to produce good consequences and acting reasonably in terms of the evidence available nevertheless, because of the unpredictability of the future, produces undesirable consequences, he has committed a wrong act. He is not, of course, morally blameworthy, but he has, nevertheless, done a wrong act. He has not done what he ought to do, so he has not succeeded in doing his duty. This variety of utilitarianism was quite foreign to Fairchild.[8] How can one be responsible for doing something that may well be beyond his power? One's duty cannot exceed his ability. For

Fairchild, if a person intends to produce good consequences and acts reasonably to achieve them, then he has done the right thing independently of what the actual consequences are. He has done what he ought to do and thus has succeeded in doing his duty. Man's duty, in short, is to want to produce good consequences and to do whatever will *probably* produce them. It is not his duty actually to produce them.

Fairchild's moral philosophy, we now see, is an interesting combination of the two traditional types of ethical theory and is well described by the rubric "intentional utilitarianism." The deontologist insists that (1) the agent's intention and (2) conformance to a formal rule determine the rightness of an act and the nature of duty. The teleologist claims that (1) the consideration of consequences and (2) the actual consequences determine the rightness of an act and the nature of duty. Fairchild's position was a combination of both points (1) and a rejection of both points (2). His intuitional utilitarianism is worth careful consideration because it helps to avoid the Millian paradox that one ought to do what he is often unable to do. There is, however, admittedly a difficulty with Fairchild's view also. It requires one to say retrospectively of an act that has produced disastrous consequences, "Yes, that is precisely what should have been done, since the evidence required it at the time." Contemporary writers on utilitarianism and moral philosophy in general might well give this problem more attention than they have.

II

Fairchild strenuously denied that he was a utilitarian. When he made this denial he had in mind particularly the utilitarian views of Paley, Taylor, and Metcalf, not those of the classical British utilitarians. Fairchild ascribed the following view to Paley, Taylor, and Metcalf.[9] Since in fact everyone is motivated only by prospects of his own happiness, he must, in order to be a moral agent, find his happiness in acting benevolently—a "higher happiness." Fairchild called this view alternately "the selfish system" and "utilitarianism." He called it the selfish

system because it claims that everyone is motivated only by prospects of his own happiness, and utilitarianism because it holds that one should act benevolently for the well-being of all. His criticism of it is skillful and devastating.

1. The selfish part of the system is wrong, he averred, because it equates all motivation with desire.[10] But if all motives are desires, he said, then all behavior is causally determined and there is no freedom of will. Acting from a sense of obligation as distinct from desire must itself constitute a motive for action if freedom of the will is to be preserved. Fairchild's criticism has an ironic aspect since both Metcalf and Taylor thought themselves staunch advocates of free will. For Fairchild this blurring of the difference between active self-agency and passive sensation, even among the critics of Edwards, must have shown how thoroughly deep-seated the confusion was.

Since Fairchild was a faculty psychologist like Mahan and most of the other members of the academic orthodoxy, he next appealed to consciousness. If one attends carefully to his consciousness he can distinguish clearly between doing good to someone for its own sake and doing good to someone because it makes one happy. Clearly only the first is benevolence. "We feel and know that benevolence is vitiated when it looks, for a motive, beyond the good itself, to some satisfaction to be derived from the action. We call such action prudence or shrewdness, not benevolence." [11] To be sure, one should derive satisfaction from acting benevolently, but if he acts to achieve this satisfaction then he has not acted benevolently. Furthermore, the selfish system, Fairchild said, undercuts any distinction between right and wrong or good and bad.

It makes the subjective motive the same in both—desire of happiness. They differ only in the means they use. But in the pursuit of an end, every man uses the means which commend themselves to his judgment, and can use no other; else he surrenders his end. The difference between the virtuous and the sinful, then, must be merely a difference of judgment, and sin is a mistake.[12]

For Fairchild this amounts to a *reductio ad absurdum*. Nor, he concluded, does this view coincide with that of the Scriptures.

How could the selfish theorist, without further absurdity, interpret the admonition of Jesus that "whoever shall lose his life for my sake shall find it"?

2. The utilitarian part of the system of Metcalf and Taylor is wrong, Fairchild thought, because it makes the utility of benevolence itself a condition of its obligatoriness.[13] They tried, in short, to give a teleological justification for acting benevolently in the first place. One should act benevolently, they said, because he thereby contributes to his higher happiness. Metcalf and Taylor missed the point that the principle of benevolence must be accepted as the fundamental moral law without further justification, a principle that itself provides the teleological justification for, and derivation of, all further specific duties. The conscience theorist, Fairchild claimed, is wrong in saying that specific duties are intuitively apprehended, but he is perfectly right in insisting upon the basic, underived nature of some moral principle—on Fairchild's view, the principle of benevolence.

III

An immediate corollary of Fairchild's principle of benevolence is that essentially man has only one duty, namely, to pursue the well-being of all, and that all other apparent duties are resolvable into this fundamental one. There are, he said, the virtues of gratitude, patriotism, veracity, fidelity, justice, humility, mercy, obedience, and so on, but they all constitute a virtue simply because they are all different manifestations of benevolence.[14] Gratitude, for example, is benevolence toward a benefactor. True gratitude occurs when a person receives a benefit, takes pleasure in it, and requites the benefactor out of love for his well-being. Patriotism is benevolence directed toward the people of one's own nation, truth telling is benevolence directed toward the well-being of all, fidelity is benevolence toward those to whom a promise was made or with whom a contract was entered upon, and so on through all the virtues. The same teleological analysis, Fairchild thought, applies to the notion of justice itself.

There is an impulse to treat every interest according to its value, and every person according to his deserts, and there is satisfaction in witnessing such a result. This characteristic of our nature is often called the principle of justice; but it becomes the virtue of justice when benevolence enters in to regulate and limit it. What is called justice becomes sin when it goes beyond the limits which benevolence appoints. To secure to a moral being his deserts is a virtuous act when benevolence requires it; it is a sinful act when a proper regard for all good forbids. . . . The only just man is the man who regards all well-being for its value and according to its value.[15]

Fairchild, however, quickly runs into trouble in his efforts to reduce all virtues to the single one of benevolence. A difficulty appears immediately in his analysis of gratitude. A person bears a special relation to his benefactor; he cherishes the well-being of his benefactor because of that special relationship and not simply because he cherishes indiscriminately the well-being of all. If he cherished the well-being of a benefactor because of his love of being in general there would be nothing unique in his attitude to count as gratitude. The same point is true of patriotism. A person bears a special relationship to his fellow countrymen; he cherishes their well-being because of that special relationship and not simply because he cherishes indiscriminately the well-being of all. If he valued the well-being of his countrymen because of his love of being in general there would be nothing unique in his attitude to count as patriotism, nothing to distinguish it from his benevolent attitude toward foreigners. Fairchild was not unaware of this problem for he wrote that "in the nature of the case, those with whom we are associated have claims upon us which others have not." "We are specially responsible for their interests," he said, because we have "special ability to serve them."[16] But he missed the point of the special claims. True to form, he gave a teleological analysis of this special relation: we have special obligation to our countrymen because we have greater means to implement their well-being. The point is rather that our special relations determine the nature of our benevolence, making it distinct from all other manifestations of benevolence.

The cases of truth telling and promise keeping present an even more fundamental difficulty for Fairchild. According to him, the only reason for telling the truth or keeping one's promise is that these acts promote well-being. The sacredness of truth "is derived from the interests of moral beings," and an agreement "in reference to a matter utterly indifferent to both parties has no binding force." [17] Fairchild, however, neglects to develop certain ominous consequences of this view. From his position it follows that one should lie and break promises if he has good evidence that doing so will produce greater good than telling the truth or keeping the promise. The trouble with this consequence is that it smacks of paternalism. It says in effect that I know what is best for you and I will act accordingly. The point is that the "good" results can be achieved only by discounting the judgment of the person or people involved as alleged beneficiaries of the act you commit. Moreover, Fairchild's teleological justification of truth telling does not seem to square with his own definite statement in another place that every person has "the right to know the truth." [18] The right to know the truth sounds like a deontological commitment and one that is difficult, in any case, to reconcile with the paternalism of teleology.

The derivation of the concept of justice given by Fairchild seems to be the weakest one of all. He did not manage to reduce it to benevolence in even the prima facie plausible way he did gratitude, patriotism, truth telling, and promise keeping. As his remarks about justice quoted earlier clearly show, Fairchild simply showed how benevolence should temper justice and not how, in fact, the latter is simply another manifestation of the former. According to Fairchild, man has the impulse to treat every interest according to its value and every person according to what he deserves. This principle of justice, he said, only becomes the virtue of justice when benevolence enters in to regulate and limit it. A critic of Fairchild might well agree that justice becomes a virtue only when benevolence limits it, but he would hasten to point out that this fact in itself would not establish that the demands of justice—that people be rewarded and punished only if they deserve it—are reduced to the demands of benevolence. The impossibility of reducing justice to benevolence seemed self-evident to an intuitionist like Mahan.[19] Why should one be equally benevolent to all? One ought to bestow those goods of life under his control to those who deserve it. Moreover, the justification of punishment can be only that someone deserved it and not that the administration of punishment will promote the well-being of society or the ultimate well-being of the individual punished. For Mahan these are beneficial consequences of punishment, to be sure, but they cannot be the justification of punishment. Punishment, like reward, can be justified only in terms of fairness, justice, and desert. To think otherwise leads to the most terrifying sort of paternalism imaginable, the sort expressed by Fairchild when he wrote that "the life of an innocent person may, in a rare emergency, be required and taken, to save the lives of many." [20]

IV

There are a number of other aspects of Fairchild's theoretical ethics that deserve consideration, but they can only be lightly touched upon. He never sufficiently understood the complexities of the calculational aspect of any teleological system. He said, to be sure, that "we have no other guide" to the right except to calculate what is productive of the good,[21] but he was never aware that, even on his own view, the production of good is not a sufficient condition for the determination of what is right and what constitutes duty. The point is that a right act must produce more good than any other act which the agent conceivably could have done. Nor was he aware that production of the good is not sufficient to define one's duty, since it is always possible that two different acts might produce equal goods. Hence both are right, but not both can be our duty. Fairchild always wrote as if moral choice were always between benevolent and malevolent alternatives when, in fact, some of the most painful decisions concern which good must be sacrificed to achieve another larger one.

Unlike most of his peers, Fairchild spent considerable time analyzing the concept "wrong" as well as the concept "right." He believed that wrong is pursued always for selfish reasons and never for its own sake. "The wrong course is pursued in spite of its wickedness," he wrote, "and not for the sake of it." [22] Fairchild, I suspect, was short-sighted in this analysis because it conflicts with another element of his system. Since the conflict comes about obliquely it is not surprising that he missed it.

Denying that wrong can be pursued for its own sake commits Fairchild to a Socratic ethic, the notion that wrong-doing is only ignorance or error, and this view, as we saw elsewhere, Fairchild rejected. According to the Socratic ethic, wrong is always pursued for selfish reasons and never for its own sake. The selfish person thinks he is acting for his own good, but he is mistaken. His real good consists in acting virtuously. Hence one who acts unjustly does so not out of malice but out of ignorance of the true good. Fairchild never realized that the only way to refute this Socratic conclusion, which he certainly wanted to do, is to insist that wrong can be done for its own sake, that people can and sometimes do act a certain way precisely because they believe it to be wrong. Only on this supposition can we make sense out of malevolence and its opposite benevolence. Without such an assumption a benevolent choice implies no merit. If it makes no sense freely to choose the wrong, then it equally makes no sense freely to choose the right. And thus genuinely benevolent action seems impossible.

Fairchild argued against both theological ethics and conscience theory in most instructive ways.[23] He saw no virtue whatever in defining "right" as "whatever God wills." If whatever God wills is right, he said, then it makes no sense to ask if God's will is right. But clearly we want to be able to do so. Moreover, we want to give as a reason why God's will is right that God always chooses the right. But this we cannot do if whatever God does is right because he did it. Moreover,

. . . we know that love to our neighbor would be duty, even if God should not require it; and in reference to many particular duties, we perceive first that they are duties, and then infer that God requires them. If duty originated in his will, the order would always be reversed.[24]

Fairchild's critique of conscience theory is clearly directed against Mahan. This critique is not the strongest part of his book, but it has redeeming features. Fairchild tried to explain away the immediacy and urgency of the dictates of conscience by resolving the notion into that of "an aesthetic conscience." This strange name is not very helpful, for what Fairchild did was to give an essentially naturalistic account of conscience—

conscience is instinctive judgment of rightness and wrongness, usually a valuable guide but always open to correction by careful investigation of likely consequences. Fairchild never made clear why this naturalistic account does not vitiate his own grounding of the principle of benevolence in conscience and intuitive insight. In one bad moment he seems to have offered his own teleological position as if that were a sufficient refutation of conscience theory:

Lastly, the rightness which is supposed to be ultimate in thought and in fact, is not ultimate. Rightness is conformity to law, and the law is the perceived obligation, and obligation arises only in the presence of the good. The good is thus the foundation of the right.[25]

He redeems this dreary performance quickly, however, by his observation that moral judgments always seem to require reasons that back them up, but that only on the benevolence view are reasons of any sort available why something is our duty—namely, because it produces some specifiable good.

Fairchild's final criticism of the conscience theory was a parting shot at Mahan. Mahan had criticized all teleological moral philosophers by saying that they were prone to make exceptions in their own favor by virtue of their calculation of goods. This criticism has a slightly *ad hominem* flavor, and Fairchild was not unwilling to reply in a similar manner. The worst feature of the conscience theory, he said, is that it leads to fanaticism. The conscience theory

. . . conveys the impression that there is righteousness which is above respect to particular and, perhaps, minute interests—that has its eye on a right which is a sure guide, forever the same, unmodified by changing circumstances and contingencies. The man who adopts the maxim ["Do right for the sake of right"] is wont to appeal to the eternal principle of rectitude in justification of his questionable course, and exhorts others to "do right if the heavens fall," careful to allay their misgivings, however, with the assurance that the heavens will not fall.[26]

Fairchild was cautious and conservative compared to Mahan and Finney, of this there can be no doubt. He was always willing to compromise on anything except the principle of benevolence, and he certainly avoided any kind of fanaticism in his conduct, courses, or administration of the college. Fairchild signaled the change of Oberlin from reform movement to conformity.[27]

V

The long section on Practical Ethics in *Moral Science* is interesting primarily because it flies off in opposite directions. It is at once extremely liberal and extremely conservative in different ways. The chapter on civil disobedience might well have been written by Thoreau or any of the other transcendentalists. It is written wholly without the qualifications introduced by Francis Wayland in his discussion of the limits of civil obedience. Fairchild presented straightforwardly and convincingly the notion of the Higher Law. God's law is supreme, and when man's law contravenes it the duty of the Christian is to obey God's law at all costs. On the other hand, the remaining chapters are highly conservative and show traces not only of paternalism but even of jingoism and manifest destiny. Oberlin had come a long way from abolition days when its name was a byword in the country for radical reform.

According to Fairchild, which form of government is best is a relative matter.[28] Not all men are responsible beings, and hence democracy is not necessarily the best form of government. Even in a democracy, immigrants and women, he averred, have no intrinsic right to vote. They have the right only if it can be demonstrated that their voting will contribute to the well-being of their community, the state, and the nation. Fairchild had a horror of the possible excesses of democracy and of individualism. The man who "occupies a favorable position," he thought, deserves to rule, and "those in an inferior position" have the obligation of obedience.[29]

The paternalism of Fairchild's notion of benevolence is further illustrated in his view of Indian policy and international law. The United States had the right, he believed, to take over Indian land because it could make better use of it for more people.

A barbarous people, occupying a vast territory as a hunting-ground, incapable of availing themselves of its agricultural resources, may be compelled to accept civilization, and surrender a portion of their domain to those who need. Their property-right is very slender, and may be extinguished sometimes against their will, but not to their real disadvantage.[30]

On international law he had this to say:

When long-continued civil strife in a nation interferes with the quiet and prosperity of other nations, these nations may have the right to compel its cessation. The propriety of the intervention will depend upon the probable results.[31]

And the paternalism of his teleological view was made explicit in his view that college administrators function *in loco parentis*.[32]

Fairchild's practical concerns contrast in a strange way with those of Bentham and Mill and illustrate beautifully the fact that there is little or no connection between concepts of moral law and commitments on specific moral issues. Utility for Bentham and Mill was a great instrument for reform, a weapon against entrenched interests defended by advocates of the conscience theory. At Oberlin, however, Fairchild was the utilitarian in theory and the conservative on practical issues, whereas Asa Mahan was the great defender of conscience theory and the ardent reformer.

6

OBERLIN REFORM

I

ASA MAHAN was Oberlin's strongest advocate of organized reform. Finney, as an evangelist and revivalist, felt that there is only one basic reform from which all others naturally flow. Convert the sinner to the ways of God, and you have regenerated his soul. Then, out of love for man and God, out of the new benevolence that is awakened in him, he will change his own behavior. He will no longer hold slaves, wage wars, indulge in vile personal habits, and so on. To be fair to Finney it is necessary to point out that he did not pursue this doctrine to an absurd extreme. He considered regeneration of souls the basic reform but was not unwilling to work directly for specific reforms as long as such activity did not interfere with basic reform. He preached occasionally against slavery, but he was never sufficiently dedicated to antislavery work to satisfy people like Lewis Tappan and Theodore Weld.[1] He even counseled Oberlin students not to become antislavery lecturers because this work would divert them from the basic reform activity, namely, preaching the word of God evangelically.[2]

Asa Mahan, on the other hand, during his fifteen years as president and professor of moral philosophy, was Oberlin's chief spokesman for organized reform movements. He was interested in revivals and evangelical preaching, but he never looked upon them as a cure-all in the way Finney did. His series of articles on "Reform" which appeared in the *Oberlin Evangelist* in 1844 is probably the best statement of the reform principles taught in his moral science class and practiced by the majority of people in the Oberlin community, by students, teachers, and townspeople alike. Oberlin as a center of reform movements far transcended the work of any of its leaders.

According to Mahan, the Christian reformer follows a reasonable alternative between conservatism and radicalism.[3] He did not advocate the *status quo* simply because it would cause trouble to fight abuses or because it had been advocated by the founding fathers, nor did he demand the immediate cessation of evil or the dissolution of existing institutions. Christian reformers, he thought, should be moderate, practical men working for "the correction of existing abuses, and the conformity of all institutions, domestic, civil, and ecclesiastical, to the fundamental ideas of universal reason, and the pattern on the mount." [4] The reformer, moreover, should never be dogmatic. Enthusiasm for the truth must never be allowed to become fanaticism. While he was president of Oberlin, Mahan introduced the practice, which became a permanent characteristic of the college, of hearing all sides of every case. Hence it was that Stephen Foster, Abby Kelley Foster, Frederick Douglass, and William Lloyd Garrison had their day at Oberlin.

The Fosters came to Oberlin in February, 1846, but they did not make a favorable impression.[5] In fact they were not met very hospitably since their meetings interrupted a revival meeting already in progress. They asked to come again in the fall, and the Oberlinites reluctantly agreed. In September one discussion between Foster and Mahan on the value of the Union lasted twelve hours, and there was a good deal of *ad hominem* argument on both sides. Garrison himself and Frederick Douglass came to Oberlin in 1847. This meeting was far more amicable—perhaps because it did not last so long. Garrison was entertained by Hamilton Hill and Professor Timothy Hudson, and he and Mahan remained unruffled on the platform. Garrison wrote to his wife that Mahan "was perfectly respectful, and submitted to our interrogations with good temper and courtesy. As a disputant, he is adroit and plausible, but neither vigorous nor profound. . . ." [6] But the Oberlin audience did not agree with the last statement. One member of the audience wrote that "the reply of Prest. Mahan was masterly and dignified, overturning and scattering to the winds every position of his opponent." [7]

Garrison, of course, was radical in precisely the ways Mahan deplored. Garrison found the Christian Church and the United States Constitution equally obnoxious because they were the dominant institutions in a society that permitted slavery not only to exist but even to expand. Garrison believed in renouncing both institutions and solving the problem of slavery by secession. He refused to believe that any significant step toward abolition could be taken through established political channels or through new channels allowed within the framework of the Constitution. Mahan, on the other hand, believed that the Christian Church, particularly through agencies like the American Missionary Association, could be made into a great antislavery instrument. And he believed that the Constitution was a great antislavery document that had been misrepresented by vested interests and corrupt judges. Moreover, Mahan, like the other Oberlin leaders, while he was a staunch supporter of peace movements, was not a complete pacifist like Garrison. Force is legitimate, Mahan believed,[8] when no other course is open and it is exercised in a righteous cause.

Garrison was not certain of the real impression he had made at Oberlin, but he said he was "abundantly satisfied" with the apparent effect.[9] In fact, he had almost no real support whatever at Oberlin except among women student leaders. Lucy Stone, Betsy Cowles, and Sallie Holley, strong advocates of equal rights for women, were all followers of Garrison's brand of abolitionism. They were, of course, favorably impressed by Garrison in the first place because he also believed in the complete equality of men and women—unlike their Oberlin professors, although here, as always, Mahan was the most radical of the Oberlinites, going further in the direction of women's rights than any of the other Oberlin leaders.

II

A possible criticism of a middle-ground view of reform like Mahan's is that it is not really a third alternative at all but is a practical equivalent of the conservative view. Mahan was willing to work for the gradual removal of evils, and he was willing to achieve his goals through established political channels or through permissible new ones. But gradualism, the criticism goes, is practically equivalent to the conservative's demand that nothing be done, since the gradualist is always "beginning to begin." And "working through established political channels," or "creating new ones," is practically equivalent to the conservative demand that nothing be done, since these channels were expressly provided to go nowhere on the issue of slavery. This criticism unfortunately is often true, but it is extremely important to see that it need not be true and assuredly does not apply to Mahan and the majority of people in the Oberlin community. The Oberlin view and practice of reform, most notably in the case of abolition, was exceedingly effective and was a living refutation of Garrison's viewpoint. Mahan's antislavery views, exemplified wholeheartedly in the activities of the Oberlin community, never degenerated into the practical equivalent of conservatism. It remained a genuine third alternative. To put the matter paradoxically, it remained a genuine alternative because within the context of their middle ground the Oberlinites were extremely radical.

The radical activity of the Oberlin community began early and took many forms. The most important was the refounding of the Oberlin Collegiate Institute in 1835 as a school that admitted Negroes to higher education on equal terms with fellow white students and permitted the free discussion of antislavery viewpoints.[10] John Jay Shipherd had founded Oberlin in 1833, and he saw the chance of turning it into a really significant institution in 1835 by attracting to it the famous evangelist Finney and the "Rebels" from the Lane Theological Seminary in Cincinnati. The Rebels, upheld by Mahan, left Lane because they were ordered to desist from abolition discussion. But none of these people would come to Oberlin unless Oberlin became a fully integrated college. Shipherd and John Keep managed to convince the trustees to admit Negroes to Oberlin, though the margin of victory was narrow. Thus Finney, Mahan, and the Lane Rebels came, and the Oberlin brand of abolitionism began in earnest. The middle-ground abolitionism advocated by Mahan was pursued in four different ways: through (1) anti-slavery societies, (2) a militant church, (3) political channels, and (4) civil disobedience.

1. In June, 1835, only months after the decision to admit Negroes to the institute, the Oberlin community formed an antislavery society with 230 members.[11] The membership grew even while new societies were formed: the Young Ladies' Anti-Slavery Society, the Female Anti-Slavery Society, and the Young Men's Anti-Slavery Society. Oberlin leaders were active in the formation of the Ohio Anti-Slavery Society. At the first meeting in Granville, where the hostility of the townspeople forced them to meet in a barn, James A. Thome, a Lane Rebel, Professor Cowles, and President Mahan spoke on various abolition themes. James G. Birney also spoke, and the Oberlin people heartily shared his views that slavery should be fought through political means. In 1837 Mahan was elected one of the Ohio managers of the American Anti-Slavery Society. "When the National Society split in 1840 most Oberlinites went with the Anti-Garrisonian wing which became the American and Foreign Anti-Slavery Society."[12] At the World's Anti-Slavery Convention in London in 1840 John Keep represented the Oberlin community, and at the international convention three years later, again in London, Amasa Walker, professor of political economy, was the delegate of the Oberlin Collegiate Institute and the Ohio Anti-Slavery Society.

In the early years, through the influence particularly of Theodore Weld, Oberlin furnished a number of lecturers and agents for the American Anti-Slavery Society and other societies. In 1835 Weld conducted a school for antislavery lecturers at Oberlin. Other Lane Rebels like Thome were his most devoted followers. Through the years fewer Oberlin students became "professional" antislavery lecturers, some being dissuaded from the task by Finney, who wanted to push revivalism and regeneration of the soul instead, but most being persuaded that they could better further the goal of abolition by teaching, founding schools for free Negroes, founding schools for runaway slaves in Canada, working through the American Missionary Association, distributing antislavery tracts, and preaching antislavery goals and methods in the pulpit. The genius of Oberlin in the antislavery movement was that almost every graduate of the institute carried forward the message and work of abolition in whatever occupation he subsequently followed.

2. Garrison looked upon the church as utterly hopeless, but the Oberlinites were leaders in the effort to turn it into a militant antislavery instrument. The Presbyterian and Congregational churches, as we have seen, were united under the Plan of Union until the 1830's when Oberlin and many other churches became wholly congregational.[13] The reasons for the split were numerous, but not least among them was the conservative attitude toward slavery and distaste for abolitionism among the orthodox Calvinists. On the Western Reserve the split was strikingly symbolized by the contrasting views of Western Reserve College at Hudson and Oberlin. "Orthodox Calvinism, the Plan of Union, conservatism with regard to the reforms of the day, distrust of revivalism, and Western Reserve College were on one side; Sanctification, Congregationalism, enthusiasm for reform, 'new measures,' and Oberlin were on the other."[14]

The Oberlin Church used numerous religious sanctions in its antislavery crusade. No slaveholder could preach or commune in the church, no transfer would be given to any church which was not antislavery, and after 1846 all fellowship was withdrawn from any people who would "lend their influence to sustain slavery."[15] The church was not denominational in a narrow sense and cooperated fully with the antislavery elements in other denominations, particularly with the Freewill Baptists and the Wesleyan Methodists. The antislavery church was in a real sense wholly nondenominational.

The Oberlin community withdrew its support from any Christian benevolent society, like the American Board of Commissioners for Foreign Missions and the American Tract Society, which was uncommitted and even unsympathetic to antislavery work. Oberlin leaders helped to found an organization that would remedy this deficiency, and thus the American Missionary Association was established.[16] Until 1860 over 90 per cent of its workers were former Oberlin students, and both of its executive secretaries—George Whipple, a Lane Rebel, and Michael Strieby—came from Oberlin.

The association published the strongly antislavery *American Missionary;* helped finance the Negro schools in Canada founded by Hiram Wilson, another Oberlinite; trained antislavery ministers; distributed antislavery tracts, particularly in the Middle West and Kentucky; provided weekday lectures and debates on the slavery issue; and actively worked to prevent extension of slavery to the territories. The association sent antislavery missionaries to the troubled areas of Kansas and exhorted ministers to speak on the duty of Christian emigration. Again the Kansas missionaries were frequently Oberlin men.

Finally, the Oberlin church strongly supported the Christian Anti-Slavery Conventions. It was important, Mahan felt, to have some strictly Christian antislavery society to offset the notion that abolitionism was exclusively the affair of nonbelievers and atheists like Garrison. In 1850 the Christian Anti-Slavery Convention met in Mahan's old church in Cincinnati, the Vine Street Church, previously the Sixth Presbyterian.[17] In 1851 the convention met in Chicago, and Finney and Mahan were elected vice-presidents and George Whipple was named one of the secretaries. Oberlin men tried to keep the movement alive, but by 1854 it had lost most of its force since by that time direct action was required in Kansas. In 1859 there was again an Ohio convention, and Oberlin men again predominated. But the cast had changed by now. Mahan had left Oberlin under unpleasant conditions, and Henry Everard Peck was the leader of the Oberlin College antislavery forces.

Peck was the outstanding orator as well as the hero of the hour because of his late experience in the Oberlin-Wellington Rescue Case. The convention was definitely a "higher law" convention, insisting that no man-made law was binding if it conflicted with God-made law; it stood for "No communion with slaveholders and no obedience to the Fugitive Slave Law." [18]

III

From 1835 until the Civil War the Oberlinites, as we have seen, spoke the truth about slavery as they saw it, but they never thought, as Francis Wayland did in his earlier years, that this mild antislavery effort was man's only duty. Even Finney, who believed that the regeneration of the soul is the fundamental reform, thought that action was necessary to meet fully man's responsibility to the antislavery movement. We have seen some of the typical Oberlin projects pursued through antislavery societies and the church, but these projects were, by and large, moderate compared with the Oberlin political activity and tactics of civil disobedience.[19]

The genius of the Oberlinites, a genius Wayland lacked, lay in their ability to act strongly in the first place and not because the onrush of political events eventually forced them to do so. They were not pushed into political activity and civil disobedience by the crush of public events but were willing to meet a difficulty where God had put it in the first place.[20] They were in open rebellion already against the Ohio Fugitive Slave Law of 1839. By the time other Americans were aroused by the federal law in 1850 the Oberlinites were veterans of passive—and sometimes not so passive—resistance. They were not fanatics who believed that any means were justified in the war against slavery, but they did believe that it was man's duty to do whatever had a reasonable chance of advancing the antislavery crusade.

Some of the students no doubt looked upon antislavery activity as a lark, and for others in the town it was a matter of momentary enthusiasm. But these groups constituted a very small minority. The sustained nature of the Oberlin antislavery movement shows beyond doubt that it was the result not of playfulness or enthusiasm but of deliberate dedication to what the Oberlin community took to be its duty. The Oberlinites were utterly matter of fact about following the demands of the Scriptures and their collective conscience. Duty required political activity and civil disobedience, and duty had to be met as a matter of course.

3. The majority of Oberlinites were originally Whigs, but they quickly became disillusioned.[21] In 1839 many members of the Whig party in the Ohio legislature, including the member elected by Oberlin votes, helped enact a strong fugitive slave law. As a result, the formation of a new political party was advocated at a meeting of the American Anti-Slavery Society in Cleveland. Both Mahan and Finney spoke in favor of this proposal. Later an antislavery nominating convention was held in Albany (April, 1840), and James G. Birney was nominated for President. The Liberal party had been formed, and the Oberlin leaders supported it in various ways. In 1848 Mahan attended the Buffalo convention when the Free Soil party was organized and Martin Van Buren nominated for President and Charles Francis Adams for Vice President. The Oberlin people were partial to Adams. Again the Oberlin leaders supported this antislavery third party, and they carried almost the whole of the community with them this time.

From the beginning Oberlin was a solid antislavery element in the new Republican party. Professors James Monroe and Henry Peck campaigned for Fremont throughout northern Ohio, and the Oberlin community voted virtually unanimously for Republican candidates. Oberlin supported Ohio Republicans like Joshua Giddings—who, as we shall see, along with George Curtis, played an important role in the Republican Convention of 1860—and produced leaders of its own like Monroe. When he came to Oberlin, Monroe had been a follower of Garrison, but he was quickly converted to the Oberlin view of reform. He represented Lorain County in the Ohio Assembly until 1860 and was a state senator from 1860 to 1862. According to Fletcher, "his outstanding achievement was the passage of the Habeus Corpus Act in 1856, an act whose purpose was to counteract the effect of the Federal Fugitive Slave Law." [22]

When the political battle centered in Kansas, Oberlin leaders (except for James H. Fairchild), unlike Wayland, had no hesitation whatever in advocating the Christian duty of emigration. The men of Oberlin organized the Kansas Emigration Aid Association of Northern Ohio, and this organization sent out small groups to Kansas in 1855 and larger ones the following year.[23] The company under the lead of Oberlinite Samuel N. Wood was well supplied with Beecher's Bibles and was attacked in the sacking of Lawrence. The association sent altogether over several hundred settlers to Kansas—some of whom, no doubt, would have gone anyway but not as easily. The propaganda value of the effort, in addition to its direct effect, was very great.

4. The Oberlin brand of civil disobedience began in 1835, when the college was refounded, and continued until the outbreak of the Civil War. John Keep, perhaps the greatest Oberlinite of all—always in the background as a trustee but always the one who held Oberlin together—phrased the Oberlin view of civil disobedience simply and dispassionately. He wrote in 1850:

> The individual must still use his own intellect and his own moral faculty, to decide for himself the path of his duty. He may owe to a court the most respectful consideration and pondering of its decisions; but when to his mind, after careful, candid examination, God appears to decide against the Court, he must act accordingly and submit peacefully to the penalty, if he cannot honorably evade it.[24]

The most frequent manifestation of civil disobedience in Oberlin was the flouting of all fugitive slave laws, state or federal. Oberlin was an extremely important part of the Underground Railroad.[25] Through the years many hundreds of runaway slaves found shelter in Oberlin, some staying indefinitely and others stopping only long enough for arrangements to be made for their passage to Canada. Oberlin had the incredible record of never losing a single runaway slave to officers of the law. The whole Oberlin community cooperated in this type of civil disobedience. "Fugitive slaves were regularly cared for in Oberlin out of Russia Township funds." [26]

Some members of the community were disobedient in more militant ways. In the autumn of 1839 Professor Thome had to go into hiding temporarily because of the role he had played in preventing an aged Negress in Kentucky from being sold into slavery.[27] And three Oberlin students even invaded the South and helped slaves escape to Illinois. George Thompson and

Calvin Fairbank were apprehended in this activity and spent substantial terms in prison. While the majority of people in the community did not approve of these radical activities at the time, they came, by 1864, to look upon Fairbank as something of a hero.[28]

The most famous and influential instance of Oberlin civil disobedience was the Wellington Rescue Case of 1858.[29] A runaway slave named John was captured and quickly taken to Wellington. John and his captors stayed at the Wadsworth House waiting for the next train out of northern Ohio. Students, faculty, and townspeople, hearing the news, spontaneously rushed to Wellington and through sheer numbers managed to rescue John without violence. But federal authority had been blatantly flouted, and the United States District Court of Cleveland took immediate action. Numerous Oberlinites were indicted, including Professor Henry Peck, associate professor of intellectual and moral philosophy, and James M. Fitch, superintendent of the Oberlin Sunday School. The arrest and trial attracted international attention, since the prosecution, wanting to vindicate the Administration, made a big issue of the Wellington Rescue Case, while the Oberlinites, wanting to arouse public opinion against the Fugitive Slave Law, dramatized their position as much as possible.

The Oberlinites used their incarceration in the Cleveland jail to good advantage. The jailer fortunately was friendly to them and allowed unrestricted visiting privileges. Professor Peck was allowed to preach to a congregation in the jail yard. And the Oberlin Sunday School went en masse to the jail one Sunday and were taught by Mr. Fitch! The leaders of the Republican party encouraged the Oberlinites and made political capital out of the trial. They staged an antislavery mass meeting in the Cleveland Public Square in front of the jail yard. Resolutions were passed and addresses were delivered by former President Mahan, Joshua Giddings, and Governor Salmon P. Chase.

The Oberlin community, however, had no intention of permitting the Wellington Rescuers to be sacrificed. The four slave-catchers were indicted for kidnaping before the Common Pleas Court of Lorain County. Clearly this court would be as completely Republican as the Cleveland court was completely Democratic. An exchange of convictions was the last thing the Southerners wanted, so both indictments were dropped and an exchange of prisoners was effected. The genius of the Oberlin group, again, was that it always operated from a position of strength. The Oberlinites were never helpless martyrs. They were expert strategists and tacticians who operated from a competitive interpretation of the law and not from lawlessness.

At the time the trial of the rescuers was in progress John Brown was visiting Ohio making preparations for his raid on Harper's Ferry.[30] One of his lieutenants, J. H. Kagi, visited the rescuers in jail. In August of 1859 John Brown, Jr., visited Oberlin, and it is likely that at this time he recruited two Oberlin Negroes, Lewis Sheridan Leary and John A. Copeland, for the raid. Leary was killed in the raid at Harper's Ferry in October, and Copeland was executed on December 16 for his participation. Professor Peck preached Copeland's funeral sermon on Christmas Day of 1859. The Oberlin community tried unsuccessfully to recover Copeland's body for burial in the Oberlin cemetery. It was clear that most Oberlinites, unlike James Fairchild, warmly sympathized with Brown and his followers. On the day of Brown's execution the chapel bell tolled for an hour, and Peck and other Oberlin leaders addressed the mass meeting on the greatness of Brown. The judgment of the student magazine was that Professor Peck had surpassed himself in eloquence. Peck, Thome, Monroe, Leary, and Copeland were the men of the hour at Oberlin.

The Oberlin attitude toward Brown seems perplexing in some ways since Brown represented anything but the middle-ground abolitionism that always characterized Oberlin. The following relevant facts, however, cast light on the matter. As a result of the younger Brown's visit, Lewis Leary asked Ralph Plumb to collect money to be used in "assisting slaves to escape." Plumb was able to collect only $17.50 for him.[31] Such behavior hardly suggests any serious support for Brown in Oberlin. After Brown's failure, capture, and death, however, many Oberlinites found in him great symbolic value and moral rectitude. Brown became symbolic of absolute justice—of the demand for immediate cessation of evil. One might not be able to follow the demands of absolute justice—and most Oberlinites thought it was not possible—but this fact, they felt, should not keep one from loving and admiring the pure voice of conscience. There were, of course, some in Oberlin who felt that Brown was objectively right in what he did, but they were in the minority. And there was one in Oberlin, namely, James Fairchild, who felt that Brown was objectively wrong in what he did because the likely consequences of it were clearly catastrophic—a probability borne out by subsequent events. Fairchild, apparently, did not realize that on his own view he should have taken into account the probable symbolic and emotional consequences of Brown's acts. The difficulty in judging the probable nature of second-order consequences is a difficulty inherent in every teleological position.

IV

After the Civil War, Oberlin College and the community were no longer a haven of civil disobedience. It might be said that Oberlin had won its point on abolitionism, and there was no longer any need for it; yet this would not be the whole story. Oberlin, in fact, after the Civil War became systematically conservative and conformed to all the required attitudes of jingoism and manifest destiny.[32] The explanation of the change—like so many explanations of Oberlin—lies in the conflicting personalities and beliefs of the Oberlin leaders. Mahan and Peck were the uncompromising reformers; Finney was a radical but unintentionally lent his support to conservative tendencies; and James H. Fairchild was the culmination of the conservative tendencies.

Mahan, as we have seen, formulated the official Oberlin middle-ground view of reform, and he was the leading Oberlin abolitionist until he left in 1850. He was also the author of Oberlin's radical view of sanctification; and, along with Professor Thome, he was willing to go much further than the rest of the Oberlin faculty in granting equal privileges to women. In addition he was the strongest advocate of the peace movement. Mahan was indeed the "No. 1 irreconcilable Oberlinite," [33] and his departure in 1850 could not but reduce the reformist zeal of Oberlin.

Finney apparently agreed with Mahan on reform principles, but his usefulness was blunted because he subordinated all his reformist work to what he considered the fundamental one of converting everybody to Christianity. Finney was always dashing off to conduct revivals even after he was appointed president of Oberlin in 1850. His frequent absences lent themselves to the development of conservative tendencies. While he was gone the conservative influences of John Morgan and James Fairchild were extremely influential in the affairs of the college.

Henry Everard Peck carried on, in a sense, the radical views of Mahan at Oberlin. He was a faculty member from 1851 to 1865 and, as we have seen, became identified, along with James Monroe, as the leading Oberlin abolitionist. Little is known about him, unfortunately, and we have only tantalizing descriptions like the following to whet our appetite for more information: "A radical and something of an eccentric, he was not always in perfect agreement with the more conservative members of the faculty." [34] Peck died in Haiti in 1867 where he was serving as minister of the United States, a position to which he was appointed immediately following the Civil War. With the passing of Peck steps toward conformity at Oberlin became easier, and they were quickly taken.

The great trend toward conservatism at Oberlin came with the election of Fairchild to the presidency.[35] The position was first offered to James Monroe, and had he accepted it the future of Oberlin, no doubt, would have been different from what it turned out to be under Fairchild. But Monroe refused, and Fairchild became the third president of Oberlin. As president his influence was largely toward conservatism, and this influence was not a surprise to those who knew him well. His conservatism had been quite evident in the past when he severely criticized Calvin Fairbank for his efforts to help slaves escape. What is more surprising is his lack of enthusiasm about Kansas emigration. One who admires Fairchild can explain the lack of enthusiasm by saying that he objected only to hastily made plans for emigration. One who does not admire Fairchild asks for evidence that Fairchild helped lay any better plans. He also held a minority opinion that Brown was morally wrong in demanding that absolute justice be met. Absolute justice, as far as Fairchild was concerned, was injustice.[36]

Fairchild, it is true, participated in the Wellington Rescue by concealing the slave John in his home for three days, but this action must not be construed to modify or qualify his conservatism. He kept the slave because he was asked to do so. One cannot help suspecting that the rescuers left John in Fairchild's home precisely because to an outsider it would seem like an unlikely place. Fairchild, Fletcher says, "represented a reaction against the zealous reformism and heresy of the early days." [37] One who admires Fairchild sees the third president as a savior, who rescued Oberlin radicalism from becoming mere raving. One who does not wholly admire Fairchild may point out that there are other ways of preventing ideology from becoming raving than by destroying it.

7

THE TRANSCENDENTALISTS

I

IN the 1880's scholars were busily occupied trying to pinpoint Emerson's significance—was he a great literary figure or a great philosopher? Lecturing in Boston in 1883 Matthew Arnold dared to suggest that he was neither; rather he was a seer, a prophet, a recorder of spiritual truth, a great teacher and helper of those who would live in the spirit.[1] The lecture caused a good deal of unfavorable comment among the admirers of Emerson and favorable comment from those he had not enchanted—"Well, I am glad to hear that! I never *did* think much of Emerson!"[2] The latter response clearly did justice neither to Emerson nor Arnold. Arnold was right in his main thesis—Emerson was not a *great* writer, and certainly he did not present a series of propositions and arguments which, taken together, could be called a philosophical *system*—and he was right in characterizing Emerson as a seer and prophet.

Unfortunately, Arnold erred in not getting across the nature and feel of Emerson's greatness as a seer. James Bradley Thayer, Emerson's attorney and cousin by marriage, thought

Arnold's comparison of Emerson to Marcus Aurelius particularly unfortunate in conveying the essence of Emerson's greatness. Marcus Aurelius was not a man possessed with a sense of the divine as Emerson was.[3] The real trouble with Arnold's lecture, he thought, was that he appeared to speak from a funded enthusiasm rather than from a fresh and present apprehension of what Emerson wrote and said.

Emerson himself would have agreed readily that he was neither a poet nor a philosopher. The pure poet spends too much time on the vehicles of his metaphors and not enough on their content. Thayer spoke for Emerson when he said:

So long as he could make, to use his own phrase, "a clean transcript of his own mind" . . . he would not imperil the freshness and truth of it by any effort at a literary setting, by elaborating the approaches to it, or attending to its due evolution, or seeking to bring his reader safely and gently back again to earth.[4]

And Emerson happily admitted he was no philosopher. The mutual consistency of claims and arguments to support them seemed irrelevant to the intuitive truths he wanted to announce. And yet, with great insight, he said to a friend, "I never was a metaphysician, but I have observed the operation of my faculties for a long time and noted them, and no metaphysician can afford to do without what I have to say." [5]

II

While he did not discuss in detail the concept of substance, Emerson nevertheless was an idealist in the sense that he denied the reality of physical substance and insisted that only mental or spiritual substance is ultimately real. The physical world, he said, is only phenomenal—"one vast picture which God paints on the instant eternity for the contemplation of the soul." [6] True, people in everyday life intuit, they think, the absolute existence of the physical world, but, Emerson claimed, the unreliability of perception shows this popular faith to be wrong. Moreover, the drift of all thought—in religion, ethics, art, and science—conspires to suggest the existence of a single, mental substance. The dualism which Emerson discusses and allowed,[7] and which subsequently misled some commentators,[8] is not the technical belief in two irreducible substances but simply the contrast between the phenomenal status of the external world and the substantial nature of the soul and oversoul. The confusion has been compounded because the term "dualism" has been used indiscriminately for almost every dichotomy in Emerson's thought—the difference between finite and infinite, relative and absolute, the soul and natural man; the conflict of good and evil, and so forth—in addition to the difference between appearance and reality.

On the problem of substance Emerson showed a curious inconsistency, which presumably would not have bothered him but is likely to disturb anyone else. Emerson routed the ordinary intuition of an independently existing external world—naïve realism—by reasons, but he thought reasons in support of his own intuitions were irrelevant. Apparently he allowed the critical function of reason to operate on some intuitions but not on others. This procedure is convenient but hardly fair. Emerson never faced up to the central problem that some criterion is required to validate true intuitions, since intuitions themselves give conflicting results.

The sources of Emerson's specific brand of "spiritualistic idealism" are numerous and include at least Platonism, Neoplatonism, German romanticism, and certain of Swedenborg's notions. The key to his idealism is his view of language and metaphor. Every metaphor, Emerson thought, literally describes some spiritual fact or announces some spiritual truth. "Every appearance in nature corresponds to some state of the mind, and that state of the mind can only be described by presenting that natural appearance as its picture." [9] This radical correspondence between visible things and thoughts, however, is not a poetic fancy but stems from the nature of ultimate reality. Things correspond to human thoughts because they themselves have a spiritual or moral side and origin; they are material manifestations of Spirit or God created according to His necessary and immutable ideas. [10] Emerson sometimes made this point by using the Neoplatonic concept of emanation—"a fact," he was fond of saying, "is the end or last issue of Spirit." [11] And, as always, he would leave it to his reader to unravel the epigram.

Had he found that many readers are unable to resist such flattery?

Following Coleridge closely, Emerson distinguished sharply the concepts of understanding and reason. The term "Understanding" referred to the capacity to apprehend the empirical and practical truths of science and ordinary life, while the term "Reason" referred to man's capacity to grasp the ultimate metaphysical truths of Spirit. According to Emerson, nature disciplines man's understanding by revealing to him specific moral truths—"a rolling stone gathers no moss"—while nature disciplines man's reason by revealing the whole correspondence between thought and things—by revealing, in short, the very essences of the spiritual philosophy. By perceiving the analogy that marries Matter and Mind, Emerson wrote, man learns the ultimate lesson of nature, namely, the unity of the Universal Spirit. We are all fragments of the divine, and hence each one implies all others and the whole. And the unity extends to thoughts as well as things: "Every universal truth which we express in words, implies or supposes every other truth." [12]

Emerson's epistemology is a simple intuitionism that follows straightforwardly from his idealistic commitments. Since each individual is an incarnation of the universal mind, or God, he can only know the truth by heeding this universal mind within himself. If he strives for truth by relying on convention, historical authority, or the judgments of others, he will not gain it. Second-handedness for Emerson, as for all the transcendentalists, was the cardinal sin. While the individual intuition is the origin of truth, however, the truth itself is not partial or particular. Each fragment of the divine, if uncorrupted by sensuous distraction, will hear the universal truth. "Speak your latent conviction, and it shall be the universal sense; for the inmost in due time becomes the outmost, and our first thought is rendered back to us by the trumpets of the Last Judgment." [13]

Emerson's view of the origin of truth, of course, quickly encounters the problem of the distorted intuition. How can one decide whether or not any intuitive deliverance is genuinely spiritual or a distortion of reality? There are only too many intuitionists who proclaim as right the most outrageous and inhuman maxims imaginable. In spite of his sneering attitude toward critical analysis, Emerson was not unaware of the problem and tried to resolve it. In later essays and in later entries in his journal he indicated that he came to appreciate more the vulnerability of the individual's conscience and recognized the need of collective opinion as a correcting influence. This crucial counterpoise, continuously formulated, tested, and transmuted, is Culture:

> Culture is the suggestion, from certain best thoughts, that a man has a range of affinities through which he can modulate the violence of any master-tones that have a droning preponderance in the scale, and succor him against himself. . . . Culture kills his exaggeration, his conceit of his village or his city. We must leave our pets at home when we go into the street, and meet men on broad grounds of good meaning and good sense.[14]

But culture, Emerson warned, should only purify the individual intuition, not replace it. One must stay on guard against second-handedness. Thus he reasserted his main thesis in the act of modifying it. Still the modification is important for the internal origin is now only a necessary criterion of truth, not a sufficient one, as it was in the original essay on "Self-Reliance."

Moreover, Emerson realized that generally, or perhaps always, there is no one individual who consistently has the pure or reliable intuition. Most men have their sane moments, but what is tragic is that all men have insane ones also. The true individual is an abstraction, exemplified not by any individual but by all of us in our best moments. The genuine impulses of virtue, Emerson felt, "are not so much to be found in a few eminent preachers, as in the better hours, the truer inspirations of all,—nay, in the sincere moments of every man." [15] Thoreau echoed the same sentiment when he wrote that "conscience not only divides states and churches, it divides families; aye, it divides the *individual,* separating the diabolical in him from the divine." [16]

The immediate corollary of Emerson's intuitionism and self-reliance is his concept of nonconformity. When the will of others, the majority will included, conflicts with the deliverance of a man's conscience, then he must stand in opposition. "Who-so would be a man, must be a nonconformist." [17] And yet Emerson never believed that nonconformity is desirable in itself. Ideally, if everyone heeded the call of the spirit, there would be a community of thought and action which, rationally and internally instituted, would be just, as well as common. It is a contingent fact that this is not so, and so the self-reliant man must speak against his fellows. But even when he speaks against a man there ought to be no breach in the solidarity of emotional life. The self-reliant man certainly ought not to exult in his opposition, at least not in its necessity, for ideally it ought not to be.

The interesting question arises, of course, of whether or not Emerson was true to the demands of his own theory. Generally I believe he was. He always insisted that the point of self-reliance is not behavior of an odd or idiosyncratic kind. Imagine, he wrote, the chaos in the railroad industry if each company used a gauge and car wheel all its own! The same point holds for the moral world: a world would be impossible if each individual invented his own rules of conduct and manners, and there were no universal moral guides. "There must be concert, there must be compromise, if you call it so." [18] He was often critical of Thoreau's behavior precisely because it made concerted moral action impossible even among self-reliant men whose intuitions of justice coincided.

If I knew only Thoreau, I should think cooperation of good men impossible. Must we always talk for victory, and never once for truth, for comfort, and joy? [19]

Henry is military . . . stubborn and implacable; always manly and wise, but rarely sweet. One would say that, as Webster could never speak without an antagonist, so Henry does not feel himself except in opposition.[20]

As for taking Thoreau's arm, I should as soon take the arm of an elm tree.[21]

Emerson clearly did not reject the ideals of cooperative moral action, compromise, and sympathetic fellow-feeling. Still, one might object, he did value solitude and isolation highly, and this appears to run counter, at least, to any high valuation of cooperation and fellow-feeling. All geniuses, Emerson wrote,[22] feel the necessity of solitude; and "the moment we meet with anybody, each becomes a fraction." Genuine understanding is a will-o'-the-wisp, he felt, and loneliness is eternal. But such solitude, Emerson also said,[23] no metaphysics can make right or tolerable; sympathy and affection are also deep urges of man and are useful in many ways. "Nothing but God is self-dependent. Man is powerful only by the multitude of his affinities." [24]

Emerson denied that the values of either solitude or society are absolute and said that the skill of living consists in subtly adjusting the claims of the two. "The conditions are met, if we keep our independence, yet do not lose our sympathy." [25] When he wrote for the public he often emphasized the values of solitude by way of needed emphasis. When he saw Thoreau, however, he felt the need of emphasis the other way. Getting away from people rather than getting on with them—even when their consciences revealed the same values—seemed to Emerson a peculiar way for a transcendentalist to act. He observed that Thoreau chose wisely for himself, no doubt, to be a bachelor of thought and nature—near to the old monks in their esthetic religion! [26] But he wrote, "I hear the account of the man who lives in the wilderness of Maine with respect, but with despair. . . . I tell him that a man was not made to live in a swamp, but a frog." [27]

III

Two of the most interesting corollaries of Emerson's intuitionism are a critique of historical religion and a defense of civil disobedience. They are equally corollaries of Parker's brand of transcendentalism; and, as we shall see, he extended them beyond what Emerson was willing to claim.

Since he believed that every individual is an incarnation of the Universal Spirit, Emerson thought every man, and not Christ only, is partly divine. Historical Christianity, unfortunately, ignores the doctrine of the oversoul and insists on the divinity of Christ as if it were a unique historical event. Historical Christianity "has dwelt, it dwells, with noxious exaggeration about the *person* of Jesus." [28] The church, Emerson felt, had lost the intuitive basis of truth, mistakenly thinking that Christ's words and divinity must be authenticated by miracles and revelation. When Jesus spoke of miracles, however, he really meant that all life is a miracle. And when the apostles claimed to be inspired they simply meant that all men were inspired. But the church changed Christ's meaning, turning "miracle" into "monster" and "inspiration" into "ritual." Emerson counseled Christian ministers to replace authority with spiritual insights of their own, to eschew coldness and formality, and to have a faith like Christ's rather than a faith in Christ. He urged ministers with liberal tendencies to remain within the church and make use of the instruments that Christianity already provides.

Emerson's critique created quite a sensation in the Boston area.[29] He had said these things to the graduating class at the Harvard Divinity School in 1838. Many professors at the school, and the Unitarian clergy in general, were terrified that such utterances might seem to be condoned by Unitarianism. While Unitarians themselves had led the fight against Calvinistic orthodoxy, nevertheless they retained much of the traditional faith. While Christ was not a deity, he was "a messenger supernaturally and uniquely endowed and sent as a special, indispensable revelation to man." [30] Moreover, the Scriptures are a source of infallible authority, and miracles are a sign of the authenticity of the revelation. Given these views, of course, the Unitarians were not likely to be happy with Emerson's address, but they reacted in quite different ways.[31]

Andrews Norton, Dexter Professor of Biblical Literature at Harvard, reacted most violently, and he has ever since been looked upon as a model of orthodoxy and illiberality. Such an appraisal is not wholly correct, for Emerson and Parker were not the unmixed heroes of the Unitarian Controversy which many historians, partial to their cause, make them out to be. After the publication of Emerson's address, Norton excoriated it in the pages of the *Boston Advertiser*. He wrote of the "craving for notoriety" exhibited by members of the New School and disparaged their ideas as the result of uncritical perusal of obscure German philosophers. The vehemence of his reply embarrassed many of the other Unitarians and puzzled them, since Norton was ordinarily a mild-mannered person, much liked personally and highly respected as a scholar. The explanation of the vehemence, however, if not its excuse, can be readily found in Norton's scholarly reputation. He valued above all else this reputation, which he had made in vindicating the authenticity of the Gospels; and, rightly or wrongly, he construed the transcendental attack on Unitarianism as an attack on his scholarship.

Norton, his critics also pointed out, strangely offered no argument to refute Emerson. But this response only showed that they missed the point of Norton's not wholly unjustifiable irritation at Emerson. What irritated him did not require argument. He simply thought it self-evident that to be legitimately called a Christian one had to believe that Christ was uniquely divine. Believe what you will—but why use language so loosely that anyone can count as a Christian as long as he loves God and man? It was simply silly for Emerson to counsel young ministers to deny any unique Christian revelation and yet to remain within the church. Emerson himself had had the good taste not to follow his own advice. He had had the decency at least to resign his pulpit when he diverged from what ordinarily goes under the name of Christianity and what the overwhelming majority of his congregation believed. Even when Norton gave his arguments, as he did in his *Discourse on the Latest Form of Infidelity,* he could be short and blunt. Christ himself said that his miracles attested his role in life. Hence, to deny this was to call Jesus either a fiend or a madman.

Other Unitarians, like Henry Ware, Jr., and Theophilus Parsons, responded more moderately to Emerson's address. They made points similar to Norton's, but without Norton's testiness; perhaps they could respond more moderately because no one would dream of thinking their scholarly reputations were being attacked. The third sort of response, made by the liberal Unitarians, irritated Norton almost as much as Emerson. Young Chandler Robbins, for example, insisted that Emerson "is a highly gifted, accomplished and holy man, and at heart and in life a Christian. . . ." [32] Norton could only shake his head sadly and say that the same could be said of a Buddhist. Was the word Christian to become wholly attenuated?

Emerson, atop Parnassus, remained silent, and in later years Theodore Parker became the main tormentor of Unitarians.[33] Parker's critique of Christianity was stronger than Emerson's and confirmed Norton's earlier wise estimate of the drift of transcendental thought toward infidelity. According to Parker, Christ, though a religious genius, was only a human being. Jesus was, in fact, mistaken about some matters, but essentially he taught what Parker called the true Absolute Religion—he taught, simply, the love of God and man. The supernatural accretions to this view through the years, Parker felt, were all false:

I do not believe in the miraculous origin of the Hebrew Church, or the Buddhist Church, or the Christian Church; nor the miraculous character of Jesus. I take not the Bible for my master, nor yet the Church; nor even Jesus of Nazareth for my master. . . . I try all things by the human faculties. . . . Has God given us anything better than our nature? [34]

Parker's justification of his position was the same as Emerson's: God is incarnate in all men and not in Jesus only. And, like Emerson, he had to reconstruct all the traditional Christian claims. When Christ said, "I am the Way, the Truth, the Life," he must have meant that what he taught was the way, the truth, the life. When the Bible speaks of Christ as the Son of God, it really means that Jesus communed with God in a way that is possible to all men. These remarks, finally, were too much even for the more liberal Unitarians. Andrew Preston Peabody, who had earlier criticized Norton for his attack on Emerson, said quite justifiably of Parker that if Absolute Religion stood independently of Jesus, if it would be true had Jesus never existed, then it was pointless for Parker to call himself a Christian.[35] It was certainly true that one ought to love God and man, but doing so hardly made one a Christian. And Peabody denied that the canonical books had been assembled by caprice or accident. Furthermore, he advanced scriptural proofs to show that traditional doctrines of Christianity had been initiated by Jesus himself. But all of these points, of course, had long before been argued by the wise old Andrews Norton.

The ministers of the Boston Association eventually retaliated against Parker's doctrines. Since church politics were congregational nothing could be done officially. But they did refuse Parker pulpit exchanges, hoping thereby to lessen his influence; and for Unitarians such a move amounted almost to excommunication. Parker, in fact, drove the association to frame what almost amounted to a creed; the Unitarians agreed at least on the supernatural origin of Christ. To have to be forced into even such a tenuous creed seems faintly ludicrous. But to deny even this and still call oneself a Christian seems even more so.

IV

A commitment to civil disobedience follows directly from the transcendental notion of the Higher Law. God's laws are known intuitively, and when civil law conflicts with this higher law it becomes man's duty, regretfully and with a realistic view of the consequences involved, to disobey the law of his land. The transcendentalists, however, were far from agreed on how far to extend the commitment to civil disobedience. Emerson was quite conservative. Sometimes he talked strongly about disobedience, but his respect for Whig leaders like Daniel Webster and Edward Everett managed to keep him rather cooperative in fact. "Although, in general, he felt that the party of the Jacksonians had the better cause, he saw that their opponents, the Whigs, had the better men." [36] On the question of slavery, of course, he had no doubts. What transcendentalist could possibly obey the Fugitive Slave Law of 1850? But compared to Thoreau, and particularly to Parker, Emerson was not strongly disobedient himself even on the matter of slavery. Parker, without doubt, was the strongest formulator and follower of the Higher Law doctrine.

One need not fear, Parker wrote, that civil disobedience will lead to anarchy or will undermine the benefits of civilized society and stable government. Followers of the Higher Law are willing, for the sake of stability, to countenance many questionable laws, but they insist that some laws are so stridently immoral that they must be openly disobeyed as well as disavowed.[37] Moreover, the person who is willing to break a law in extreme cases is the very person who can be counted upon to be the strongest upholder of law in general and unlikely to break it for selfish reasons. Finally, any person who would obey any law whatever just because it is a law cannot be trusted. What horrors have not been produced throughout the ages under the loathsome excuse that one was simply obeying orders of lawfully constituted superiors?

Parker in practice was both militantly and successfully disobedient to all aspects of the law that countenanced slavery.[38] He was certainly one of the most effective of the abolitionists, and since his power was great he was taken quite seriously by antislavery politicians. He helped William and Ellen Craft escape from slave hunters and by threats drove the latter out of Boston. Then he went home and wrote President Fillmore what he had done, challenging him to enforce the Fugitive Slave Law. But Parker was not always so successful. Shadrach also escaped, but Frederic Wilkins and Anthony Burns were marched back to slavery from Massachusetts. These events, Parker knew, strengthened the antislavery forces because the return of the slaves infuriated masses of people who had been uncommitted before. He was delighted when Burns, purchased from his master, immediately enrolled in Oberlin College.

Parker's commitment to the Higher Law, and his acceptance of its consequences, made him a highly influential preacher and lecturer. His success as a preacher, in fact, was clearly due to his positive emphasis on the doctrine of the soul, the Higher Law, and civil disobedience, rather than to his negative assaults on the supernatural aspects of Christianity. Many who did not share his specific views on religion loved him for his antislavery views and fought valiantly beside him. And "fought" is precisely the word that applies to Parker. As the carriage sped through the streets of Brookline he sat next to Ellen Craft with a hatchet in his hand, and when threats were directed toward him he kept a loaded pistol in his desk.

Henry David Thoreau is, no doubt, the most famous proponent of the doctrine of civil disobedience. Thoreau, as everyone knows, refused to pay his taxes by way of protest against the Mexican War and the expansion of slavery. Never has a famous act accomplished so little, since Thoreau had to leave jail when friends paid his taxes. Yet for many people the act has become highly significant as a symbol of passive resistance to injustice. There is no doubt that it can be so construed, and that Thoreau so intended it. But to rest content with this view of Thoreau's civil disobedience is to miss the truly radical nature of his political thought.

Thoreau pushed the transcendental doctrine to its most extreme position, far beyond what the other followers of the Higher Law were willing to claim.[39] He believed that all civil law that covered moral concerns was an unwarranted encroachment on the rights of an individual. A majority vote does not establish what is true or right. In the ideal state each individual would pattern his conduct on his own insights into Universal Truth. The result would be universal moral behavior, and there would be no need of civil government at all. Thoreau, in short, was an anarchist: if that government is best which governs least, then that government is absolutely best which does not govern at all. The ideal state is one in which there is no need of government, except for the exercise of practical affairs that are not matters of conscience.

Thoreau sometimes had sufficient practical sense to realize how utopian his view was, although he never fully appreciated how odd his talk sounded to people who took a dimmer view than he of the present and likely future motivations of man. How can anyone really believe that anarchy, fine-sounding as it is in principle, is even remotely possible in fact? And Thoreau never had the slightest appreciation of the social nature and necessities of men. He never took to heart the wise insight of Emerson that man is powerful only by the multitude of his affinities. His individualism was extreme because he thought of the individual and society as always at war with each other. The notion of a community that would not only condition individuals but would also provide the context for cooperative endeavor through which individuals could grow spiritually never seemed to occur to him. "Thoreau," Emerson observed, "goes to a house to say with little preface what he has just read or observed, delivers it in a lump, is quite inattentive to any comment or thought which any of the company offer on the matter, nay, is merely interrupted by it, and when he has finished his report departs with precipitation." [40]

V

The whole burden of transcendentalism, in a way, is antiutilitarian. Since transcendentalism is intuitive and utilitarianism empirical, the followers of each are implicitly critical of the other. But the transcendentalists offered little first-rate specific criticisms of utility. The one notable exception is James Bradley Thayer, Weld Professor of Law at Harvard and expert on the law of evidence. We learn of his critique of utility primarily from unpublished notebooks and from unsigned articles in the *North American Review* later identified as his.[41]

Thayer should not be called literally a transcendentalist since he was only a youth during the height of the transcendentalist-Unitarian controversy. Yet he was close to Emerson both personally and philosophically. Thayer's wife was a cousin of Emerson, and Thayer served in later years as Emerson's attorney and stockbroker.[42] He accompanied Emerson on his famous journey to Yosemite and wrote an account of it called *Western Journey with Mr. Emerson*. The philosophical influence of Emerson is fully apparent in his criticism of utility and shows forth, here and there, in his legal and educational papers.

From his life-long friend Chauncey Wright, Thayer learned to avoid the fallacious and shop-worn criticisms of Bentham and Mill. He was convinced that Mill successfully disposed of the traditional criticisms that utilitarianism is godless, that it does not allow for self-sacrifice, that it is simply the doctrine of expedience, that happiness is unattainable, and so on. Thayer was poorly impressed by Carlyle's attitude toward utility and was almost equally unimpressed by Whewell and Sedgwick. Thayer wrote:

Towards these writers he [Mill] shows an asperity and curtness of which he makes mention in the Preface to this collection; and which is justified by the ignorance that they display of the real points in dispute, the looseness with which they use language, and the unworthy superciliousness of their tone.[43]

Thayer, as we shall see, offered more interesting criticisms of Mill than most of these contemporaries.

Thayer had grave doubts about the way Mill justified his basic moral commitment to general happiness. His most fully developed criticism of Mill centers around the latter's now famous "proof" of the greatest happiness principle. The point of putting the quotation marks around the word proof for Mill is that his argument is not a logical proof but an argument designed to show that it is reasonable to follow the utilitarian principle. Mill, convinced of the correctness of a teleological ethic, wanted to show why utility is the most reasonable version of the teleological viewpoint.

Mill's argument has three parts: (1) the happiness of any individual is intrinsically good; (2) the general happiness is intrinsically good; and (3) nothing else, in fact, is experienced to be, or is, intrinsically good.[44] Hence general happiness is the only teleological criterion of right. Thayer, however, detected several crucial difficulties with steps (2) and (3) in Mill's "proof." Concerning the second point Mill had written:

> No reason can be given why the general happiness is desirable, except that each person, so far as he believes it to be attainable, desires his own happiness. This, however, being a fact, we have not only all proof which the case admits of, but all which it is possible to require, that happiness is a good: that each person's happiness is a good to that person, and the general happiness, therefore, a good to the aggregate of all persons.[45]

Thayer believed that this argument contains a simple *non sequitur*. From the fact that everyone desires his own happiness it does not follow that everyone desires the general happiness. Mill replied to this sort of criticism in the following way: "I merely meant in this particular sentence to argue that, since A's happiness is a good, B's a good, C's a good, etc., the sum of all these goods must be a good." [46] The point of the argument supposedly is to show that since general happiness is a good people ought to desire it whether, in fact, they do or not. Thayer, however, saw further difficulty with part (2). "Where is the evidence that the happiness of one man is as desirable as the happiness of another? . . . that the happiness of all persons is commensurate, so that 'the truths of arithmetic are applicable to the valuation' of it." [47] Thayer firmly believed that some people deserve happiness more than others, and that it is one's duty to act accordingly. The notion of justice, he felt, was more basic than the notion of general happiness in still another way. The greatest happiness concept has no moral significance unless it is amended to read, "One should try to produce the greatest amount of happiness evenly or justly distributed."

Thayer also criticized part (3) of Mill's "proof." In (3) Mill tried to show that only happiness is experienced as intrinsically good. To be sure, he said, other things like virtue are experienced as intrinsically good, but only because they have been associated with happiness and hence have become a part of it. But Mill did not stop with his argument from associationistic psychology; his final argument was introspective in nature. He wrote:

And now to decide whether this is really so; whether mankind do desire nothing for itself but that which is a pleasure to them, or of which the absence is a pain. . . . It can only be determined by practiced self-consciousness and self-observation, assisted by observation of others. I believe that these sources of evidence, impartially consulted, will declare that desiring a thing and finding it pleasant, aversion to it and thinking of it as painful, are phenomena entirely inseparable, or rather two parts of the same phenomenon; in strictness of language, two different modes of naming the same psychological fact: that to think of an object as desirable (unless for the sake of its consequences), and to think of it as pleasant are one and the same thing. . . .[48]

Concerning this argument Thayer wrote that

. . . one is aware of the same sort of error that is observable in the reasonings of what is called the "Selfish School" of moralists; namely, that of straining and misusing language, looking at things from a wrong point of view and (if one may say so without begging the question) measuring things by a standard which is inapplicable.[49]

Thayer's reference to the Selfish School is extremely appropriate and deserves amplification.

Hobbes, for one, had tried to break down the distinction between selfish and unselfish acts, arguing that in reality all acts are selfish. If I do not give a beggar a coin but use it myself, although I have all I need, I am directly selfish; but if I give the coin to the beggar I am still selfish, albeit indirectly, since I am only avoiding the guilty feeling I certainly would have if I ignored a needy person. But, Thayer was saying in effect, it is certainly straining and misusing language to talk this way. Moreover, what gain is there in talking about direct and indirect selfishness when it simply makes the same distinction we would ordinarily mark out by the words selfish and unselfish. Things are what they are, not something else—and, of course, Thayer had Bishop Butler in mind here.[50] The same point, he felt, applies to Mill. It is straining and misusing language to say that what we ordinarily call desirable is really pleasant or that the two terms refer to the same thing. Things are what they are, and not something else. At this point, it is interesting to note, Thayer was criticizing Mill in the same way G. E. Moore did years later.[51] Both men, in essence, were accusing Mill of illegitimately defining a moral notion by a naturalistic one. Thayer, however, unlike Moore, never claimed that Mill committed this fallacy— if fallacy it is—in part (1) of his argument.

Thayer had a larger, more pervasive dissatisfaction with Mill, as well as with Bentham, than any of the criticisms so far examined would indicate. And this pervasive dissatisfaction resulted almost wholly from the influence of Emerson. Mill, he thought,[52] lacked imagination—if one takes this word to refer to "the instinctive insight of a sensitive nature." Like a true Englishman, Mill warned this type of imagination off the ground. "And yet, on every subject which is a part of the science of man, there is especial need of resorting to these delicate sources of suggestion by which, as from 'the convolutions of a smooth-lipped shell,' we get 'authentic tidings of invisible things.' " [53] Emerson, Thayer felt, more than anyone else, had that "instinctive insight of a sensitive nature" that Mill lacked, and he, if anyone, certainly had "authentic tidings of invisible things." Writing in the *Boston Daily Advertiser* after Arnold's lecture, Thayer observed that Emerson

. . . was flooded and full to overflowing all through his life with a sense of the presence, the omnipresence, and the instant operation of what he called "the over-soul." His apprehension and acceptance of this was no merely intellectual matter; it was something that penetrated into the substance of his being, and moved him like a vital force; it was this, with its related beliefs, that gave such power to his speech and such charm to his character, as of one who had already entered upon the immortal life. . . .[54]

8

GEORGE WILLIAM CURTIS

G E O R G E   C U R T I S   knew most of the transcendentalists
and was closely associated with Emerson, George Ripley,
and Theodore Parker. He knew Thoreau well enough to help
him build his cabin on Walden Pond. His philosophical views
were most directly influenced by Emerson, but his views on
social reform reflected, in the long run, a more active brand of
transcendentalism than Emerson's. More than most of the transcendentalists he translated his philosophical principles into
consistent and intelligent reform movements. Curtis, like
Parker, was a remarkably interesting practical transcendentalist.[1] Some philosophies, perhaps, carry stronger motivations to
action than others—a view which is itself one of the tenets of
transcendentalism—but, nevertheless, these philosophies, like
any others, can be accepted and yet remain inoperative in a
pervasive way in a person's life. Curtis and Parker are the happy
exceptions among the transcendentalists.

I

At Mr. Hartshorne's school in Providence, George and his brother Burrill first came under the spell of Emerson. The Sage of Concord read his essay on "The Oversoul," and the youths were no doubt captivated more by the manner and charm of the speaker than by the substance of what he had to say—although there can be little doubt that the substance was not wholly lost on them. After the first meeting with Emerson, Burrill wrote, "He seemed to speak as an inhabitant of heaven, and with the inspiration and authority of a prophet." [2] They heard him lecture frequently and later became well acquainted with him.

In 1842 the Curtis brothers decided to continue their education at George Ripley's Brook Farm, near West Roxbury, Massachusetts. In deference to their father's wishes, they went as boarders, not as members of the community. Apparently their father, president of the Bank of Commerce in New York City, caught the faint aroma of Ripley's later socialism in the word community! George learned a good deal about music, literature, and philosophy from George and Sophia Ripley, George Bradford, John Dwight, and Charles Dana; and he listened, sometimes attentively and sometimes not, to the nonresident philosophers—Parker, Hedge, Margaret Fuller, and Emerson—who were always drifting in and out of Brook Farm. Emerson again fascinated the impressionable young men above all others. But Brook Farm, of course, was not all music and philosophy. George picnicked and masqueraded with the wonderfully motley crowd of farmers, mechanics, and reformers, all of whom "were thrown into convulsions of laughter at the sight of G. W. C. dressed as Fanny Elssler, making courtesies and pirouetting down the path. . . ." [3]

The Curtises did not return to Brook Farm after Ripley turned to Fourierism but went instead to Concord in 1844 to labor half days at farming and continue their studies at will, the ideal they kept from Brook Farm days. During their second season in Concord they stayed on a farm near Walden Pond and lived quite simply, studying sometimes and spending many afternoons boating or roaming the woods. George renewed his acquaintance with Emerson, "meeting him sometimes on musical evenings at the Hoars, sometimes at his own home where George went to talk or to borrow books." [4] During this time he also helped Thoreau build his cabin and became friendly with Nathaniel Hawthorne, whom he had met earlier at Brook Farm and who was at this time living in the Old Manse in Concord. Curtis also saw Bronson Alcott, Ellery Channing, and Henry Thoreau at the little noted and short-lived Monday evening club that met in Emerson's study. In a passage that exhibits a literary genius he did not always sustain, Curtis describes the first meeting of the club:

I went, the first Monday evening, very much as Ixion may have gone to his banquet. The philosophers sat dignified and erect. There was a constrained but very amiable silence, which had the impertinence of a tacit inquiry, seeming to ask, "Who will now proceed to say the finest thing that has ever been said?" It was quite involuntary and unavoidable, for the members lacked that fluent social genius without which a club is impossible. I vaguely remember that the Orphic Alcott invaded the Sahara of silence with a solemn "saying," to which, after due pause, the honorable member for Blackberry Pastures [Thoreau] responded by some keen and graphic observation—while the Olympian host [Emerson], anxious that so much good material should be spun into something, beamed smiling encouragement upon all parties. But the conversation became more and more staccato. Miles Coverdale [Hawthorne], a statue of night and silence, sat, a little removed, under a portrait of Dante, gazing imperturbably upon the group; and as he sat in the shadow, his dark eyes and hair and suit of sables made him, in that society, the black thread of mystery which he weaved into his stories, while the shifting presence of the Brook Farmer [Bradford] played like heat-lightning around the room.[5]

Probably no other youth in Curtis' generation had such a rich opportunity for philosophical and literary education. The influence, however, was quite uneven. He listened to Orphic Alcott's sayings with an incredulous smile and spoke of them with an irreverent laugh. The influence of Emerson, on the other hand, was extensive. Curtis' biographers emphasize this influence almost to the exclusion of the other transcendentalists, although

Curtis did, in fact, also come under the influence of Ripley and Parker on the nature and importance of reform movements.

Ripley's rationale of Brook Farm, even before its Fourieristic phase, was based on the necessity of organized social reform. The way society is organized, he thought, stifles the realization of man's intuitive power and self-reliance. It is necessary to create a social and intellectual climate in which self-realization will be truly possible. "Thus, while Emerson retired to Parnassus, Ripley was forced to wade into the mire of social reform." [6] And Brook Farm, it must be remembered, was not an end in itself for Ripley, but a symbol and a pattern for the over-all reform of society.

Curtis, however, while he was at Brook Farm and later, firmly believed that the transcendental doctrines of self-reliance and the perfectibility of the soul committed one to a negative position on organized social reform. Political agitation and social manipulation, he felt, could attain nothing significant; the only effective reform was regeneration of the individual heart and soul. Furthermore, one ought not to interfere in God's work, trying to bring about or hasten the appearance of something that might not be in His plan at all or that was meant to appear gradually. "Reform," he wrote, "becomes at last a practical atheism and, so far as organized, loses souls . . . and the wise man lends himself to no organization." And in a jocular fashion he added: "Reform is organized distrust. It says to the universe fresh from God's hands, 'You are a miserable business; lo! I will make you fairer!' and so deputes some Fourier or Robert Owen to improve the bungling work of the creator." [7] Curtis, moreover, with youthful enthusiasm denied simply and naïvely that there is any social basis of evil. "As Fourier seems to me to have postponed his life, in finding out how to live, so I often felt it was with Mr. Ripley. Besides, I feel that our evils are entirely individual, not social. What is society but the shadow of the single men behind it." [8]

Nevertheless, less than ten years later Curtis had dedicated himself to numerous important and fundamental organized reforms—the abolition of slavery, the increase of women's rights, rehabilitative penology, and the securement and extension of civil service. Curtis had realized that it is cold comfort for a slave to know that his future will be secure when his master's heart is regenerated. And even though God is directing things, might not the efforts of man be instruments of His actions? Seen in this light, organized reform no longer seemed like practical atheism. But for Curtis organized reform was always a piecemeal way of removing specific evils, never a wholesale way of bringing about the millennium. He never accepted Ripley's Brook Farm ideal of recreating a whole society along utopian lines. Among the transcendentalists there was a continuum between extremes on the question of reform. Emerson and Ripley are the opposite extremes: a skeptic about organized reform on the one hand, a utopian reformer on the other. Curtis and Parker fall between these extremes: while not being utopian, they realized the importance of organized reform in fighting specific evils.

The cause of Curtis' change in attitude about reform is complex; it was partly his own intensely practical temperament, but it was largely also the influence of the Francis Shaw family whose daughter, Anna, Curtis married.[9] The Shaws commanded his admiration and inspired his love so that their aims and ideals either became his own or, where they coincided with his own, strengthened and stimulated them. The Shaws were strong antislavery people, and they communicated their moral enthusiasm to Curtis, who became one of the most influential and levelheaded of the abolitionists. Like William Lloyd Garrison, however, the Shaws could not say, "This one injustice only will I fight," but they were attracted by every important, fundamental reform. Thus, Curtis, in sharp contrast with his earlier views, came to accept the necessity of organized social reform in principle. The Shaws, in turn, reflected the influence and ardor of Theodore Parker, whose church they had attended in West Roxbury. So, although he never explicitly acknowledged it, Curtis departed in one way from the paths of Emerson and followed the example of the more activistic brand of transcendentalism. But, as we have seen, he did not follow Ripley either.

The true symbol of Curtis' transcendentalism is neither Walden Pond nor Brook Farm. The true symbol is Emerson's concept of "The American Scholar at Work."

II

In his early years Curtis reflected in his writing many of the familiar Emersonian themes—the importance of the scholar, compensation, self-reliance, and the spirituality of nature. To Isaac Hecker he wrote:

Men are like the ocean, each drop is necessary to each, but the single drop is perfect and represents the whole.—Every soul is necessary to my soul, but mine is not ripe and matured till it has naturally separated from every other and stands cool and alone.[10]

The spirituality of nature was, perhaps, his favorite theme in those early days: "Nature continually reminds me that she is only that graceful aspect which He assumes because my eyes cannot suffer his pure glory." There are, however, no original insights in these renditions of transcendental themes. Curtis was wholly dominated by Emerson's thought and had accepted his beliefs ready made. He was, in fact, a second-hand transcendentalist; he had simply taken over his beliefs from the transcendentalist society in which he lived, and they had not, as yet, gone deeply into his own being.

In his later satires and romances Curtis emphasized the importance of avoiding sham and artificiality, another pervasive theme that runs through much of the transcendental literature.[12] In *The Potiphar Papers* he lambasted the phoniness of contemporary New York society, whose members staged huge balls, built tremendous homes, paid lip service to religion, learned a few appropriate French phrases, wore Parisian styles, and stocked their libraries with leather covers that had no books inside! Like other transcendentalists, Curtis took particular delight in satirizing the clergy who preached only on safe topics and enjoyed the luxurious hospitality of parishioners. The satire is sometimes heavy, but there are some good passages. He continued this stream of satire in the only novel he ever wrote, *Trumps,* a dismal failure from almost every point of view.

Prue and I had more merit than any of Curtis' earlier work, and parts of it still read well. It is sometimes sentimental, but it exhibits a graceful, flowing style missing in his earlier works. He also demonstrates real ability in evoking local color; his description of the Providence dock area, for example, is very well done. The theme of *Prue and I*, one suspects, was suggested by Thoreau in chapter ii of *Walden*. The real owner of a farm, wrote Thoreau, is not necessarily the one who pays taxes on the land but the one who knows and loves the meadows well. Curtis presented this view by saying that a man is rich when he owns a beautiful sunset or a "castle in Spain." The pleasures of the imagination, for Curtis, were supreme; like Thoreau, he never tired of extolling the philosophy of plain living and high thinking. Curtis was still reflecting the transcendentalism of someone else, but he was fast approaching the time when he would make his own contribution to the spiritual philosophy.

Curtis' major contribution, which appeared mainly in his antislavery lectures on the Lyceum circuit, was his theory of conscience. For Curtis conscience was simply the word of God in man and needed no supplementation by natural theology and historical religion.[13] With much care and detail he drew numerous corollaries from his conscience theory—the doctrine of human rights, the role of civil government, the principle of liberty, the nature of true patriotism, the "good fight" interpretation of history, and the role of the American scholar. Curtis was at his best when he defended these notions and consistently applied them to the practical political problems of his age. He became one of the most effective of the abolitionists and, in post-Civil War days, a skillful advocate of civil service reform. He had become a practical transcendentalist; and it was then that his transcendentalism became more than youthful mouthings of his mentor's views—that he ceased being Emerson's man and became his own.

Since he was more interested in ethics than in metaphysics, Curtis called "the fragment of the Universal Mind" simply "man's conscience." God writes the universal rule of right and the love of God upon man's perception, "and we call it conscience, or God in him." [14] To be sure, the dictates of conscience are sometimes partial, fragmentary, or distorted. They are often warped by self-interest, passion, and weakness;[15] but if a man's conscience is healthy and able to function in an unobstructed way then the results are absolute and universal. Every man then discovers the same moral truth.

The most crucial revelation of any conscience that is free of passion, weakness, and self-interest, Curtis felt, is simple and unambiguous: it tells us to treat everyone as moral equals. Morally everyone is to count for one, never more nor less. In the moral realm, he believed, there is no room for caste. Specifically, conscience informs us that all men have equal rights to life, liberty, and the pursuit of happiness. These rights belong to men as human beings, not because they are members of some civil society. Consequently, the function of civil government is to insure the largest exercise of these rights by every man commensurate with the largest exercise of the same rights by every other individual. No individual's rights should be infringed upon except for criminal action—that is, when he transgresses the rights that another has equally with him.

The laws of society, indeed, deprive man of liberty, and even of life, but only when by crime they have become injurious to society. The deprivation of the life or liberty of the individual under other circumstances is the outrage of those rights which are instinctively perceived by every man, but are beyond argument or proof.[16]

Curtis believed steadfastly that the moral doctrine he advocated was nothing more nor less than the American principle of liberty formulated most forcefully by Samuel Adams and James Otis, two of the fathers of the Revolution for whom he had particular reverence. The very root of the American principle of liberty, he said, is the equality of human rights based upon our common humanity.

The ultimate scope of that doctrine is the absolute personal and political freedom of every man: the right that is to say, of every man to think and speak and act, subject to the equal rights of other men, protected in their exercise by common consent, or law. It declares that men are to be deprived of personal liberty only for crime, and that political liberty is the only sure guarantee of personal freedom. These are the postulates of our civilization.[17]

The true American patriot, Curtis continued, is the one who gives complete allegiance to the American principle of liberty and eschews the notion of "my country right or wrong." To say "my country right or wrong" is like uttering the words of a thief who chuckles, "My fortune, however acquired." [18] In short, a man's country is not simply a strip of land; some mountains, rivers, and woods. It is a principle, and true patriotism is fidelity to that principle. Since the American principle is the principle of liberty, the true American patriot is dedicated to the universal doctrine of conscience and human rights.

The Civil War, Curtis believed, was the supreme test of the American principle of liberty. Did the Civil War prove the impracticability of the American principle, or did it show the evil fruit of infidelity to that principle? Curtis thought it proved the latter.[19] Political infidelity—lack of loyalty to the principle of human rights—all through the nineteenth century had the Civil War as its direct result. Slavery seemed on the way out, but suddenly the cotton gin made cotton and slave labor very valuable. The South began to think that slavery was perhaps not a moral evil, after all. John Calhoun justified it by the United States Constitution, and Richard Fuller justified it by the Bible. And State Street in Boston concurred. Trade with the South was profitable, and the northern merchants sighed and said they were not responsible for slavery. The abolitionists, to be sure, tried to rouse the conscience of the North, but Garrison was dragged through the streets in Boston, and Lovejoy was murdered in Alton, Illinois. "Serves them right," the North muttered, "for meddling in other people's business." The ministry was singularly quiet; instead of talking about the sins of America they talked about Sodom and Gomorrah. Not everyone was corrupted because of self-interest; many more from fear. "Talk against slavery and we will leave the Union," shouted the South. Webster and Clay jumped to compromise; Calhoun indeed was their master in every way. They never realized that, while it is possible to compromise on details, it is never possible to compromise on principle and retain any moral content whatever. The Civil War, Curtis sadly concluded, was the result of the northerner's political infidelity—his disloyalty to the principles of human rights, to the principles of Sam and John Adams and James Otis, to the principles of American liberty.

Curtis interpreted the course of all history in terms of conflict between the principle of liberty, on the one hand, and the influence of greed, passion, weakness, cowardice, callousness, and an ability to rationalize away the suffering of others, on the other hand.[20] The "good fight" is between advocates of the greatest amount of personal freedom commensurate with the freedom of others, on the one hand, and those who would impose their own greed and passion or their own ideologies and vested interests on other people, on the other hand. Curtis wanted no controls on human freedom beyond what was necessary for mutual self-realization; he loathed the imposition of limits on some people as a result of what other people believed or wanted. In the good fight, Curtis said, liberty at times advances and at other times retreats, but it gains overall in strength. The good fight, moreover, knows no limits in time or place. It is the same fight in which Leonidas was a warrior at Thermopylae, Galileo at Pisa, and Lincoln at Gettysburg. Their adversaries have been legion, but highly representative are Torquemada, Philip II of Spain, and the "scientific" scholars who try to prove the physical and mental inferiority of Negroes. Curtis summed it up in an oversimplified but refreshingly direct way: we are all either Butternuts or Bluecoats!

The role of the scholar, Curtis thought, was particularly important in fighting the good fight on whatever front the enemy was engaged at the moment.[21] The true scholar is not, he said, what the popular imagination sometimes conceives him to be: a person with all the weaknesses of a woman but none of her charms. Neither is the true scholar simply the knowledgeable man, but he is the *wise* man, the one who can skillfully apply whatever he knows to the better management of life. The very nature of the scholar, of the wise man, fits him for such a task. He is the one who supposedly more than any other rises above the muck of passion, greed, and ignorance, and who can follow out the dictates of conscience in the fight for universal liberty. The ideal scholar is Milton, not Roger Ascham. The scholar often enough fails to participate in the good fight through fear, but Curtis exhorted him to enter the lists by holding up to his view the transcendental claims of conscience.

III

Curtis' interpretation of history as exhibiting the continuous episodes of the good fight has a number of interesting implications for a current debate among American historians. From 1912 until approximately 1945, American historians under the influence of Charles Beard, Frederick Jackson Turner, and Vernon Parrington viewed their past as a series of conflicts and extolled the underdog and the value of reform. Recently there has been a sharp reinterpretation of America's past, and the emergence of the consensus school of American history. These historians view America's past as homogeneous, placid, and tranquil. Like de Tocqueville, they see America as a happy land, adventurous in manner but nonexperimental at heart. They frown on reform. The interesting aspect of Curtis' view of history, as we shall see, is that it suggests that there is something right and something wrong about both these contemporary views.

Beard, Turner, and Parrington viewed American history along dramatic lines: there were turning points, big convulsive movements, in which progress toward democratic goals occurred and the entrenched economic interests were overthrown.[22] Such convulsive turning points were the American Revolution, the Revolution of 1800 when Jefferson came to power, the rise of democracy under Jackson, the Civil War, the Industrial Revolution, and the Populist Revolt. These crises suggest that American history, like the histories of all nations, is not smooth and continuous but jagged and discontinuous. The path of American history, in short, like that of all nations, is the result of struggle and conflict.

Each of the members of the conflict school interpreted the struggle somewhat differently. Beard pictured it as the struggle of class against class or between different competing economic interests. Turner saw the conflict as the frontier versus the settled areas of the East, country versus city, and farmers versus merchants. Parrington interpreted all of American intellectual history as a struggle between human rights and property rights, or between Jeffersonian and Hamiltonian ideologies.

In contrast to the conflict school, the new consensus school, including Louis Hartz, Richard Hofstadter, and Daniel Boorstin, minimizes the conflict in America's past.[23] These historians see a quiet and unexciting past, free of convulsions like the French and Russian revolutions. In America "classes have turned into myths, sections have lost their solidarity, ideologies have vaporized into climates of opinion." [24] The American Revolution turns out to have been no crusade for human rights but simply a "reluctant resistance of sober Englishmen" to what they took to be infringements of their traditional liberties. Jefferson and Jackson were hardly democratic reconstructionists; they merely wanted to restore the stable simplicity of America's earlier years. The Populists were not reformers or ideologists either; they can best be understood as rural capitalists who had family quarrels with other capitalists. The Civil War, to be sure, is difficult to explain away. But the fact that Americans have been so preoccupied with this event suggests that it is a surrogate for fundamental conflict and struggle in the American past.

The consensus school, however, is far less unified than the conflict school. Hartz and Hofstadter are sometimes critical of the consensus they find, while Boorstin erects his own ideology upon it. The genius of American politics, he says, consists in not having any political philosophy or ideology. Man becomes interested in political theory only when he becomes dissatisfied with political facts. Our success as a nation has thus precluded the need of political philosophy. Boorstin, however, is anti-intellectual in a more pervasive way. He not only believes that America has flourished because it scrapped European philosophical blueprints for Utopia, but he is happy to find that American political life exhibits no theory or ideas at all. The genius of Americans is not to have any articulated system of thought but to deal in a piecemeal and practical way with each problem as it comes along. The unarticulated source of Boorstin's distaste for systems of ideas is this: holding a system of beliefs commits one to certain actions on principle. Hence, when a new problem arises, one is committed to acting toward it in an antecedently determined way, rather than judging in terms of what might be most expedient for the specific circumstances. Bluntly stated, to act from ideas causes trouble; it prevents compromise; it prevents sliding through a tough problem by insisting upon ideal demands.

The implications of Curtis' view of history is that each of the contemporary views is partially right and partially wrong. The conflict school is right in insisting upon conflict but wrong in locating the conflict between stable classes, areas, and ideologies. Its members are right in insisting upon conflict but wrong in locating it within a political context. Curtis himself emphasized that there is a consensus in the United States about the desirability of its political system. But within this system the fundamental moral conflict that has always existed, with its specific political repercussions, still exists. Parrington was closest to the mark, but he still mistook the nature of the fundamental moral conflict in America as elsewhere. The conflict is not between human rights and property rights; people without property can be as bigoted as those with property, and vice versa. The fundamental moral conflict, the good fight as Curtis viewed it, is between advocates of the greatest amount of personal freedom commensurate with the freedom of others, on the one hand, and those who would impose their own ideologies and vested interests on other people, on the other hand. As we have seen, Curtis wanted no controls on human freedom beyond what is necessary for mutual self-realization. And Americans like Sam Adams and James Otis who fought for this type of liberalism were his heroes. He loathed the imposition of limits on some people as a result of what other people believed or wanted; and Americans like Calhoun, Fuller, Conkling, and Blaine—who, he thought, exemplified this illiberalism—were for him the scoundrels of American history. The conflict school historians were right in viewing historical figures as heroes and scoundrels; they simply did not have the right formula for finding them.

The implications of Curtis' view for the consensus school are equally clear. The consensus school is right in denying competitive political ideologies, but it is wrong in missing the real conflict, which is moral rather than political in nature—

although, needless to say, the moral conflict has constant repercussions of a political sort within the uncontested political framework. The consensus school is obviously wrong in minimizing conflict in America's past. Certainly conflict was there; the difficult point is to identify and characterize it correctly.

The most interesting implications of Curtis' view are those which are relevant to Boorstin's particular ideology. Horror of reform, for Curtis, was just as wrong as reconstructive ideology. Curtis urged no wholesale reforms—he was no Ripley—but he urged the crucial need of piecemeal reform of evils to protect that very system so loved by conservatives. And Curtis was anything but anti-intellectual. His whole life consisted in acting consistently on his transcendental principles. Far from finding the genius of American politics in its mindlessness, he found the tragedy in its past due to the abandonment of acting on principle—abandonment of the American principle of liberty. The Civil War, far from being a surrogate for the conflicts that never existed elsewhere, becomes a symbol both for the very nature of America's moral conflict and for its omnipresence.

Finally, Boorstin's notion of social expediency is repugnant to the whole of Curtis' thought. Curtis would admit that acting on principle rules out social expediency, but he would hardly have apologized for this fact. What is social expediency but the willingness to accept an injustice to someone else because it would cause trouble generally to fight it? Curtis believed that compromises on matters of detail were perfectly proper, but that compromise on principles was impossible without losing the moral content of the principles. And he believed that compromising moral principles—infidelity to the doctrine of human rights—led to far worse consequences in the long run than adherence to principles. On this point we can hear him saying firmly with the aging Francis Wayland: the best place to meet a difficulty is just where God puts it. If we avoid it now, we will meet it later in a still more terrifying way.

9

THE GOOD FIGHT

I

AMONG the transcendentalists George Curtis became one of the most widely read proponents of reform and one of the most effective abolitionists. He fought the propaganda war through the pages of Harper publications and on the Lyceum platform and fought the actual battles through political channels and civil disobedience.

Curtis wrote antislavery articles and editorials for *Harper's Magazine* and *Harper's Weekly*. The *Weekly* reached a large audience and was extremely influential in forming public opinion. Curtis eventually became its political editor, and his sphere of influence was thus considerably enlarged.

But Curtis fought slavery most effectively through numerous appearances on the Lyceum platform. He delivered countless antislavery speeches and was counted one of the most influential speakers on the circuit. "The Duty of the American Scholar," delivered at Wesleyan University in the summer of 1856, first drew attention to his oratorical ability. Kansas, he told the students, is America's Thermopylae. It was a scholarly speech, but it had power, too: "The fight is fierce—the issue is with God." The speech was published in the *New York Weekly Tribune* and issued separately as a pamphlet.[1]

Its influence was enormous, and Curtis became almost overnight the most effective of the younger abolitionists. But the road to victory was full of pitfalls. Chief Justice Taney rendered the Dred Scott decision; more work was necessary. Curtis traveled widely, giving his addresses on "Patriotism," "The American Doctrine of Liberty," "Political Infidelity," and "The Present Aspect of the Slavery Question." [2]

The climax of Curtis' antislavery effort came in 1859 with his delivery of "The Present Aspect of the Slavery Question" in Philadelphia. He had delivered it at Plymouth Church in Brooklyn in October without incident, and he was scheduled to deliver it again in Philadelphia on December 15.[3] By December passion was running high, for John Brown had struck his blow and was then waiting to be hanged. The Anti-Slavery Society of Pennsylvania was meeting in Philadelphia at the time Curtis was to appear—although his appearance was not connected with the meeting of this society. On December 14 handbills were distributed calling for a mass meeting at National Hall to prevent Curtis from speaking. A mob of thousands appeared, and trouble was not long in coming. Parts of the audience repeatedly tried to storm the platform but were repulsed. The milling mob outside threw stones and acid through the windows; one woman was burned. Then the mob tried to set fire to the hall, forgetting, apparently, about their cohorts inside. Chief of Police Ruggles, who was a Democrat but no slavery man, had been busily arresting rioters and putting them in boxcars in a warehouse under the hall. When the attempts were made to fire the hall, Ruggles climbed on top of a car and calmly said that if the hall caught fire every effort would be made to save the people inside at the expense of the human freight in the boxcars. The attempt to fire the hall was not renewed. Curtis at that very moment was saying:

The country *does* want rest, we all want rest. Our very civilization wants it—and we mean that it shall have it. It shall have rest—repose—refreshment of soul and reinvigoration of faculty. And that rest shall not be a poison that pacifies restlessness in death, nor shall it be any kind of anodyne or patting or propping or bolstering—as if a man with a cancer in his breast would *be* well if only he said he was so and wore a clean shirt and kept his shoes tied.[4]

Curtis also fought slavery through existing political channels or, where such channels did not exist, by helping to create new ones. He was a charter member of the Republican party and actively campaigned for the election of Fremont in 1856. In May, 1860, he went to Chicago as a delegate to the Republican National Convention, and there he exercised influence in a most unexpected way. Curtis went to the convention as a staunch advocate of Senator Seward of New York, the strongest candidate. Yet in an accidental way he helped bring about the nomination of Lincoln, for which he was, later, heartily grateful.[5]

The antislavery element of the Republican party wanted a strong statement against slavery in the 1860 platform while professional politicians like Thurlow Weed of New York, fearing that such forthrightness would be political suicide, advocated a noncommittal policy. Joshua Giddings of Ohio, a strong antislavery man and friend of Oberlin, proposed to add to the platform the preamble of the Declaration of Independence. Giddings' motion was lost, and Giddings was about to leave the hall in despair. Wondering whether the Republican party was any different from the Democratic and Whig parties, Curtis decided to find out immediately. He was given the floor to speak but was met with jeers and catcalls. He waited for order, and finally, when he could be heard, spoke more eloquently than ever before. He dared the representatives of the party of freedom, meeting in a free state, in a hall dedicated to liberty, to deny the equal rights of man and to reject the doctrine of the Declaration. "The speech fell like a spark upon tinder, and the amendment was adopted with a shout of enthusiasm more unanimous and deafening than the yells with which it had been previously rejected." [6]

In defending Giddings, Curtis was fighting the conservative forces of his own state headed by Thurlow Weed, and Weed, it must be remembered, was the leader of Seward's forces. Thus, indirectly Curtis worked against Seward, for whom he had nothing but respect and whom he supported for the nomination. It is difficult to assess the importance of Curtis' speech in sidetracking Seward's bid, and the exact nature of the role it played has never been fully explored. But the incident nicely exhibits the importance of *accident,* along with social, economic, and rational forces, in determining the flow of historical events, a factor to which historians generally find it difficult to do justice.

The nature of Curtis' civil disobedience was systematically to flout the Fugitive Slave Law. He did much to encourage Underground Railroad activity, although he never actively tried to release slaves captured in the North or help slaves to escape from the South. He was a perfect example of the passive resistance strain in the civil disobedience movement.

II

This brief survey of Curtis' activity should be sufficient to show that Curtis was not a radical abolitionist or outside the mainstream of American tradition and to support the view that he was one of the most reasonable and level-headed of the abolitionists. Curtis, like Parker, was far less radical than Garrison on the question of preserving the Union. Like the Oberlinites, Curtis did not look upon the Constitution as an evil document and viewed the dissolution of the Union as an odd remedy for slavery—financially catastrophic to all the states and no help to the slaves who would remain in bondage. Dissolution might ease the conscience of people like Garrison, who felt guilty about participation in a Union that permitted slavery, but objectively it would produce no good for anyone. It is true that Curtis, as a youth, had suggested dissolution of the Union as the only solution to the slavery issue; but in his mature years, when he was in the midst of his antislavery effort, he was a staunch advocate of its preservation.[7]

Curtis, moreover, was less radical than Parker within the framework of their agreement. Curtis was happy to disobey the Fugitive Slave Law but unwilling to use force as Parker did. He would not counsel mass insurrection of the slaves because he knew such a procedure would be suicidal, and he never himself used force to release runaway slaves once captured. Unlike

Parker, he worked through established political channels to fight slavery and when these proved insufficient helped establish new ones; as we have seen, he was vitally active in establishing the new Republican party. Unlike Parker, he realized that while the individual conscience is the motive power of politics this power will accomplish nothing unless it is harnessed into a united effort through political machinery. Curtis, in short, among all the transcendentalists, represented essentially the Oberlin viewpoint of militant moderation, of "radical" involvement in passive resistance and politics.

Thus, it should be apparent that Curtis pursued his abolitionist goal in nonrevolutionary and yet effective ways, but it might be useful, given the rigid stereotype of the abolitionist as a radical, to emphasize the point further by mentioning other evidence of Curtis' conservatism in later years.

When radicals like Phillips denounced Lincoln's cautious management of the war, Curtis wrote:

But the President of the United States cannot rightfully do what he thinks the people ought to wish but what he honestly thinks they do wish, for that only will stand. Gen. Butler could not govern this country, as he governed New Orleans. Andrew Jackson would have landed us in perdition two years ago. Honesty, fidelity, sagacity, and patience will carry us through. Do you know anyone who has more of them than Abraham Lincoln? [8]

Curtis criticized some of the German liberals who had come to this country for not understanding the American principle of liberty under law. "The truth seems to be that the European democrats who come among us have very little conception of constitutional liberty. They are rather for absolute liberty, and if they cannot have their own way entirely seem almost ready to lose everything." [9] In 1872, when Carl Schurz joined the Liberal Republicans because he was disgusted with Grant's foreign policy and civil service scandals, Curtis, although equally disgusted, remained steadfast. He was slow to move; he bolted the Republican party only years later when Blaine was nominated. In the disputed Tilden-Hayes election Curtis again emphasized the importance of the concept of liberty under law: we have institutions to settle this problem, he insisted, without bringing to the surface again the hatreds of the Civil War.[10] Several historians have credited his dramatic speech—full of the doctrine of moderation—at a dinner in New York City, where many prominent men of both parties were present, as an important aid in calming the rising tide of passion.[11] And, finally, he had grave reservations about Wendell Phillips' immoderate eulogy of the French Revolution:

When an orator calls the French Revolution "the greatest, the most unmixed, the most unstained and wholly perfect blessing Europe has had in modern times, unless, perhaps, we may possibly except the Reformation," there will be those who differ—who will grant the beneficent results of revolution, as of wild storms of nature, but who will hesitate to call a movement of which the September days, the noyades, and the bloody fury of a brutal mob were incidents, the most unmixed and the most unstained of blessings.[12]

While in the present context Curtis' moderation has been emphasized, it would be an error to overestimate it. Curtis' moderation, like that of the Oberlinites, never spilled over into an advocacy of social expediency but remained a halfway house between extremes. The notion of social expediency, Curtis saw clearly, entails an extremely cautious policy toward injustice if trying to get rid of it would be likely to lead to major trouble. "Be realistic and compromise with the ideal," says the proponent of this point of view. The opposite response, Curtis knew, is radical: a demand for the immediate cessation of injustice, for an immediate closer approximation of the ideal in our world. "The demands of conscience must be met *now*," says the proponent of this point of view, best represented, Curtis thought, by Wendell Phillips and Parker. These men, he felt, unlike the others, had real virtue. They were the pure voice of conscience, and he loved them for it even though he did not agree with their methods of bringing about what conscience dictated.[13] He felt, moreover, that their strong stand was useful for getting a hearing for justice. One must sometimes speak bluntly to be heard at all. Curtis himself, however, eschewed both extremes of social expediency and radical action. He demanded and fought for greater justice in the world no matter how painful the results might be, but he was willing to try to achieve it gradually, by established and nonrevolutionary means. But he was never a moral hypocrite. He never used the plea of moderation as an excuse for doing nothing. He never dallied around beginning to begin, and he beautifully castigated the illicit use of the plea of moderation in his "Easy does it, Guv'nur" article.[14] Let us try to achieve justice within the established order, Curtis said, but if the choice is forced upon us of giving up the quest for justice or fighting—why, I for one must choose to fight.

III

Curtis' abolitionist view led him into a famous indictment of Nathaniel Hawthorne, an indictment he hated to make because he felt close to Hawthorne on personal grounds. Curtis was a frequent visitor at the Old Manse during the three years Hawthorne lived there, and Anna Shaw was sometimes a week-end guest of the Hawthornes. Through the ensuing years Curtis lost neither his affection for the man Hawthorne nor his admiration of his friend's literary talents; but, like other transcendentalists and abolitionists, he was shocked by Hawthorne's views on slavery and his political affiliation with Franklin Pierce. After Hawthorne's death, when other friends wrote only conventional eulogies even though they loathed Hawthorne's politics, Curtis wrote honestly and even caustically about the life and writings of Miles Coverdale. Hawthorne's publisher refused to let this piece appear in the pages of the *Atlantic* but Charles Eliot Norton, irritated both by Hawthorne's politics and by James T. Field's censorship, published it in the *North American Review*.[15] Some people who had been shocked by Hawthorne's politics were equally shocked that Curtis should mention the matter now that Hawthorne was dead. Others felt that Curtis' article was a far better tribute than the conventional eulogies delivered by friends who believed one should never speak ill of the dead. But was there evil to speak of Hawthorne? Curtis thought so, but certain recent commentators think otherwise.[16] The contrasting moral views in this debate provide us with another parable for our times.

The two things that particularly bothered the transcendentalists were certain aspects of Hawthorne's campaign biography of

Pierce in 1852 and his dedication of *Our Old Home* to Pierce in 1863. Pierce's views on slavery in 1852 were well known: he believed that any effort toward emancipation was wrong because unconstitutional, disruptive of the sacred Union, and, even if successful, harmful to the Negro. The real shock for the transcendentalists was that Hawthorne, in his biography of Pierce, presented these views sympathetically and, in effect, agreed with them. "These were his real sentiments, Hawthorne told Bridge, and he did not regret that they were on record even though, as he put it, 'hundreds of friends at the north dropped off' from him 'like autumn leaves.' " [17] Mrs. Hawthorne defensively wrote to her transcendentalist friends, "If you knew General Pierce as we know him, you would be the first to respect him." [18]

Hawthorne's *Our Old Home* was published by Ticknor and Fields in September, 1863, and was dedicated to Pierce, by then one of the most hated of the Copperheads. Pierce's view throughout the war was that the North should withdraw from the war and return to the prewar *status quo*. Many readers inferred from Hawthorne's dedication that he still agreed with the political views of his old friend; but, in fact, he held a much weaker view. While he always thought that the war could have been avoided, he always longed, once it started, for the military success of the North. But he felt that the Union he had loved so well could never be recovered. Even if the South lost, it could never be incorporated into a whole Union again. Hence the goal of the war should be to salvage the border states of Maryland, Virginia, Kentucky, and Missouri. These states, he argued, were fully capable of becoming free states; "he would 'fight to the death' for their reclamation and 'let the rest go.' " [19]

In addition to these two items there was ample evidence in Hawthorne's talk and letters to indicate his distaste for antislavery activity. Commenting on needed reforms in the maritime fleet, he wrote to Ticknor about Sumner, "Had he busied himself about this, instead of Abolitionism, he would have done good service to his country and have escaped Brooks' cudgel." [20] And he longed to talk to those who, unlike the abolitionist, are able to hear two sides of a question.[21] It was quite clear to his friends on many counts that Hawthorne was critical of all antislavery activity, if not actively proslavery. To George Curtis this attitude and viewpoint seemed morally wrong. Unlike Hawthorne's other friends, he felt he must speak the truth as he saw it. The outcome of the Civil War was still very much in doubt, and views like Hawthorne's should not go unchallenged. So he wrote the article that Norton published in the *North American Review*.

From the beginning, Curtis felt, Hawthorne exhibited an inability to be completely in sympathy with, or possessed by, a passion, a spiritual truth, or a moral endeavor. Even his first romance, published anonymously, was "a cold analysis of passion." [22] He turned Hawthorne's description of one of his characters onto the author himself; he "cannot come close enough to human beings to be warmed by them. . . ." [23] Moreover, Hawthorne had no special political, religious, or patriotic affinity with the Puritan spirit that inspired all his greatest work. "It was solely a fascination of the intellect." [24] Unfortunately, while he did justice to its stern and melancholy features he never showed "a deep, completely sympathetic appreciation of the fine moral heroism, the spiritual grandeur, which overhung that gloomy life. . . ." [25]

Hawthorne's trouble, Curtis felt, was that he saw human beings simply as psychological phenomena and was never committed to anything. "In his simplest and sweetest passages he still seems to be studying and curiously observing, rather than sympathizing. You cannot help feeling that the author is always looking askance both at his characters and you, the reader. . . ." [26] And in his life:

He treated his companions as he treated himself and all the personages in history or experience with which he dealt, merely as phenomena to be analysed and described, with no more private malice or personal emotion than the sun, which would have photographed them, warts and all. [27]

Hawthorne exhibited toward reform movements, Curtis wrote, a skeptical courtesy rather than hopeful cordiality:

He does not chide you if you spend effort and life itself in the ardent van of progress, but he simply asks, "Is six so much better than a half a dozen?" He will not quarrel with you if you expect the millennium to-morrow. He only says, with that glimmering smile, "so soon?" [28]

It was not spiritual pride at work here, Curtis averred, but simply an inability to feel the need of commitment to *something,* however fruitless, if for no other reason than to save one's own soul. Hawthorne, Curtis firmly believed, was not unlike Donatello in *The Marble Faun*—"alas! is he human?" one wonders with a pang of doubt.[29]

Hawthorne's inability to be committed on crucial moral issues, Curtis continued, was grotesquely exhibited during the Civil War. "What other man of equal power, who was not intellectually constituted precisely as Hawthorne was, could have stood merely perplexed and bewildered, harassed by the inability of positive sympathy, in the vast conflict which tosses us all in its terrible vortex?" [30] He was pained to see his friend "merely impatient or confounded" by the war and even seeming "to insinuate that it would have been better if the war had been avoided, even at that countless cost to human welfare by which alone the avoidance was possible." [31] Must Hawthorne always be a spectator of life and never a participant?

Curtis' criticism takes on added interest if one looks for a moment at Hawthorne's tales and romances. A recurring theme is that the greatest evil possible is the isolation and alienation of men, the breakdown of the chain of human sympathy and love. Hawthorne repeated this theme in "The Gentle Boy," "Rappacini's Daughter," "Lady Elenore's Mantle," "The Birthmark," "Ethan Brand," and *The Scarlet Letter.* Hawthorne varied the cause of the breakdown of human love and sympathy: sometimes it was fanaticism and self-righteousness; other times, pride of social rank, wealth, or power; or, finally, a disinterested, merely theoretic intellect. According to Curtis, Hawthorne himself stood convicted by his own standards for he was the best example of all of a disinterested, merely theoretic intellect.

Randall Stewart is one of the recent commentators who defends Hawthorne against the type of charge made by Curtis. According to Stewart, Hawthorne's disinterest was simply that of the serious artist at work. To be sure, as he listened to a sad story he was thinking of the literary possibilities of the story and hurried to record it in his diary. However, "the North Adams journal should be regarded primarily as an artist's sketchbook and not as a diary of private emotion." [32] But the man was never completely subdued by the artist, Stewart assures his reader, for his emotion sometimes breaks through the restraint.

Hawthorne was not indifferent to the evils of the world, Stewart continues; he simply doubted the permanence of the effects of external reforms. He advanced the Puritan argument that the regeneration of the individual's soul is necessary for a permanently better world. Moreover, Hawthorne felt that reformers were little better than crackpots and monomaniacs. Some worshiped the potato, others thought that beards had spiritual significance, while everywhere the abolitionist brandished his one idea like an iron flail. Stewart admits that "the juxtaposition of the abolitionist with Shakers and vegetarians must have been shocking to some," but adds that from Hawthorne's point of view they all "made the mistake of concentrating on only one aspect of the problem, and that a superficial one." [33] Unfortunately, also, reformers did not know "what they were up against." [34] They were too naïve about what could be achieved in this complex world. Stewart sees a great deal of wisdom in Hawthorne's view of reform:

> Hawthorne opposed his own skepticism to the faith in reform. He foresaw that prohibitory statutes (like the Maine liquor law) would not prevent the consumption of alcohol. He foresaw, too, that the emancipation of the Negro—though regarded by abolitionists like Whittier as a final and complete solution—would not solve the tangled, deep-seated problem of race relations.[35]

Organized reform according to Hawthorne, and Stewart agrees, is not fundamental. It gets rid of symptoms only and does not get to the cause of the difficulty: man's evil heart. "And unless they hit upon some method of purifying that foul cavern," he continued, "forth from it will reissue all the shapes of wrong and misery—the same old shapes or worse ones—which they have taken such a vast deal of trouble to consume to ashes." [36] Hawthorne, like Edwards, Stewart says, believed that true reform comes only when men's souls are regenerated.

The answers to Stewart will be quite different depending upon the details of the view of reform held by the people who answer. But almost everyone who holds a moderate position on reform can agree on certain points. No doubt a permanently good world could be achieved by the regeneration of men's hearts. Unfortunately, widespread regeneration seems as unlikely as ever. Hence, the insistence upon waiting for it can only be understood as an excuse for doing nothing in order to avoid causing trouble to those who do not already have it, or, worse yet, as a screen for vested interests. Moreover, even if regeneration were possible, what do we do in the meantime? Do we need to continue to live with the injustice without any effort to remove its symptoms? It seems perfectly reasonable to take aspirin while waiting for a doctor to diagnose the cause of a headache and remedy it. Even if we cannot reconstruct the world according to our heart's desire, we can still try to mitigate specific evils in a piecemeal way. Of course the world is complex, and we sometimes unintentionally produce bad results in trying to bring about even piecemeal reforms. But the same holds true for everyone's practical and prudential calculations in the workaday world. Sometimes calculations go awry here too. But we usually manage to avoid catastrophe and, in any case, there is no significant rational alternative. No doubt Curtis was sometimes overly optimistic about what reform movements could achieve. But he was no fatuous optimist. He believed that even if reform efforts accomplished nothing, it was better to make the effort than to learn to live comfortably with injustice to someone else.

10

CHAUNCEY WRIGHT

A F T E R 1860 philosophical thinking in America occurred in
a scientific rather than a religious context. After that date
philosophy was primarily a series of different responses to Darwin's epochal work.[1] Some writers like John Fiske and E. L.
Youmans generalized evolutionary concepts into "cosmic metaphysics," while other writers pressed them into extreme forms of
"social Darwinism." Chauncey Wright's response to the *Origin
of Species,* however, was quite different. For him the important
thing was not to use Darwin's work for speculative purposes in
philosophy but to analyze carefully the logical structure of biological explanations. Such analysis is significant in its own right,
he felt, as well as helpful in pointing up the uselessness of the
speculative appropriation of Darwin's thought. It is important to
understand in detail Wright's response to Darwinism because he
was America's first technical philosopher of science and ushered
in the Golden Age of philosophy in America.

Although the context of philosophy after 1860 was scientific,
interest in moral philosophy was as great as ever. Utilitarianism

continued to be a topic of interest, but now the views of Bentham and Mill rather than those of Paley, Finney, or Fairchild were most discussed. Wright was a staunch advocate of J. S. Mill's brand of the greatest happiness principle and never tired of defending it against what he took to be unjust criticism. Nevertheless he was not a blind follower of Mill but, as we shall see, developed a more cautious and negative view of reform than is usually associated with Millian liberalism. It was a pessimistic view more akin to some strands of contemporary liberalism than to anything that came before it. However it was not a nihilistic view and reflects in part the good sense of his friend George William Curtis.

I

Wright lived most of his life in Cambridge, Massachusetts, where, after graduation from Harvard, he was employed as a mathematician by the United States *Nautical Almanac*.[2] Twice he was a lecturer at Harvard, once in psychology and once in physics, but was never successful as a teacher. His real career was that of village philosopher of old Cambridge. In private conversation he was brilliant, influencing older friends like Charles Eliot Norton and E. W. Gurney and younger friends like C. S. Peirce, William James, and Oliver Wendell Holmes, Jr.

Wright's intellectual career was launched, so to speak, when he was elected to membership in the American Academy of Arts and Sciences at the meeting of January 25, 1860.[3] This event was symbolically and materially important, for Wright was elected just in time to attend the great debate on Darwinism between his friend Asa Gray and Louis Agassiz, in whose Cambridge school for girls Wright had taught. Impressed with Gray's exactness of thought and his way of keeping scientific discussion free of metaphysical speculation, as well as with Darwin's new book, Wright was quickly counted among the Darwinians. No doubt as a result of Gray's ascendancy in the academy, Wright was elected recording secretary of this learned society on May 26, 1863, and served in this office until May 24, 1870.[4]

Gray quickly recognized Wright's great ability in science and mathematics and set him to work on the problems of phyllotaxy, that is, the arrangements of leaves on the stem of a plant.[5] The mathematical ratios exhibited by the arrangements of leaves had led to much idealistic speculation among German biologists, one of whom, Alexander Braun, was the brother-in-law of Louis Agassiz. Wright completely reworked the idealistic system of phyllotaxy into one derived by natural selection. On Wright's view, "leaves were arranged about a stem to economize space and have good exposure to light, being based on two plans perhaps derived from fronds of *algae*." [6] Wright's long, technical article was published in the *Memoirs of the American Academy of Arts and Sciences* and was reprinted in several other places.[7] "Joined together," writes A. H. Dupree, "Gray and Wright thus proceeded with the destruction of the world of Agassiz and the erection of the world of Darwin in a brilliant and almost forgotten line of research." [8]

By December, 1860, Gray was trying through Darwin to get Huxley to publish an article by Wright in the *Natural History Review*. Darwin and Huxley decided not to publish the article, and this has led one commentator to say that Wright was rejected by the inner circle of Darwinism.[9] This conclusion is wrong, however, for Wright was handsomely accepted by Darwin himself in later years. Darwin was impressed particularly by the critical ability displayed by Wright in his critique of St. George Mivart's *Genesis of Species* in 1871. Mivart, an English biologist, had accepted the fact of evolution but had rejected Darwin's natural selection explanation of it. Wright criticized Mivart's argument and sent a copy of his paper to Darwin. To Darwin he wrote, "My special purpose has been to contribute to the theory by *placing* it in its proper relations to philosophical inquiries in general." [10] The scholar of Down replied that he liked the paper very much. In fact, "I have hardly ever in my life received an article which has given me so much satisfaction as the review which you have been so kind as to send me." [11] Darwin, with Wright's consent, reprinted the article, with an additional appendix, and distributed it in England.[12] Darwin's recognition of Wright prompted Mivart to reply; and Wright, who needed the stimulus of discussion, continued to write long essays on Darwin's work.

Wright's adherence to Darwin's view was not accidental; he had a long acquaintance with the evolutionary point of view and early showed a predilection to view it favorably. He had read Robert Chambers' *Vestiges of the Natural History of Creation,* which defended an evolutionary point of view, as a high-school student in Northampton, and while at Harvard he had written a paper for Dr. James Walker on brute and human intellect which exhibited the specific influence of this controversial book.[13] It is true, however, that while Wright was impressed by the evolutionary point of view he was not impressed, after becoming acquainted with Gray, with the sort of arguments advanced by Chambers. Even before his friendship with Gray he had noticed that the real scientists, like Baron Cuvier, seemed to be against the derivation hypothesis, and this checked his enthusiasm. However, the appearance of Darwin's work removed all his doubts. Darwin not only established the fact of evolution with scientific skill and care but also offered an attractive explanation of it in terms of natural selection. Darwin avoided all the teleological elements present in previous evolutionary theory, and this fact recommended his work immediately. Wright held a Galilean conception of science, and nothing that departed from this model was likely to win his allegiance.

II

In addition to his contribution to phyllotaxy, Wright also collaborated with Jeffries Wyman, professor of zoology at Harvard College, in an effort to explain cell structure in beehives.[14] His most important contribution to the discussion of natural selection, however, was not scientific in nature but a matter of logical analysis. In his definition and defense of Darwinism, Wright tried to clarify the meaning of basic concepts and to explain the logical structure of explanations in biology. His three major essays on Darwin's work, all of which appeared in the *North American Review* and were later reprinted in *Philosophical Discussions,* were "Limits of Natural Selection," "The Genesis of Species," and "Evolution by Natural Selection." The first of these essays he wrote in defense of natural selection against the limits placed upon it by Alfred Russel Wallace, coauthor of the concept, and the latter two against what he took to be the errors of St. George Mivart, a Jesuit naturalist, who accepted evolution as a fact but rejected natural selection as its explanation. Since Wright was answering specific objections his essays have a piecemeal and disorganized appearance. But they contain, in spite of this, fundamental philosophical insights.

1. Wright contributed in an essential way to the logical analysis of the species concept. In discussions about species in scientific circles in Cambridge it was fashionable to say that on Agassiz' theory species were real and fundamental while on Darwin's view they were conventional and arbitrary. Wright felt that this way of stating the difference between the two obscured the issue rather than clarified it.

According to Wright,[15] classes or species of anything may be called real or fundamental when the individuals composing the class have a cluster of characteristics in common. On the other hand, a class may be called conventional or arbitrary when the individuals composing the class have only the characteristics in common which formed the basis of classification. On this view "mammal" is a real or fundamental class while the class of individuals composed of people whose last names begin with the letters *A* through *D* is a conventional or arbitrary one. Given these senses of the crucial terms, Wright said, we can see that the species concept for Darwin is just as real and fundamental as it is for a nonevolutionist. The species concept for Darwin can be said to be arbitrary or conventional only in the following sense. Since characteristics vary on a continuum, it is arbitrary where the continuum is divided to produce a species. But within any such cross section it still remains true that there is a cluster of characteristics exhibited just as surely as a cluster is exhibited in the species of nonevolutionists.

2. Wright warned that one should not expect the explanatory power of natural selection to be as great as that of physical concepts like acceleration, momentum, and force.[16] The concept of natural selection is used to explain a concrete series of events, the origin of species, not a highly controlled and artificial series

of laboratory events. Explanations in terms of natural selection are more like the explanations found in meteorology and physical geology, sciences that apply general principles to the actual workings of concrete nature. Again, natural selection might be compared to the fundamental laws of political economy, which can be demonstrated as actually at work in the production of prices in the market but are not sufficiently detailed for prediction. As in natural selection, there is too much missing evidence.

Discouraged by these difficulties, some biologists try to explain everything by a transcendental philosophical hypothesis. Such biologists simply exhibit their own lack of resources in finding the unknown incidental causes through which the principles act. In short, Wright believed that the principle of natural selection has a high probability of being true, but that the application of it in detail to all the complexities of organic life requires the same skill the meteorologist needs in applying the principles of physics to the concrete course of nature. Mivart, Wright thought, singularly lacked appreciation and understanding of such skills.

3. Any sciences of the geophysical type that deal with a concrete series of events, Wright said, run into the problems of causal complexity and irregularity. In a concrete series of events causal chains are intermingled most intimately; and this complexity, unfathomed in precise detail, generally gives the appearance of irregularity and hence suggests the possibility of uncaused events. But irregularity is an appearance only and not reality, Wright thought, and the suggestion of uncaused events is unfortunate. Irregularity for Wright indicates not an abridgment of causality but only an abridgment, because of causal complexity, of our knowledge of it.[17]

Wright's younger friend C. S. Peirce was also interested in the notion of irregularity but interpreted it quite differently. The occurrence of things by absolute chance was Peirce's explanation of the irregularity in the world; chance for him was ontologically irreducible—"an objective reality, operative in the cosmos."[18] This view of absolute chance, or the notion that some events are uncaused, was Peirce's doctrine of tychism, and no view could be farther removed from Wright's belief in the

universality of causality. Hence it is puzzling to find one commentator suggesting that Wright anticipated Peirce's tychism.[19]
Wright and Peirce, to be sure, both emphasized the notion of
irregularity in concrete events, but they interpreted the concept
in radically different ways. Wright, to use Peirce's later phrase,
was a hidebound necessitarian.

Peirce strenuously objected to the necessitarian view, which
he characterized in the following way.[20] According to the necessitarian, if one knew all the laws of the universe and knew the
exact state of the universe at any moment, then he could predict
the occurrence of every subsequent event in the universe and
could predict every characteristic of these events. But if this
universal determinism were true, Peirce continued, then there
would be no novelty in the universe; everything to come would
be built in, so to speak, from the beginning. But, clearly, there is
novelty in the universe; hence universal determinism must be
wrong. Wright realized the significance of this sort of argument
long before Peirce advanced it, and he thought he had an
acceptable answer to it. He felt that it was possible both to be a
necessitarian and to allow in a certain sense for novelty in the
world. His discussion of this point depends upon his interesting
distinction between two different senses of "explanation."

According to Wright,[21] one way of explaining an event is to
state the cause of its occurrence. One explains the falling of a
stone, for example, by pointing out that it was left unsupported
above the surface of the earth. However, the nature of this cause
is wholly unlike the nature of its effect. There is nothing in the
notion of being unsupported that suggests, in an a priori way,
falling. One simply has to experience their constant conjunction
and hence conclude that they are causally related. The second
way of explaining an event, he continued, is to state the cause of
its occurrence and, at the same time, to analyze or decompose it
into its constituents. Wright said that this sort of explanation is
the most perfect and occurs only in mechanics. In addition
to the parallelogram of forces, he had in mind Newton's solution
to the n-body problem. In this most perfect sort of explanation
there is nothing new in the result; it is the sum of its constituents. Hence, given the constituents one can predict the occur-

rence and characteristics of the resultants. One does not have to experience the conjunction of constituents and resultants to establish causality. Given the one, the other *must* occur. The reason it must occur is precisely that there is nothing new in the effect.

The application of Wright's distinction to the necessitarian issue occurs in the following way. The determinist should not claim that if he had sufficient knowledge he could predict the first occurrence and the characteristics of every event. Wright believed that this sort of prediction occurs only for limited events in mechanics. The first occurrence of most events—to say nothing of their characteristics—cannot be predicted; hence such events and characteristics are genuinely new or novel. Consequently, one can be a determinist and still account for novelty. According to Wright:

. . . the power of flight in the first birds, for example, is only involved potentially in previous phenomena. In the same way, no act of self-consciousness, however elementary, may have been realized before man's first self-conscious act in the animal world; yet the act may have been involved potentially in pre-existing powers or causes. The derivation of this power, supposing it to have been observed by a finite angelic . . . intelligence, could not have been foreseen to be involved in the mental causes, on the conjunction of which it might, nevertheless, have been seen to depend.[22]

But, one might argue, even though the determinist can account for novelty in some sense, he still has a difficulty. Since he believes that all events are caused, he still has to believe that everything is built in from the beginning. Wright, however, rejected this sort of argument. "In the beginning," he felt, were the magical words of Christianity or of any theistic belief, and he rejected on various grounds, epistemological and ethical, this cosmology.[23] For Wright there was no beginning of the universe. Like Aristotle, he believed the universe to be uncreated and eternal.

III

Much of Wright's written work was devoted to criticizing the speculative appropriations of Darwin's thought. The speculative appropriations, he felt, occurred mostly in philosophy, but Darwin's work had speculative repercussions even in scientific cosmology. Spencer, he thought, was the worst offender on both counts, generalizing biological evolution into cosmic metaphysics, on the one hand, and allowing it to determine his judgment about the nebular hypothesis, on the other. One of the first articles Wright wrote was an attack on Spencer's work, and the day he died he was still writing against his prime antagonist.

1. Wright's most extensive criticism of Spencer appears in a long article published in the *North American Review* for April, 1865,[24] where, in addition, he presented his own analysis of the logic of science. What irritated Wright most about Spencer was his claim to have a "scientific" philosophy when, he felt certain, Spencer knew precious little about the structure of scientific inference. According to Wright:

> Nothing justifies the development of abstract principles in science but their utility in enlarging our concrete knowledge of nature. The ideas on which mathematical Mechanics and the Calculus are founded, the morphological ideas of Natural History, and the theories of Chemistry are such working ideas,—finders, not merely summaries of truth.[25]

But, Wright claimed, this is not the value we find in Spencer's speculations. For example, Spencer defines psychology as the study of ideas and posits as the test of the reality of an idea "the inconceivableness of its negation." But, Wright said, Spencer "makes little explicit use of his postulate. . . . It is one of those unproductive principles which Positivism condemns; and he develops others equally useless, except in the mental discipline there may be in following their evolution." [26]

Wright also claimed that Spencer's Law of Evolution, the change from homogeneity to heterogeneity through differentiation and integration, applied universally to the movement of nature, is a resurgence of teleology in scientific thinking. This is not, to be sure, a teleology of final causes or happy denouements, but a teleology that imposes upon the world an order that the mythic instinct is inclined to: "something having a beginning, a middle, and an end,—an epic poem, a dramatic representation, a story, a cosmogony." [27]

Spencer related his Law of Evolution to the fundamental scientific ideas of space, time, matter, and force; and again Wright criticized him for viewing scientific principles as summaries instead of working hypotheses. "To all the ideas which he adopts from science he adds a new sense, or rather a vagueness, so as to make them descriptive of as much as possible." [28] One example of this procedure is his translation of the physicist's "conservation of force" into the "persistence of force." In losing their precision and definiteness, Wright said, scientific principles lose their predictive value, their capacity to discover new facts (as the law of gravity led to the discovery of Uranus), in which their real value lies.

Terms which the real physicist knows how to use as the terms of mathematical formulas . . . terms which have been of inestimable service both in formulating and finding out the secrets of nature, are appropriated by Mr. Spencer to the further elaboration of his vague definitions, and to the abstract description of as much in real nature as they may happen to apply to. . . . Out of mathematical formulas these terms lose their definiteness and their utility. [29]

Philosophers after Wright generalized his "working hypothesis" interpretation of scientific principles into various pragmatic "theories" of mind, meaning, and truth. Peirce, for example, claimed that all empirical propositions, not simply the theoretical ones of science, have the nature of hypotheses. Thus, a simple sentence like "This diamond is hard" is a hypothesis which predicts that if I rub the diamond across glass it will cut the glass, if I rub glass across it the glass will not cut it, etc. The whole meaning of the sentence for Peirce is the set of such *possible* sensory experiences. The meaning of any concept used in a sentence is simply the sum of sensory consequences it entails if true. [30]

Wright, however, never interpreted sentences like "This diamond is hard" as a hypothesis. For him only sentences that contain theoretical words—such as "This object is in uniform motion"—count as hypotheses. Nor did he ever suggest that the meaning of a sentence consists in its whole set of experienceable consequences; he only insisted that theoretical terms, to be admissible scientific notions, must have some sensory credentials, either by yielding sensory consequences themselves or by yielding such consequences in conjunction with other theoretical terms.[31] Wright, in short, was offering a criterion of meaningfulness for scientific terms; he was not offering an analysis of the meaning of terms, either scientific or ordinary. And it is interesting to note that Wright was offering a liberal criterion of meaningfulness for scientific terms. He did not require that every theoretical word have an empirical consequence, but only that the whole theoretical system must have empirical consequences of a specific kind.

2. Wright's criticism of Spencer's defense of the nebular hypothesis and an account of his own scientific cosmology appeared in the *North American Review* for July, 1864.[32] Wright felt that Spencer uncritically accepted the nebular hypothesis, in spite of its scientific difficulties, because it fitted neatly into his evolutionary cosmology, exhibiting, as it did, the subtle teleology of dramatic unity. Wright claimed that the production of systems of worlds, like ordinary weather, shows on the whole no development or any discernible tendency whatever but is a doing and undoing without end—a kind of weather, "cosmical weather." He based his ateleological view on what he called the principle of countermovements, "a principle in accordance with which there is no action in nature to which there is not some counter-action," which he contended is a likely generalization from the laws and facts of science.[33]

Wright worked out a technical and elaborate hypothesis about the nature of cosmical weather,[34] a system that exhibited the principle of countermovements and avoided what he believed to be the teleological elements of the nebular hypothesis. Briefly, Wright, impressed with the conservation of energy principle, accounted for the origin of the sun's heat and the positions and movements of planets by the first law of thermodynamics and the conservation of angular momentum. The spiral fall of meteors into the sun, he thought, is the cause of its heat. The sun does not rapidly increase in size, he suggested, because the heat of the sun is reconverted into mechanical energy. Some of the heat is consumed in vaporizing the meteors and parts of the mass of the sun, while the rest is expended in further heating, expanding, and thus lifting the gaseous material to the heights from whence it spiraled into the sun. There it cools and condenses, and the cycle begins again.

Wright apparently thought that mechanical energy and heat energy are not only convertible but also reversible. He was not unaware of the second law of thermodynamics, however, at least not when he wrote "The Philosophy of Herbert Spencer" a year later.[35] In a section of this article devoted to the nebular hypothesis, Wright says that the most obvious objection to his hypothesis is Thomson's theory that there is a universal tendency in nature to the dissipation of mechanical energy:

. . . a theory well founded, nay, demonstrated, if we only follow this energy as far as the present limits of science extend. But to a true Aristotelian this theory, so far from suggesting a dramatic *dénouement*, such as the ultimate death of nature, only propounds new problems. What becomes of the sun's dynamic energy, and whence do the bodies come which support this wasting power? [36]

IV

None of the essays published in Wright's lifetime dealt with moral issues, but he was, nonetheless, deeply interested in the nature of moral law. His defense and applications of Mill's version of utilitarianism are to be found in his long and frequent letters to Charles Eliot, Grace, and Jane Norton during one of their long sojourns in Europe. These letters were eventually included in *Letters of Chauncey Wright,* edited by James Bradley Thayer,[37] although unfortunately they were shortened and frequently emended. The original letters are preserved in the Norton Collection at Houghton Library, Harvard University.[38]

Wright accepted the utilitarian view of moral law because it was required by his theory of knowledge. To know which types of acts are right or wrong the utilitarian examines consequences; and this procedure, he felt, unlike the intuitions of conscience, lends itself to the tests and corrections of common or "public" experience.[39] The rightness of an act, he contended, is wholly determined by the nature of its consequences without any reference whatsoever to what seemed likely to the agent at the time he acted. If a person intends to help someone but in fact hurts him, he has acted *wrongly* even though, as a person, he is not morally *blameworthy*. Wright's view, thus, makes an interesting contrast with Fairchild's. The latter claimed that if a person intends to help someone and acts reasonably in terms of the available evidence, then, in spite of the actual consequences, he has both acted *rightly* and is morally praiseworthy. Wright's view has the difficulty that it makes it impossible for man to do his duty unless he is omniscient, while Fairchild's view unfortunately requires that we say retrospectively of an act which has had disastrous consequences that nevertheless it should have been done. Neither alternative seems quite right, and nothing Fairchild or Wright said on the problem successfully removed the puzzle.

While Wright never conceded anything to the deontologist as Fairchild did, nevertheless he did not ignore the importance of good intentions in moral judgment. He simply felt that this importance could be accounted for adequately within a utilitarian framework. In Wright's words:

. . . What is called the conscience, or strong and compelling aversions to certain classes of actions and admirations or approvals of other classes, should be respected and carefully fostered, even though in some matters it leads wrong; since a faulty conscience is more useful or less harmful on the whole than unprincipled conduct. . . .[40]

Like all nineteenth-century utilitarian moralists, Wright faced the following challenge: Can you distinguish between higher-order and lower-order pleasures, or—as ministers liked to put the question—between spiritual and beastly pleasures? Does the utilitarian endorse the greatest amount of beastly pleasure for all concerned or the greatest amount of spiritual happiness for the greatest number?

Bentham adroitly answered the challenge by saying that it is a false dichotomy. The point is to achieve the maximum amount of mutually consistent pleasures for the greatest number. The so-called spiritual pleasures *are* higher-order precisely because, and only because, they are more productive of maximum pleasure than are sensuous ones. But, he claimed, there is no intrinsic difference among pleasures.[41] The pleasures of the board and the book, qua pleasures, are precisely the same. J. S. Mill, however, insisted that there is a qualitative as well as an instrumental difference between types of pleasure. Any person capable of experiencing both spiritual and sensuous pleasures would invariably refuse a life of complete sensuous pleasure if it entailed giving up the sometimes painful but spiritually significant life of man. Who would choose to be a blissful pig at the expense of giving up the possibility of spiritual contentment?

Wright thought that Bentham answered the ministers' challenge well. They offer indeed a false dichotomy! What the utilitarian endorses is the maximum amount of mutually consistent "spiritual" and "beastly" pleasures. Sometimes the latter run wild and make over-all satisfaction impossible and so must be checked by rational effort. But this outcome is not always the case. Sometimes the two go perfectly well together. They are not in principle opposed. One may enjoy his glass of wine while he reads the latest installment of a Dickens novel.

On the question of qualitative difference Wright thought Mill was correct. It might be added, however, that he was never sufficiently impressed with Mill's "blissful pig" way of arguing the point even to mention it in his discussions. Wright discussed this issue in various contexts and always came to the conclusion that there is a "preferability in kind" among pleasures, a qualitative difference among them which cannot be explained away as simply instrumental differences.[42] Esthetic experiences, for example, he thought, have a certain *experienced* dignity, a felt place in the spiritual hierarchy which sensuous pleasures lack. As we shall see, Wright had to urge this point upon his friend Charles Norton when the latter felt that utilitarianism—a position he ultimately adopted under Wright's influence—did not do justice to esthetic value.

The bulk of Wright's discussion of the principle of utility took the form of defending it against what he took to be misinterpretation and hasty criticism. He was convinced that the low quality of argument against this view reflected a blind distaste for it in some quarters.

1. Critics sometimes said that utilitarianism, based on pleasure, as it is, does not take seriously the basic moral concepts of

unselfishness and self-sacrifice. Wright points out that following the principle of utility *entails* acting unselfishly. A utilitarian must decide the rightness of an act in terms of its over-all good consequences, not simply the good consequences for himself. Moreover, the utilitarian must be willing to sacrifice himself if an occasion objectively demands it. He only insists that the sacrifice must produce over-all good and not be pointless or gratuitous. Self-sacrifice must be realistic and take into account likely consequences. Self-sacrifice, in short, is not intrinsically good—as the romantic moralist believes—but only instrumentally so.[43]

2. Another criticism of utility was that sometimes an act that produces over-all happiness is nevertheless immoral. Consider the following case. A district attorney uncovers new evidence that shows a habitual criminal innocent in the particular case for which he is being tried. It would be beneficial to society if the evidence were suppressed and the criminal convicted, but such a course of action would be manifestly immoral. To this sort of criticism the adherents of Millian utilitarianism have always had a stock reply, a type of reply that seemed adequate to Wright. The district attorney should not suppress the evidence because it might become public knowledge and have catastrophic effects on the public's confidence in the courts of law. This standard utilitarian reply, however, has been called in question by W. D. Ross and other recent "rule utilitarians," and requires further refinements if it is to meet their telling criticism. How can it possibly be the case that an act is wrong if people might find out about it but presumably right if they did not?[44]

3. Critics of the greatest happiness principle say that a person who needs to reach a moral decision does not have time to calculate the likely consequences of alternative acts. The time for decision would be gone while he was still busy calculating. J. S. Mill had replied that this criticism would be the same as saying that a Christian is unable to apply his moral principles because he would not have time to read the Bible before deciding. Presumably the Christian has read his Bible beforehand and can act quickly in standard cases. In like manner presumably the utilitarian has learned from past experience and can apply

what he has learned quickly and adequately to present similar cases.

Wright met this sort of criticism by emphasizing the importance of moral rules. Moral rules have been "naturally selected" precisely because following them produces over-all beneficial consequences for any society. Hence, instead of taking the time to calculate consequences in a specific case, the best plan of action usually is to apply quickly the appropriate moral rule. Wright urged strongly the importance of habit in successful moral action.[45] Acting from habit rather than from specific calculation usually produces the best results and hence is justified by an over-all utilitarian point of view.[46]

4. Intuitionist critics objected that there was no reason for accepting the principle of utility itself. An intuitionist says he can "see" that his basic moral principle is the right one, but how can a utilitarian justify his position? Mill had tried to show that while the principle of utility is not based on intuition, and cannot be "proved," nevertheless there are reasons that can be advanced for accepting it. That is the burden of chapter iv of his *Utilitarianism*. And yet, as we have seen, Wright's friend James Bradley Thayer effectively criticized Mill's performance— criticized it in a way that requires an answer from a serious student of Mill. One expects to have the answer from Wright and is surprised to discover that, far from answering Thayer's criticism, Wright nowhere in his letters or essays even considers the general question of justifying the principle of utility. The only way to explain this surprising fact, I suspect, is that Wright did not take seriously the possibility of arguing directly for the acceptance of any philosophical position. The answer to both Mill and Thayer implicit in all his writings is this: the only way to establish any philosophical position is indirectly—that is, by showing that the system in question explains all the relevant data, makes all the relevant distinctions, and is not demonstrably inconsistent, and that all alternative systems can be shown to be deficient in one or more of these respects. One must admit that this procedure does seem to be the main thrust of philosophical dialectic.

11

PRACTICAL PROBLEMS

W R I G H T ' S views on organized reform were intermediate between the two opposed views popular in the middle
of the nineteenth century. Emerson represented a negative attitude toward reform while George Ripley defended the reconstructionist viewpoint. Wright's alternative, as we shall see, was,
in principle if not in action, much like that of the Oberlinites
and George W. Curtis—although, unlike theirs, his was primarily negative in nature.

I

Emerson felt that his doctrine of self-reliance and the perfectibility of the soul committed him to a negative position on
organized reform. Political agitation and social manipulation
could attain nothing significant; the only effective reform was
regeneration of the individual heart and soul. As we have seen,
this was also the view of the early Wayland and of Finney and
Hawthorne. Ripley, on the other hand, felt that the very structure of society stifles the realization of man's self-reliance and

blocks the perfectibility of his soul. It is necessary, he thought, to create a social and intellectual climate in which self-realization would in fact be a realistic possibility.[1] Brook Farm became the symbol of his reconstructionist views.

Wright certainly could not agree with either of these alternatives. He clearly could not agree with Emerson or Finney, since one would wait until doomsday for the regeneration of men's hearts. On the other hand, he had no enthusiasm for trying to reconstruct society in any fundamental way either.[2] Utilitarian reason, he felt, is but a crude guide for life; and even well-thought-out systems of law contain little positive wisdom. Take the case of marriage. Marriages resulting from accident or because of momentary passion often have sad consequences, and society would like to avoid them. But planned marriages through religious, legal, and social restrictions, he thought, would have far worse results. "Not to legislate," he wrote, "is often the wisest principle of legislation." [3]

. . . No law-givers, no private counsellors, are at all equal to the subtle skill of nature, shown in the survival of the fittest; which, though a rough remedy for evils that wisdom, if it existed, might forestall, is one which wisdom has not yet equalled. The ancient state of Sparta, whose law-givers undertook to do the work of nature in selection, perished in consequence; and nature selected those ancient communities whose principles of freedom and humanity to the weak seemed opposed to her Dracontic laws. *Not to help* natural selection is the human way, strong in its weakness, of gaining the favor of this fatal power. . . .[4]

While Wright was convinced that utilitarian reason could do little by way of reconstructing society, he felt that it could do much through legislation and social reform to alleviate the suffering and injustice that occur within the framework of a democratic society. While one cannot bring about the millennium, one can try, with reasonable assurance of success, to reform the social and economic conditions that lead to misery and despair. Different things make people happy, but an empty stomach generally leads to misery. While he accepted the rights and laws of private property and ownership,[5] Wright felt that such rights had got out of hand. To a sometimes frightening extent the laws of property had given rise not to increased gains for many people but to a large and permanent class of unproductive consumers—in which case the laws of property had become simply legalized robbery and should be amended or abrogated through legislation inspired by utilitarian principles.[6]

Another injustice in American society which he thought could be remedied was the subjugation of women. He felt that women were unjustly deprived of the vote and of legal equality, conditions that could be rectified through social and religious, as well as political, reform.[7] Here was an evil which, for utilitarian reasons, should be removed without further delay. He willingly admitted, on utilitarian grounds, that restrictive laws are often necessary. But, he continued, laws that infringe on the rights of individuals without being necessary for security are impertinent and defeat the larger utilitarian goals.

. . . Believing as I do, that human beings generally, even children, have hitherto been much more in subjection to authority than they ought to be (both directly and indirectly, or through the sanctions of punishments and rewards) . . . and seeing that, so far as women are treated differently from men, it is mainly in consequence of some traditional and prevailing sentiments, which are not justified by any more obvious utility than an unreasoning conservatism,—I am in general ready to protest against this present state of things and in favor of larger liberty. . . . [However] it is under the rights of individuals . . . that I would place the rights of women; and it seems to me that those who agitate specially for the latter are not usually actuated by the true principle of liberty, since what they demand is not equal exemption of all persons from oppression . . . but . . . an increase of the range of authority by conferring it equally on all.[8]

Grace Norton, in replying to Wright, doubted that women are really "subjected" in any important sense. After all, she wrote, the force of character and wide experience rather than the fact of sex determine the ruler and the ruled in all immediate personal relations.[9] And she might have added, as some people did, that they determine also the ruler and the ruled in a political sense also. Napoleon's mother was an influential woman even though she did not vote. Wright agreed with Grace Norton in part but noted that

. . . men have so arranged the affairs of life that, for the most part, they or their sex have the best opportunities for acquiring these qualifications for ruling. . . . No doubt, a prince is better able to rule than a peasant, and therefore has a better right; still society is just as responsible for the peasant's subjection, since it has made the inequality by the difference in their education.[10]

The application of this point to the Negroes during the Reconstruction Period in which Wright wrote is painfully clear.

By way of summary, Wright rejected both extreme views of reform. The notions of regeneration and reconstruction seemed equally utopian to him, although, of course, for different reasons. He did not believe that one can reconstruct society, but he did urge the need of piecemeal reform of existing evils. Even in the latter case, Wright offered certain cryptic advice to all social workers whose first question is, "What do we do about it?" They should ponder carefully, he said, these Delphic answers: "Keep knowledge at nurse as long as possible; cherish its grounds, reasons, and questions; draw conclusions only when the necessity of decision compels." "Let not your love of your neighbor mistake itself for a knowledge of him." "Don't mistake an aesthetic preference, on the one hand, for a moral judgment; nor let generous feeling, on the other hand, corrupt either justice or good taste." [11]

II

Wright was too much impressed with the complexity of human behavior to make a good reconstructionist. In this respect his views on utility departed substantially from those of Bentham. Consider the following moral problem. Should a doctor tell his patient that he is seriously ill or lie to him? The answer, for Bentham, would be wholly contextual and rationally to be decided. If the doctor had good reason to believe that knowledge of his condition would not be detrimental to the patient, then he should tell him the truth. However, if he had good reason to believe that knowledge of his condition would itself worsen the patient's health, then the doctor, on rational utilitarian grounds, has the duty to lie.

Wright, however, felt that specific cases are often so complex that it is difficult to calculate what the likely results will be. If the doctor lies to his patient in order to avoid some painful consequences he may inadvertently introduce others. Out of ignorance of his true condition the patient may do something extremely damaging to his health. Should the doctor lie and have a nurse keep close watch? Obviously such attention would be inconsistent with the doctor's reassurances that the patient was not seriously ill. This feeling for the complexity of events led Wright to ascribe far more importance to traditional moral rules than Bentham did. Wright felt that careful adherence to moral rules like "one ought to tell the truth" produces better consequences in the long run than calculated contextual breaking of them. In fact, as we have seen, Wright felt that these moral rules survive precisely because they have utility [12] and hence should be followed closely unless we have good evidence that following one would produce disastrous consequences. He would not, obviously, require one to tell the truth to a maniac who, pursuing someone with a knife, stops to ask which way his quarry has fled!

Wright, in general, came to hold a utilitarian view quite far removed from that of Bentham. Wright was not only a second-order utilitarian—that is, one who believes that following traditional moral rules will produce better results in the long run than habitually breaking them—but he also stressed the great practical importance of acting from habit and instinct rather than by directly calculating the likely consequences in each specific context. Acting from habit and instinct, he felt, often produces better results than the explicit attempt to calculate what good results will likely follow in a given case. According to Wright, the reliance of utilitarianism

. . . on the forces of habit and instinct is not for rational guidance, but for practical efficacy; yet these are so important to its aims, that they are not safely to be disregarded, or unnecessarily opposed, or weakened by substituting for them habitually the calculations of expediency.[13]

Wright further elaborated this point in a letter to Grace Norton:

Utilitarianism needs to be supplemented, in order to meet misunderstandings, by a Philosophy of Habit, and to lay down among its practical principles that, since motives are effective, not in proportion to their usefulness or reasonableness, but rather to their singleness or instinctiveness, therefore it is reasonable to foster and to rely practically on the force of proper habits and just, natural inclinations.[14]

While Wright stressed the complexity of human behavior and the importance of traditional moral rules, and emphasized the importance of habit and instinct to the utilitarian, nevertheless he was not unsympathetic to certain aspects of Bentham's reform notions. Wright might best be understood as stressing the negative part of Bentham's views on reform. While Wright was pessimistic about the possibilities of positive reform, he believed that much could be done to get rid of the evils that occur in the existing framework of a democratic society. Wright claimed, with some of the same spirit of reform that pervaded Bentham's work, that utility is crucially important in practice as a standard for correcting a whole world of abuses that have been perpetrated by various tyrants under the guise of the dictates of conscience.

Such are the self-sanctioned prejudices, time-sanctioned iniquities, religious absurdities, all of which can claim the same grounds of justification as those on which the intuitive morality would base the ten commandments; namely, that most people, or at least somebody, *feels* them to be right. That *somebody,* say the pope, should be infallible in his feelings, is a necessary corner-stone of this philosophy, and most of the unorthodox or radical advocates of it claim this infallibility for themselves; but it follows from their principles that in cases of dispute some pope,—whether the Roman pontiff or not,—some holiest man, must be the final arbiter.[15]

The results of such arbitrariness, Wright felt, are generally restrictive of human liberty, and the great role of utilitarianism is the negative one of breaking down such restrictions whenever they occur—even in a democratic society.

III

An understanding of Wright's views on reform helps one to evaluate J. B. Thayer's criticism of his moral life. Thayer was

Wright's lifelong friend and editor of his *Letters,* and hence any criticism he offers must be taken quite seriously. In chapter ix of the *Letters* Thayer wrote, with apparent reluctance, that Wright had

. . . insensibly permitted the scientific habit—that habit which, as he himself has acutely said, refuses to acknowledge any burden of proof—to creep into the region of conduct; unobservant, in his own case, of those laws of life by which conduct of some sort is forced on men, and even inaction is made to count for action. His disorder was not that of Hamlet, where enterprises of great moment sicken from too much thinking: it was the more subtle difficulty of a mind, healthful and vigorous in its speculative activity, which is content to have no enterprises at all, and to decline the unremovable burden of ordering its own life. He had suffered little, except in one grievous particular, from the goads of experience; and he knew little of the hard exigencies of practical affairs, or of the strifes, the griefs, the longings, and the needs of the passionate seeker after moral perfection.[16]

Thayer is apparently making four separate criticisms of Wright, namely, (1) that he suspended judgment on moral matters, always waiting for further evidence, until the chance for action was past; (2) that he never had any moral enterprises at all or got involved in any reform movement; (3) that he even declined the unremovable burden of ordering his own life; and (4) that he lacked a longing for moral perfection. Each criticism, as we shall see, requires careful consideration in order to do justice to both Wright and Thayer.

1. Wright certainly had verbal commitments on numerous moral matters. He was in favor of greater legal rights for women and thought that they should be granted the right to vote, but he never, as far as the records show, did anything at all to bring about these moral goals. But it seems highly unlikely that the reason he never did anything was because he was waiting for further evidence either about the desirability of the goals or the best way to bring them about. The best estimate, I suspect, is that Wright was fully aware of his own impotence in fighting such public moral battles. The notion of Wright's speaking in public or working through political organizations is simply ab-

surd to anyone aware of the shyness and melancholy that were the defining characteristics of his personality.[17]

2. In the light of Wright's views on reform, we can see clearly why he was in one way legitimately content not to have moral enterprises and undertake reform. According to Wright, the more we try to order our own and others' lives positively, the more likely we are to create unexpected unhappy consequences. Moral meddling, in short, is usually a dangerous thing. To be sure, Thayer's criticism would be valid if Wright had done nothing to alleviate the suffering and misery of the world, a legitimate goal of reform on his own utilitarian view. He could not hope to be a warrior in any public reforms; he was not emotionally equipped for it. Political or social efforts to achieve reform were closed to him. But where personal effort to relieve suffering was required in small and unobtrusive ways, Wright was certain to be close at hand. To the crippled and exhausted Susan Lesley, Wright's care of her daughter Mary was a godsend.[18] To the frail Mrs. Ann Lyman in her gloomy depression he was the only anchor to reality.[19] He took Gurney to tea with her daily so that she would have the intellectual atmosphere she loved so dearly. To Mary Walker, runaway slave, he was steadfast friend in all daily matters, large or small, and trusted ally in trying to help her rescue the members of her family still held in slavery.[20] None of these friends would have found in Wright one who was content to have no moral enterprises at all.

There is a sense, however, in which Thayer's complaint in a weaker way legitimately applies to Wright. Wright seemed unable to get involved systematically or as a matter of principle in any moral effort. His moral enterprises, personal as they were, came to him by the accidents of association, and such enterprises, once aroused, disappeared as soon as the personal claims were gone.

3. Thayer's notion that his dear friend declined the unremovable burden of ordering his own life really misses the point. Wright did not decline to order his life; he was hopelessly and tragically unable to do so.[21] Because of his loneliness and poor work habits he smoked and drank more than was wise.[22] His feeling of impotence about the Civil War added to his gloom,

and he stayed up later than ever, ate more irregularly, and drank more copiously. The climax was reached in 1863 when he bruised the instep of his right foot. The wound became infected and the symptoms were threatening, but Dr. Wyman finally checked the danger. An even worse bout with depression and overindulgence occurred in 1869.[23] His friend Gurney was no longer available for Socratic talks, and the Nortons left for an extended stay in Europe. His *Almanac* work fell greatly in arrears, and eventually he gave it up. He absented himself from his clubs, had no interest left in writing or talking philosophy, and excused himself from the invitations of his other friends. But his friends were not to be put off so easily. Unobtrusively they rallied around him and rescued him from his gloominess. He returned to his traditional occupation as the Socratic sage of old Cambridge. As always, old friends and new sought him out for brilliant conversations. Wright was of that lonely and gentle kind who, unable to order his own life, helped give beautiful order to the lives of others.

4. The very notion of longing for moral perfection seems inappropriate when applied to Wright. Thayer, as we have seen, was a transcendentalist and a great admirer of Emerson, and his notion of a self-realizational ethics comes from this source. For Wright these ideas were utterly romantic. What we need in this workaday world, Wright felt, is not such grandiose notions as moral perfection but some hard-headed consideration of consequences directed toward the removal of the very tangible evils of life. Wright may not have been a passionate seeker after moral perfection, but he had a good eye for the needs of worthy people like Susan Lesley, Mary Walker, and Mrs. Lyman.

12

CHARLES ELIOT NORTON

C H A R L E S Eliot Norton is well known for his Dante scholarship, his other literary commentary and criticism, and his studies in the history of fine art. He translated *The New Life* and *The Divine Comedy* and published significant studies of the work of Dante, Donne, Ruskin, Gray, Michelangelo, Holbein, and Turner, among many others.[1] He spent much of his time in Europe from 1868 to 1873, collecting material for his important *Historical Studies of Church Building in the Middle Ages;* and on his return to America he inaugurated courses at Harvard on the history of fine arts, in which venture he was extremely successful and influential.[2]

Norton's thought and effort, however, were by no means confined to the arts; he was ardently interested in moral and social problems, both practically and philosophically. He published articles on a wide range of topics, including, among others, religious liberty, the church and state, immorality in politics, the poverty of England, the Indian Revolt, dwellings and schools for the poor, model lodging houses, and the work of the sanitary commissions.[3] He not only wrote about, but worked for, the social reforms he believed in. Moreover, the moral element was never absent from Norton's work in the fine arts. When his eldest son, in a serious jest, suggested as a title for his father's lectures, "Modern Morals as Illustrated by the Art of the Ancients," Norton good-naturedly agreed! [4]

While he published much on practical moral issues, Norton published little, particularly in later years, on fundamental issues in moral and social philosophy. To discover his mature views one needs to read his *Letters* carefully and to peruse certain crucial parts of his unpublished correspondence. From these sources the picture of Norton as a Mill-Wright type of utilitarian and liberal clearly emerges, although his views of liberalism and reform were even more touched by pessimism than Wright's. Norton's utilitarianism, liberalism, and skepticism will come as a surprise to many scholars who know him only as the devotee of Dante; the author of the conservative *Considerations on Some Recent Social Theories,* written early in his career; and the confrere of Emerson, Longfellow, Ruskin, Arnold, and Carlyle. Norton more than most thinkers suffers in interpretation by association.

I

Norton's *Letters,* published soon after his death, are a rich mine of material for the literary, social, and political historian of the nineteenth century; and some of his biographical sketches show a high order of literary ability.[5] In his *Letters* one might expect to find his ethical and esthetic peregrinations in detail; but this is not so. He apparently talked more than he wrote about these matters; still there are enough explicit analyses and direct statements in the *Letters,* and even more in his unpublished correspondence, to make it possible to piece together his philosophical puzzles and principles.

There are a number of signposts in the *Letters* that indicate to a careful reader where Norton's philosophical predilections lay, although the reader usually misses them because he is not expecting them amidst the fascinating character portraits of Carlyle, Ruskin, Emerson, Mill, Longfellow, and Curtis. In a letter to his philosopher friend Chauncey Wright, to whom he owed much of his utilitarianism and skepticism, Norton wrote:

Once a week comes the best of all possible journals, "The Nation," and I find it at once the support and the disappointment of my Americanism. I am American only so far as our political and social systems are, to use your favorite phrase, in accordance with the principles of utilitarianism, and there are plainly many efforts to be made and many disappointments and failures to be achieved before the accordance becomes in any good degree complete.[6]

Norton was struck with the discontent of the lower classes in Europe in 1869 and the complaints of the workers—raised in the heated discussions of the conventions and committees of the trade societies—about division of property, rights of labor, and rates of wages.

Much of the talk is helpless enough,—vague, wild, and ignorant to the last degree,—but not the less dangerous for that. Some of it is strong, full of abstract sense, and quite unanswerable from the point of view of one who believes in and aims at the ultimate greatest good of the greatest number.[7]

While Norton did not write a great deal about utilitarian theory, it crops up often in his discussions of morality and of related topics with his American friends Ephraim Gurney and Chauncey Wright and with the English follower of Mill, John Morley, who was at the time (1870) editor of *The Fortnightly Review*.

In belief and opinion I agree with [Morley] more nearly than with most men. . . . Religion, utilitarianism, the modern view of Morals, political opinion in England, and the United States, were some of the subjects on which we talked. To record such talk is difficult, perhaps not worth while, but is not without effect in carrying forward and defining one's own thought.[8]

Norton saw Mill occasionally, too, and was much drawn to him. "My feeling for him has in it a very tender element mingled with respect"; and, "If one saw much of him affection would soon equal respect for him." [9]

In Norton's unpublished correspondence one does find some

utilitarian analysis; and, surprisingly enough, Norton took a more radical position on some issues, namely, property and wealth, than Mill did. During his extended European trip (1868–73), when he had talked and corresponded with Mill and Morley and was stimulated by social conditions to moral speculation, he wrote this letter to Chauncey Wright:

VILLA SPANNOCHI, SIENA
September 13, 1870

. . . In one of your late letters you discussed, if you remember, some of the conditions of the "rights" so called of property. The same subject is touched upon in Mill's article in the June *Fortnightly* on the Land Question. One sentence of his seemed to me to imply the dangerous doctrine of a "sacred" right of private individuals over other property than land. He says distinctly (p. 842) that it is just and expedient that individuals should be permitted to exercise absolute control,—the *jus utendi et abutendi*—over movable wealth. In writing to him I ventured to question this doctrine, and I quoted a sentence from your letter. I wrote to the effect that private property seemed to me sacred in no other sense than all institutions on which the order and progress of society depend are sacred; that so far as it is private its use alone can make it sacred; and that it was in no wise just or expedient that private individuals should exercise absolute control, extending to an unrestricted *Jus abutendi* over any kind of property; and that the convention to this effect seemed to [be] injurious to the real interests of society. I quote now from Mill's reply. "I agree in the main with all that you say respecting the limitation of the right of property even in movable wealth. I never meant to say that this right should be altogether unlimited, nor to ascribe to it sacredness in any other sense than that all the necessary conditions of human happiness are sacred. I do not, indeed, quite agree with your friend Mr. Wright when in the passage quoted and concurred in by you, he seems to say that from the utilitarian point of view the right of private ownership is founded *solely* on the motives it affords to the increase of public wealth; because independently of those motives, the feeling of security of possession and enjoyment, which could not (in the state of advancement mankind have yet reached) be had without private ownership, is of the very greatest importance as an element of human happiness. But this is probably a difference rather of expression than of opinion between us.

There is, however, this great practical difference between the case of movable wealth, and that of land, that, so long as land is allowed to be private property (and I cannot regard its private appropriation as a permanent institution) society seems to me bound to provide that the proprietor shall only make such uses of it as shall not essentially interfere with its utility to the public: while in the case of capital and movable property generally, though society has the same right, yet the interest of society would in general be better consulted by laws restrictive of the acquisition of too great masses of property, than by attempting to regulate its use. I have in my Political Economy proposed limitations of the right of ownership so far as the power of bequest is part of it on the express ground of its being injurious to society that enormous fortunes should be possessed by gift or inheritance."—All this is interesting and is as complete a statement as a letter is likely to contain,—and it is a pity that in writing for the *Fortnightly,* Mill was not a little more precise in his statement on a subject of so much importance, and on which his opinions are likely to be cited as authoritative.[10]

At the very time Norton made this analysis, however, he felt a conflict between his utilitarian ethical views, with their social, political, and economic corollaries, and his esthetic interests. He felt that utilitarianism did not do justice to esthetic value and, in fact, ignored the whole feeling and passionate side of man's nature. He wrote to Carlyle:

I have not read Mill's "Autobiography." One who knows anything of the "Vita Nuova" and of the "Divine Comedy" may be pardoned if he smile compassionately at poor Mill's experience of love. There is room for improvement, doubtless, in the regulation of our passions, but to regulate them out of existence is to go too far.[11]

Norton, in part, may here be playing up to Carlyle's view of the Mill-Taylor marriage; yet hints of his theoretical quandary occur elsewhere in his published letters. He loved the grace and picturesqueness of the Villa Spannochi; it had, in a sense, become a symbol for him of the charm and esthetic excellence of old Italy which, unfortunately, he believed, the new Italy was losing in the process of achieving utilitarian aims, of making advances in politics and commerce.

Italy in losing tyrants, in becoming constitutional, in taking to trade, is doing what she can to spoil her charm. The railroad whistle just behind the church of Santa Maria Novella, or just beyond the Campo Santo at Pisa, sounds precisely as it sounds on the Back Bay. . . .[12]

But his explicit criticism of the greatest happiness principle—its lack of concern with esthetic values—occurs in some unpublished correspondence with Chauncey Wright.

VILLA SPANNOCHI, SIENA
June 12, 1870

. . . All that you say of the weak side of the old times when concentration of passion, of interest, or of faith secured the development of strong individual characters, and the production of admirable works of art and of learning, I am quite ready to accede to. But I think we have no reason to be satisfied with a philosophy or system of life which is content simply with a high general level of humanity, and neither provides for nor desires the production of marked individualities or high and strongly defined characters. As compared with the men of the 13*th* Centy, those of the 19*th* are deficient in character, that is, in exercise of will, and play of motive, and susceptibility to passion. No doubt "utilitarian reason must govern the modern world,"—but how can utilitarian reason supply to us that which makes up the poetry and highest delight of life. There is a delight beyond that of being reasonable, or of being generous;—it is the enjoyment of what is passionately desired, accomplished or felt. It belongs to a different range of spiritual conditions. I doubt if there is anything in America on which so much feeling has been expended as Benvenuto Cellini's Perseus, or Michael Angelo's Night and Day. I doubt if there is any such unselfish happiness as that which the best Gothic artists felt (not thro' devout passion, but thro' plain aesthetic joy) in the successful solution of the problems they had to solve. It was the delight in beauty joined with the excitement of genuine scientific achievement. Now the sense of beauty is a part of human nature from which some of the purest, most refining and most elevating joys spring. It is wholly unscientific and for any direct result un-utilitarian. It seems to belong in the highest degree only to passionate natures, or to natures readily susceptible to passion. It is cultivable, and is connected with peculiarities of physical organization, and of race.—The "modern world," the utilitarian world, America, seem to leave it out of account, and seem to be cultivating and developing a type of man in whom the capacity for passion of a poetic order is carefully limited.[13]

Wright reassured Norton that, at least as far as utilitarian theory is concerned, there is certainly no antagonism between utilitarian and esthetic goals.[14] Quite to the contrary: the teleological or instrumental derivation of moral value presupposes a class of intrinsic goods, which it is our moral duty to try to procure; and this class of intrinsic goods contains all "ultimate sources of pleasure of whatever rank or intensity." Esthetic experience and feeling are ultimate ends, and as immediate sources of human happiness or excellence they are their own positive standards and sanctions. Utility does not prescribe ultimate ends or dictate what motivation must be; it only tests in a negative fashion the things that are experienced as intrinsically good—"checking their consistency with other interests and feelings, and with the maximum of all in all sentient beings measured both by intensity and rank." [15]

Esthetic pleasures, Wright indicated, generally turn out to be morally unobjectionable because their "broad (mental) relationships would be likely enough to insure that consistency with the maximum of excellence or happiness or well-being. . . ." [16] Moreover, esthetic pleasures, and some passions, have in the realm of ends-in-themselves an intrinsic dignity, a preferability in kind, distinct from other sources of pleasure. This intrinsic rank or preferability must not be confused with moral rank, which is derivative or instrumental in nature, but nevertheless must be taken account of in the derivation of moral values themselves. In short, according to Wright, there is between utility and beauty an antithesis that is sometimes mistaken for antagonism; actually, the beautiful, along with other sources of happiness of whatever rank, constitutes the grounds of utility.

Norton's puzzlement about the connection of art and morality and his fear that his utilitarian ethics was antagonistic to his esthetic interests apparently were resolved and allayed by Wright's analysis—to some extent, at any rate. He thereafter referred to "utilitarian ends, using the epithet in its best and largest significance." [17] Moreover, in later years Norton became acquainted with Mill's St. Andrew's Address, in which Mill stressed the importance of esthetic education for the creation of "whole" men; Norton was, of course, favorably impressed by this address and quoted from it in his own paper on "The History of the Fine Arts" (1895):

Mill went on to speak of a third division of human culture, "not less needful," he said, "to the completeness of the human being," "the culture which comes through poetry and art, and may be described

as the education of the feelings, and the cultivation of the beautiful." And this, he declared, "deserves to be regarded in a far more
serious light than is the custom in these countries," that is, in Great
Britain. . . . It was about seven years after the delivery of Mill's
address that the chair of the history of art which I have the honor to
occupy was established at Harvard, and, so far as I know, it was the
first of its kind in our country. By its establishment this great branch
of the humanities was recognized as having an equal position in the
scheme of college or university studies with the other branches, and
as needful a function as any of them in the work of education. It
was a noticeable step in educational progress.[18]

Norton's part in these educational advances through his writing,
teaching, and editing has not yet been sufficiently recognized;
yet it can hardly be overemphasized.

II

Somehow Norton has become associated in the minds of
some writers with the Emersonian tradition in American literature and philosophy,[19] partly, perhaps, because he greatly admired Emerson, praising his worth and significance,[20] and edited
the Carlyle-Emerson correspondence; partly because he was the
close friend of George William Curtis, with whom he shared so
many ideas and characteristics that people have assumed these
included Curtis' transcendental principles, which he emphasized
in *Harper's Weekly* and *Monthly;* and partly because his philosophical and religious beliefs, which are clearly not in agreement
with Emerson's or in the Genteel Tradition, are subordinated by
the editors in the biographical part of Norton's *Letters.* True,
Norton did not often make his theoretical views explicit; but still
there are enough analyses and direct statements in his letters for
anyone to see clearly that he was, besides a utilitarian in ethics,
a skeptic on metaphysical problems, an agnostic on religious
questions, and a pessimist on the outcome of social and political
issues.

Norton's diatribes against metaphysical philosophy, that is, as
la recherche de l'absolu—he had a good opinion of the naturalistic relativism of Santayana—occur frequently in his letters.[21]
He informed Carlyle, for example, that Emerson

. . . is to read a lecture this month at a "Summer School of Philosophy" at Concord of which your old acquaintance, the potato-and-apple Evangelist, Alcott, is the High-Priest. The teaching is marvelous; and the intuitionists have it all their own way, and the contradictoriness of the intuitions of the different sages is the supreme test and evidence of their truth. Is not truth polygonal? Are not the ego and the non-ego resolvable in the last analysis into a single affirmation? You know the kind from of old. All the doctors of this Faculty are not to be found in the New World. The only novel development is that we have female sages. . . .[22]

To Goldwin Smith, he wrote:

Your conception of "conscience" as a "faculty" (?) that bears testimony that is to be trusted to things of the spirit, in regard to which the reason is silent, has too much of the intuitional to be acceptable to a disciple of Locke and Hume. But why dwell on differences? Here we are, old men, near the end of life, and waiting the end without anxiety or a shadow of fear; perplexed indeed by the mighty mystery of existence and of the universe, and happy in the conviction that the chief lesson of life is that of love.[23]

The editors of Norton's *Letters* use E. W. Gurney's description of another friend to characterize Norton's skepticism:

[He] was by intellectual temperament a sceptic, in the best sense of the term, an on-looker who is interested neither to prove nor to disprove, but to judge; and, when there is insufficient material for judging, to hold his mind in suspense,—a suspense, however, which contains no element of pain. Upon his chart of the Universe, the *terra incognita* of the not-proven that stretched between the firm ground of the proved and the void of the disproved, included some of the chief beliefs to which mankind has clung; but it should be said also that he admitted the entire rightfulness of the claim of Faith to take possession of any portion of this territory, provided she did it in her own name: there might even be much solid and goodly land there, and not mere mirage of tradition and the emotions; he denied only that it lay within the range of man's experience, and therefore of knowledge in the sense in which he understood and used that term.[24]

Norton's religious agnosticism, of course, was a corollary of his philosophical skepticism; but, again, one is not prepared for it, for was he not the son of Andrews Norton? Andrews Norton, with his usual acumen, had attacked transcendentalism at its first flowering, particularly Emerson's and Ripley's criticisms of historical religion, calling it the German heresy.[25] Nevertheless, his son came to believe that the transcendentalists did not cut to the heart of the matter, did not go far enough in their criticism of historical religion. He agreed entirely with Leslie Stephen's arguments in the "Agnostic's Apology" and wrote to Stephen that he could not see

. . . how any man accustomed to use his reason can resist the force of your argument,—unless, indeed, like Lowell, he reject reason in favor of sentiment, or of something which he called intuition. Such a position is possible as we have known,—but as Montaigne says: "Ces choses-là nous les trouverions autant ou plus incroyables qu'aulcunes autres." [26]

Later he wrote to Stephen about Benjamin Jowett's apparent turn away from traditional religious views:

At the close of his life he had not much left of the old-fashioned religious faith. He was like an old dowager who has found out that her heirloom diamonds are after all only paste, yet still goes on wearing them to make a show in the world, which has begun to suspect them, and because she herself is fond of them from old association. When he comes to writing of God as "the great overruling law of progress in the world, whether personal or impersonal," he does not differ much from Mat Arnold.[27]

Yet, of course, as Donald Reay asserts,[28] Norton never tried to shake the convictions of anyone; he felt that if anyone came to share his religious views it must be because of the merits of those views.

Norton's pessimism about the outcome of social and political issues in the latter part of the nineteenth century, and about the moral growth of humanity, was well known during his lifetime. To Dr. Holmes, he wrote, "I find every biography,—even this of a man so happy by nature and by circumstance as Emerson,—a pathetic record;—so much of hindrance in life, the best achievement so far from absolutely good. 'What a piece of work is a man!' " [29] Paradoxically, Norton held that the out-and-out pessimist is cheerful "even though nature herself play false, and uses loaded dice against him in the game." The reason? "Darwinism has helped us a good deal. You expect less of men when you look at them not as a little lower than the angels, but as a little higher than the anthropoid apes." [30] His pessimism was not unmitigated, however; he allowed a refuge from pessimism in "the good men and women at any time existing in the world,—they keep faith and happiness alive . . ."; [31] and was not unwilling to acknowledge the likelihood of some small progress but at terrible costs. Apart from his pessimistic doubts on particular issues, he was mainly interested, in his pessimistic stand, to deny Neoplatonic optimism and the ultimate harmony solution to the problem of evil. Indeed, his distaste for optimism in this technical sense was one of the main roots of his distaste for the type of idealistic and religious system that produced it. In his later years he wrote to Moorfield Storey:

What you say of getting comfort from Emerson's "Diary" interests me much. I doubt if such comfort as one may derive from such faith as his and such doctrine, is other than a modified Stoical attitude of mind, at least for one who does not, like Emerson, indulge in an optimism that rejects the evidence of facts. In one of the recently published letters of Darwin he says, "What a book a Devil's-chaplain might write on the clumsy, wasteful, blundering, low and horribly cruel works of nature." It is plain, I think, to the student of history, that the same principle holds in the world as in the material universe. "This is a moral world and eternally destroys what is not moral" may be accepted as a truth, but the root of "what is not moral" is as vital and everlasting as the root of what is moral. And though we may be sure that retribution is always certain as a consequence of error and crime, the retribution is often so remote, often falling on the innocent, often taking the form of new error or crime, that the criminal, be he man or nation, does not recognize its connection with his sin, and in many instances seems to his own view to escape altogether from punishment for it. In a large sense the moral law prevails in the long run, and man, perhaps, slowly improves, but how "blundering, wasteful and horribly cruel" seems the process! [32]

Norton's pessimism, beginning early in life,[33] was not only theoretical but also temperamental and is only one facet of a highly complex personality, which is frequently a study in contrasts. A thoroughgoing psychological analysis of Norton's character would be a rewarding and profitable task. The Norton legend pictures him as a cultivated gentleman but, unfortunately, genteel too. It was Richard Watson Gilder who wanted

Huckleberry Finn expurgated [34]—the height of the Genteel Tradition and the nadir of literary evaluation; but it was Norton who said he would be sorry to know that any woman had looked beyond the title page of *Leaves of Grass*.[35] Yet Norton was certainly not a kid-glove character. He may have seemed overly nice in some ways to people of other temperaments; but his condemnation of America's part in the Spanish-American War, and his weathering of the resultant contumely showered on him for this and other controversial stands, including his part in the Liberal Republican movement that helped defeat Blaine in the election of 1884, took a good deal more courage than most people had in his day, to say nothing of our own.

13

THE CONSERVATIVE TRADITION

A RECENT commentator has classified Charles Eliot
Norton as a political conservative in the tradition of Edmund Burke, and a sentimental Federalist.[1] This estimate of
Norton is very wide of the mark and constitutes further evidence
that Norton, more than most thinkers, has been classified and
categorized more than he has been understood.[2] At one period
in his life Norton was genuinely a Burkean, but he radically
altered his political philosophy in later life just as he altered all
the rest of his philosophy. Commentators in this area again have
missed the essential impact on Norton of Wright. Norton and
Wright cannot be classified neatly: they are not Burkeans, or
Enlightenment or transcendental liberals, and certainly not a
laissez-faire blend of these ingredients. They were anything but
reconstructionists, but they did value reform in a negative sense.
Except for their emphasis on negative reform, they shared much
the same in-between views on reform and politics as those of
their mutual friend George Curtis.

The reason for the misclassification of Norton as a Burkean is, no doubt, complex. Part of it probably is due to Norton's deep pessimism. Pessimism is usually taken as a sign of classical conservatism, and optimism as a sign of liberalism. Unfortunately, in this case the usual inference fails. Norton's pessimism was so deep that it undercut the whole foundation of conservatism. Whatever the cause of the misclassification, however, it is important to set the record straight—not only for the sake of historical accuracy, but also for the sake of the larger philosophical issues involved which each generation has to reargue for itself. The record can best be set straight by, first, tracing out the development of Norton's political philosophy and, second, analyzing the structure of his mature position, showing its affinities with, and differences from, the major traditions.

I

From his ancestors and parents Norton received a firm belief in the importance of some sort of an elite. He was the descendant of John Norton (the younger), one of the last of the hell-and-damnation Puritan ministers.[3] Crucial with him, of course, was the notion that there is an elect, predestined from all eternity to inherit the Kingdom of God, while the rest of mankind is condemned to hell. Andrews Norton, the father of Charles, emphatically broke with this Puritan background, but he nevertheless kept, in a subtle way, the notion of an elite. As we have seen, like most nineteenth-century American Unitarians, he remained close to orthodox Christianity. He did not accept the concept of the Holy Trinity, but he still believed Christ to be "an intermediate divine being, a messenger supernaturally and uniquely endowed and sent as a special, indispensable revelation to man." [4] He also insisted upon the importance of miracles as signs of the existence of God. The existence and point of miracles, however, can be established only by reason and scholarly investigation; this is, in short, the domain of the specialist, the intellectual elite. The masses should defer to religious authorities, Andrews Norton said, because the interpretation of Christian revelation lay beyond the ability of most men.[5] His notion of an elite was not a religious, moral, or political one but simply the notion that superiorly endowed human beings had the duty to lead the masses in all areas of life. This notion of an intellectual and spiritual elite Andrews Norton passed on to his son Charles, and it never ceased to be a strong influence in his life. It was, however, later to be transformed by the utilitarian views of J. S. Mill and Chauncey Wright.

Charles Norton was elected to Phi Beta Kappa at Harvard and graduated with distinction in Greek, Latin, and political economy. As a result of his study of political economy he showed an enthusiasm for social reform, but among friends of the family this enthusiasm was viewed as a youthful conceit which, no doubt, would not last. And, indeed, the enthusiasm did not seem to last long. After several years in business Norton became noticeably more conservative in his political views, and he began to doubt seriously the ability of the masses to help themselves through political and economic reform.

In 1849 Norton sailed to India as supercargo on a Bullard and Lee ship. When he arrived he was shocked by the way the British treated the natives; as an American he was unable to countenance the caste system. The English used the Indians for their own gain, living in handsome houses while the exploited ones lived in hovels. But when Norton became better acquainted with the Indian population he did not like what he discovered there either—the masses in the abstract were all right, but in fact, he felt, they turn out to be shiftless, dishonest, and ignorant.[6] Norton now saw the British in a better light. They were building hospitals and schools and were trying to help the Indian people to better themselves economically. After all, he was inclined to think, this situation might be symptomatic. Perhaps the masses can never help themselves; perhaps there must be an elite with the know-how and integrity to lead the masses to something better.

About five years later Norton's "perhaps" had congealed to a firm belief. In 1853 he published anonymously a book called *Considerations on Some Recent Social Theories,* in which he articulated a Burkean type of political philosophy.[7] There are two main themes in the book—namely, that leadership and power should be vested in the intellectual and moral elite, and that social and economic progress of the masses must occur through the regeneration of men rather than by the rational reconstruction of society. Norton was full of sympathy with the masses but had little faith in them. Since they were without counsel, restraint, or education, they must be led by the educated few who had been blessed with opportunities. Moreover, the plight of the poor would not be corrected by the utopian reforms and social experiments advocated by Saint-Simon, Fourier, Robert Owen, and Etienne Cabet. These social theorists, Norton felt, had an oversimplified notion of what reform could accomplish. The structure of society was far too complex and delicate to be dealt with in such a wholesale and cavalier manner. So Norton, after all, had got rid of his youthful enthusiasm for social reform. But this was hardly surprising to the friends of the family, who looked on him as the descendant of John and Andrews Norton.

In 1855, in poor health, Norton left for Europe. He spent much time in Italy, a country whose art and people he came to love dearly, and eventually published a little book which deserves to be far better known than it is, *Notes of Travel and Study in Italy*. It has little unity, but there are a number of recurring elements—a condemnation of Catholicism, social and political criticism, and an embryonic art theory that reflects the influence of Ruskin. His denunciations of the Catholic Church in Italy were strong. He was shocked beyond measure at these opening lines of a prayer: *"Vi adoro, Sacratissima Piaga del Piede sinistro del mio Gesù. Vi compatisco del dolore acerbissimo Sofferto."* [8] But his main criticism centered on what he took to be the antidemocratic bias of the Church. The American notion that freedom of feeling, thought, and speech are fundamental rights, "privileges of liberty," he felt the Catholic Church skillfully destroyed.[9] The excellence of America, Norton wrote, is the existence of the most unlimited freedom consistent with the existence of society. The emphasis in these statements, and the love of Jefferson and Samuel Adams that they reflect, is scarcely Burkean in nature, and makes it quite clear that Norton had not as yet written the final version of his political philosophy.

Upon his return to America, Norton became involved in various journalistic projects—he wrote for the newly established *Atlantic Monthly;* was coeditor, along with James Russell Lowell, of the *North American Review;* helped E. L. Godkin to found the *Nation;* and, during the Civil War, was editor of the Loyal Publication Society.[10] It was during these journalistic years that Norton's friendship with Chauncey Wright began. The depth of the friendship and the great extent of Wright's influence on Norton are not adequately reflected in the biographical sections of Norton's *Letters* or in any of the other accounts of Norton's life. Wright's influence on Norton, however, was well known at the time. An unpublished letter reveals exactly how matters stood. A friend of Wright, Charles Salter, mentioned Wright's name to the Reverend Charles Grinnell of Charlestown and received this reply: "He is, is he not, the one who led Charles Norton astray?" [11] Without intending to influence his friend, Wright changed the whole course of Norton's thought. As we have seen, Norton abandoned the Christian Unitarianism of his father and became a skeptic on metaphysical issues, an agnostic on religious questions, and a utilitarian in moral philosophy.[12]

At this point in Norton's career the source of the error in classifying him as a follower of Burke and a sentimental Federalist becomes clear. Norton's newly acquired skepticism, agnosticism, and utilitarianism obviously are not compatible with the classical conservative political philosophy that he had, with varying degrees of enthusiasm, espoused in previous years. Commentators miss the shift in Norton's viewpoint—a shift easy to miss, to be sure, since Norton never heralded his new view as he had the old one in his *Considerations of Some Recent Social Theories.* His final view on political philosophy must be reconstructed from unpublished letters and certain portions of the Norton-Howe volume.[13] Not only is this view worth analysis in its own right, but such analysis itself helps to demonstrate the extremely rough nature of such classifications as liberalism, conservatism, and laissez-faire conservatism.

II

The best way to get an understanding of Norton's mature views is to contrast them with the main tenets of classical conservatism. But here there is a difficulty heralded by all recent commentators. Conservatives by and large do not like the notion of ideology and hence dislike stating their general principles. Yet there is still a loose set of beliefs which taken together define the classical conservative position. They are not a set of necessary conditions for a conservative viewpoint, but any conservative will accept a large number of these beliefs.[14]

The classical conservative generally believes that there is a natural stratification into classes, and that the higher classes —the good, the rich, and the wise—should constitute a ruling aristocracy, one which is alive to its responsibilities toward the less fortunate. He denies that man has certain rights simply by being born; he insists that the rights of man are earned and not given. The conservative views private property as the bulwark of order and liberty. The man with property has something at stake, something to lose; hence his judgment is careful and measured. He emphasizes the importance of stable institutions and the values of traditional beliefs, symbols, and rituals.

Deeply embedded in the conservative's thinking is a commitment to organized religion (preferably Christian) and a conviction that such religious beliefs are important to the stability of society. He believes in the existence of immutable principles of universal justice and dislikes any hint that right is dependent upon the different needs of various societies and cultures. The conservative, finally, exhibits a pessimistic attitude about the nature and prospects of man. He views man as tinged with sin and showing a corrupt nature, and he does not believe that man is continually progressing toward a more ideal state. Man's reason is very fallible, and hence it is wise to avoid tinkering with institutions and trying to institute reforms. The conservative, in short, "tends to react rather than act, to say no rather than yes, to counsel caution rather than adventure, [and] to rationalize suffering and evil rather than to move boldly against them. . . ." [15]

If this characterization of the Burkean tradition is correct, then it follows clearly that Norton's early views represent the mainstream of classical conservatism. However, after his basic philosophical shift to skepticism and utilitarianism, Norton either abandoned or seriously modified almost every one of these claims.

In his mature years Norton was quite willing to admit that there is a natural stratification into classes, but he did not believe that the rich, the wise, or anyone else should constitute a ruling aristocracy. Norton was a thoroughgoing democrat in the sense that he believed that every man should count for one morally, legally, and politically; but he was not at all a democrat in the larger sense of believing that "everybody is just as good as everybody else." He heartily rejected the notion that all people are equally significant and valuable in every way. He strongly approved of Whitman's political democracy, but he was revolted by Whitman's wiping out of all natural distinctions: "By God! I will accept nothing which all cannot have their counterpart of on the same terms." The double aspects of democracy in Whitman, and Norton's acceptance of one and rejection of the other, explain Norton's ambivalent attitude toward *Leaves of Grass.* And Norton's acceptance and rejection throw into bold relief precisely the kind of democrat he was: a political but not a social one, a critical and not a romantic one, a cautious and not a maudlin one.

While Norton did not believe that the wise or good should constitute a ruling aristocracy, he did believe that they had the *duty* to be leaders in a democracy. Norton's rude awakening came when he discovered that these were not, by and large, the kind of leaders chosen in a democracy. He constantly railed against this shortcoming in the country he loved so much. But his bitter disappointment did not lead him to reject his country or the democratic concept it represented. He did not sentimentally yearn for any aristocratic replacement of democracy. He simply did his best to raise the standards of his country and came to realize that if he had not hoped for so much from his beloved country he would not have been so bitterly disappointed.

In later years Norton never claimed that the rights of man are not innately his but must be earned. On the contrary, according to Norton, no government can bestow on any individual the right to life, liberty, and the pursuit of happiness because such rights are not within the authority of government to bestow. The point of a democratic government is to safeguard such rights, not bestow them.[16] As a utilitarian, Norton believed that each man's happiness, insofar as it is compatible with that of others, is intrinsically good, and hence that he has a right to pursue it. He has the duty to pursue the happiness of others insofar as it is also compatible with the general good. Hence the ideas of right and duty for Norton, as for any careful moral philosopher, are correlative and cannot be advocated absolutely or separately.

Norton's views on property were not even remotely like those in the conservative tradition. He never emphasized that private property is the bulwark of order and liberty. Quite to the contrary, he felt that the privileges of wealth must be sharply circumscribed by utilitarian considerations. Norton, as we have seen, advocated to Mill an exclusively stewardship concept of wealth. The only justification for private wealth, Norton felt, was the motives it afforded to the increase of public wealth.[17] Mill, in fact, thought this view a little extreme and replied that "independently of those motives, the feeling of security of possession and enjoyment, which could not (in the state of advancement mankind have yet reached) be had without private ownership, is of the very greatest importance as an element of human happiness."[18]

Norton never abandoned his appreciation of stable institutions, but such appreciation hardly makes him a classical conservative. This criterion is certainly suspect, since the alternative to it is not liberalism but idiocy. No one, it may be assumed, prefers in principle to live in an unstable society. The crucial point in Norton's mind was the nature of the stable institutions. He would not have altered radically any of the political institutions of his country, but he accepted these institutions because in principle he felt them to be good and right—he did not value them simply because they gave stability. The worst tyrannies could also be very stable. He was quite skeptical, however, as to whether America was using its institutions intelligently. Mediocrity, corruption, and laissez-faire ideology were doing their best to keep American political institutions at ebb tide.[19]

Originally Norton had been committed to Unitarian Christianity and absolute moral standards, but, as we have seen, he completely abandoned these conservative characteristics in later life. He was influenced not only by Wright's agnosticism but also by Leslie Stephen's arguments in the "Agnostic's Apology." [20] He came to believe that anything that is to qualify as knowledge must be publicly verifiable, and religious assertions, he thought, notoriously lacked these characteristics. Even more fundamentally for Norton, the theistic world view foundered on the problem of evil. An all-powerful, all-good God is not consistent with the enormous amount of gratuitous suffering in our world. Norton, moreover, had little faith in the kind of stability that religious beliefs, even if false, lend to government, based as they generally are on selfish motives.[21] Would the mass of people act with utter abandon if the sanctions of heaven and hell were removed? He never answered this specific question, although it is quite clear that he was not impressed by people's behavior even under such sanctions.

On the issue of moral absolutism, Norton's utilitarianism required that telling the truth, keeping promises, and so on are not absolute duties apprehended by conscience but are derived from, and justified by, consideration of the tendencies of such acts to produce good consequences. Moreover, since the utilitarian determines the right by the good, and since the good is relative to the different needs of men in different societies, it follows that what is considered right will vary from society to society. The only moral commitment that does not vary is the ultimate concept of right stated in the principle of utility—the greatest good for the greatest number in any society.

Norton continued to the end to have a pessimistic attitude about the nature and prospects of man, but his was not the pessimism of a Burkean. By the latter part of the nineteenth century, Norton's pessimism cut so deep that it included almost everything. He was not a classical conservative; he was a Chauncey Wright Darwinian. He was not pessimistic because he thought man had a sinful nature; he was pessimistic rather because he knew that men were only a little higher than the anthropoid apes.[22] With this deep-seated pessimism Norton approached, although he never explicitly formulated, a naturalistic justification of democracy—so different in kind from the transcendentalist justification. There are a few genuinely good people "who keep faith and happiness alive," and a few genuinely bad, but the majority of men have their good moments and their bad. A democracy, then, has this advantage: it gives the good moments, represented by different people at different times, a chance to operate. The reverse, of course, is also true. But, when the bad moments are represented by the majority, evil at least has not won by default and there is the chance of future redress.

Norton certainly did not believe that man is continually progressing toward a more ideal state. He was not an Enlightenment or transcendental liberal who was optimistic about progress, but this does not mean he was not a liberal of another sort. He was willing to acknowledge the likelihood of some small progress, but at terrible costs. "In a large sense the moral law prevails in the long run, and man, perhaps, slowly improves, but how 'blundering, wasteful and horribly cruel' seems the process!" [23] But even if there were no discernible progress at all, it would still be man's only dignity to make the effort.

Norton clearly gave up the Burkean horror of reform without embracing the reconstructionist views of liberals like George Ripley. Norton rejected the notion of wholesale reform, but not because he thought the economical and social life in America were excellent—far from it. His point was that we do not know enough to change things radically for the better; life is too complex and involved to be reconstructed.[24] Nevertheless, he urged the piecemeal reform of positive evils. It may be impossible to bring about the millennium by reform, but it is not impossible to correct the most flagrant and obvious evils of our world.

In his views on reform Norton was reflecting the utilitarianism of Chauncey Wright. Wright, as we have seen, felt that we often do not know enough about likely consequences in specific cases to make realistic judgments. It is wise to rely on the traditional moral rules generally because they have come into being and are justified by their long-run and over-all utilitarian value. One does not, of course, tell the truth if the consequences clearly would be disastrous. But one should tell the truth, and so on for all other moral rules, unless he has very strong evidence that not breaking them would lead to disastrous consequences.[25] Norton found that such a justification for taking rules and tradition seriously within the liberal tradition suited him exactly.

Finally, and most important of all, there is the question of rationalizing suffering and evil instead of moving decisively against them. Some historians seem to make the ability to rationalize evil a sort of ultimate characteristic of the conservative temper. In the early years Norton quite easily rationalized suffering simply because he held a theistic view of the universe. Historians unfortunately never see the connection between several of the characteristics of conservatism that they list. The conservative's ability to rationalize evil, and his antireform attitude, are closely related to his acceptance of traditional theistic beliefs. The basis of this relationship is the ultimate harmony solution to the problem of evil.

Christians, like all theists, have long pondered why there should be so much apparently gratuitous evil in the world if God is all-powerful and all-good. Their favorite answer is "ultimate harmony." [26] Man has a fragmentary viewpoint—he sees isolated events as evil; but God, who sees the over-all pattern, knows how these apparently evil events fit into an ultimate good. "Whatever is, is right," even though man cannot see the rightness of it. If whatever is, is right, moreover, it follows that one should not meddle with affairs; he should not try to reform the world but should wait until God's time comes. Hence the theistic world view is the basis of the conservative's ability to rationalize the existence of suffering and evil.

When Norton abandoned his theism, he also abandoned his ability to rationalize injustice and his negative attitude toward organized reform. Since he no longer believed in God and the resultant ultimate harmony, he decided that it was his duty to fight for the only justice men will ever have, namely, what man himself can do to remove the bonds of slavery, fill empty stomachs, and enable people to live in decent houses. It is a hard fight and an endless one, producing only meager results, but to abandon it would violate the most fundamental demand of moral law, whether that law be conceived along utilitarian or deontological lines—a type of law supremely imperative, Norton felt, because there is no one, not even a God, to enforce it.

NOTES

CHAPTER 1. INTRODUCTION

1. Robert S. Fletcher, *A History of Oberlin College* (2 vols.; Oberlin, Ohio, 1943), Vol. I, chap. xxx.

2. William G. McLoughlin's Introduction to the John Harvard Library edition of Charles Grandison Finney's *Lectures on Revivals of Religion* (Cambridge, Mass.: Harvard University Press, 1960).

3. *Ibid.*, p. xxi.

4. Herbert Schneider, *A History of American Philosophy* (2nd ed.; New York: Columbia University Press, 1963), chap. iv; and Joseph L. Blau, *Men and Movements in American Philosophy* (New York: Prentice-Hall, 1952), chap. iii.

5. Schneider, *A History of American Philosophy*, pp. 202–7.

6. *Ibid.*

7. See Francis Wayland's *The Elements of Moral Science* (rev. ed.; Boston: Gould and Lincoln, 1870); Asa Mahan's *Science of Moral Philosophy* (Oberlin, Ohio: J. M. Fitch, 1848, 1884); and James H. Fairchild's *Moral Science* (rev. ed.; New York: Butler, Sheldon and Co., 1892).

8. William R. Hutchison, *The Transcendentalist Ministers* (New Haven, Conn.: Yale University Press, 1959). See pages 219–21 for bibliographical guides to the study of Unitarianism.

9. *Ibid.*, pp. 1–21.

10. E. H. Madden, "George William Curtis: Practical Transcendentalist," *The Personalist*, XL (1959), 369–79.

11. McLoughlin, Introduction to *Lectures on Revivals of Religion*, p. xl.

12. Blau, *Men and Movements in American Philosophy*, chap. v; Schneider, *A History of American Philosophy*, chap. vi; Philip P. Wiener, *Evolution and the Founders of Pragmatism* (Cambridge, Mass.: Harvard University Press, 1949); and Max H. Fisch, "Evolution in American Philosophy," *Philosophical Review*, LVI (1947), 357–73.

13. Cf. E. H. Madden, *Chauncey Wright and the Foundations of Pragmatism* (Seattle: University of Washington Press, 1963) and *Chauncey Wright* (New York: Washington Square Press, 1964).

14. Cf. E. H. Madden, "Charles Eliot Norton on Art and Morals," *Journal of the History of Ideas,* XVIII (1957), 430–38.

15. Cf. Clinton Rossiter, *Conservatism in America* (2nd ed., rev.; New York: Alfred A. Knopf and Random House, 1962), p. 159.

16. E. H. Madden, "Francis Wayland and the Limits of Moral Responsibility," *Proceedings of the American Philosophical Society,* CVI (1962), 348–59.

17. Fletcher, *A History of Oberlin College,* Vol. II, chap. li.

18. Henry Steele Commager, *Theodore Parker* (Boston: Beacon Press, 1960), p. 215.

19. George William Curtis, *Literary and Social Essays* (New York: Harper and Bros., 1894), pp. 61–93.

20. *The Letters of Charles Eliot Norton,* edited by Sara Norton and M. A. De Wolfe Howe (2 vols.; Boston: Houghton Mifflin Co., 1904), I, 221–23.

CHAPTER 2. FRANCIS WAYLAND

1. Cf. William R. Hutchison, *The Transcendentalist Ministers* (New Haven, Conn.: Yale University Press, 1959), p. 22; and Joseph L. Blau, *Men and Movements in American Philosophy* (New York: Prentice-Hall, 1952), p. 110.

2. Cf. William G. McLoughlin's Introduction to the John Harvard Library edition of C. G. Finney's *Lectures on Revivals of Religion* (Cambridge, Mass.: Harvard University Press, 1960).

3. Cf. Robert S. Fletcher, *A History of Oberlin College* (2 vols.; Oberlin, Ohio, 1943), II, 701.

4. Cf. Francis Wayland, *The Elements of Moral Science,* ed. Joseph Blau (John Harvard Library edition; Cambridge, Mass.: Harvard University Press, 1964), particularly pp. 29–41; Asa Mahan, *Science of Moral Philosophy* (Oberlin, Ohio: J. M. Fitch, 1848, 1884); McLoughlin, Introduction to *Lectures on Revivals of Religion,* pp. xxi–lii; and Fletcher, *A History of Oberlin College,* I, 472.

5. Reverend Dr. Hoby, Reminiscences of Wayland, 1-U, W36 let, MSS, Special Collections Room, John Hay Library, Brown University. Cf. E. H. Madden, "Francis Wayland and the Limits of Moral Responsibility," *Proceedings of the American Philosophical Society,* CVI (1962), 348–59.

6. Isaac Davis, Reminiscences of Wayland, 1-U, W36 let, MSS.

7. Cf. Blau's edition of Wayland's *The Elements of Moral Science*, pp. 29–41, 367–70. (Professor Blau's comparisons of different editions on crucial points are exceedingly helpful.)

8. *Ibid.*, p. 369.

9. *Ibid.*, pp. 30–31.

10. *Ibid.*, p. 31.

11. *Ibid.*, pp. 369–70.

12. *Ibid.*, p. 370.

13. *Ibid.*, pp. 26–29, 367–68.

14. *Ibid.*, pp. 36–41.

15. *Ibid.*, pp. 107–21.

16. *Ibid.*, p. 110.

17. Mahan, *Science of Moral Philosophy,* p. 92.

18. *Ibid.*

19. *Ibid.*, p. 85.

20. *Ibid.*, pp. 89–90.

21. Wayland, *The Elements of Moral Science,* ed. Blau, pp. 43–46. (The example is mine, but the point is Wayland's.)

22. *Ibid.*, pp. 43–44.

23. *Ibid.*

24. *Ibid.*, p. 81.

25. *Ibid.*, pp. 81–82.

26. *Ibid.*, p. 85.

27. *Ibid.*, pp. 46–47.

28. Adapted from a view expressed by G. E. Moore in his *Ethics* (London: Oxford University Press, 1949), p. 21. The only change is the substitution of "good" for "pleasure."

29. Wayland, *The Elements of Moral Science,* ed. Blau, pp. 122–35.

30. *Ibid.*, p. 129.

31. Thomas Paine, *The Age of Reason,* ed. Alburey Castell (New York: Liberal Arts Press, 1948), pp. 16–17.

32. Wayland, *The Elements of Moral Science,* ed. Blau, p. 130.

33. *Ibid.*, pp. 129–35.

34. Cf. Paine's *Age of Reason.*

35. Wayland, *The Elements of Moral Science,* ed. Blau, pp. 124–25, 133.

36. *Ibid.*, p. 133.

37. Cf. Wayland's *University Sermons,* p. 7.

CHAPTER 3. THE ISSUE OF CIVIL DISOBEDIENCE

1. Cf. E. H. Madden, "Francis Wayland and the Limits of Moral Responsibility," *Proceedings of the American Philosophical Society,* CVI (1962), 348–59; and Joseph L. Blau's Introduction to his edition of Wayland's *The Elements of Moral Science* (John Harvard Library; Cambridge, Mass.: Harvard University Press, 1964).

2. Madden, "Francis Wayland and the Limits of Moral Responsibility," pp. 352–59.

3. Wayland, *Elements of Moral Science* (Boston, 1853), pp. 206–16.

4. Wayland, *The Limitations of Human Responsibility* (2nd ed.; New York: D. Appleton and Co., 1838), particularly pp. 167–96, although the whole book is relevant to the topic. The first edition of *Limitations* was also published in 1838 (Boston: Gould, Kendall, and Lincoln). The second edition is practically identical with the first; the only difference is several additional footnotes in the second edition.

5. *Ibid.,* p. 172.

6. *Ibid.,* p. 173.

7. *Ibid.,* p. 193.

8. This view permeates the whole of *The Limitations of Human Responsibility.*

9. *Limitations,* p. 109.

10. Cf. James O. Murray, *Francis Wayland* (Boston: Houghton Mifflin and Co., 1891), p. 209.

11. For a concise statement of Parker's views cf. Henry Steele Commager's *Theodore Parker* (Boston: Beacon Press, 1960), chap. x. For Curtis' views cf. his *Orations and Addresses,* ed. Charles Eliot Norton (3 vols.; New York: Harper and Bros., 1894), I, 3–177.

12. Cf. Commager, *Theodore Parker,* pp. 205–13.

13. Curtis, *Orations and Addresses,* I, 53 ff.

14. Cf. Madden, "George William Curtis: Practical Transcendentalist," *The Personalist,* XL (1959), 369–79.

15. Cf. Curtis, *Orations and Addresses,* I, 90.

16. On this point I am representing what seems to me implicit in the views of Parker and Curtis rather than any explicit argument of theirs.

17. Curtis, *Orations and Addresses,* I, 83.

18. *Ibid.*

19. Murray, *Francis Wayland*, p. 213.

20. Francis Wayland, Jr., and H. L. Wayland, *A Memoir of the Life and Labors of Francis Wayland* (2 vols.; New York: Sheldon and Co., 1867), II, 55.

21. Wayland, *University Sermons* (3rd ed.; Boston: Gould, Kendall, and Lincoln, 1850), pp. 267–68.

22. *Ibid.,* pp. 268–69.

23. *Ibid.,* p. 270.

24. *Ibid.,* p. 283.

25. Cf. Wayland and Wayland, *A Memoir of the Life and Labors of Francis Wayland,* II, 58. He also favored the adoption of the Wilmot Proviso.

26. *Ibid.,* pp. 155–56.

27. *Ibid.,* p. 332.

28. Murray, *Francis Wayland,* pp. 238–39.

29. Wayland and Wayland, *A Memoir of the Life and Labors of Francis Wayland,* II, 134–35.

30. Murray, *Francis Wayland,* 139–40.

31. Wayland and Wayland, *A Memoir of the Life and Labors of Francis Wayland,* II, 135.

32. Murray, *Francis Wayland,* p. 118.

33. *Ibid.*

34. *Ibid.,* p. 145.

35. Wayland, *Elements of Moral Science* (revised and improved ed.; Boston: Gould and Lincoln, 1870), p. 210.

36. Letter to Dr. Potter, Providence, November 25, 1856, 1-U, W36, MSS, Brown University Archives.

37. Wayland, *Elements of Moral Science* (1870 ed.), p. 215.

38. *Ibid.* (1853 ed.), p. 393.

39. *Ibid.* (1870 ed.), p. 394.

40. Cf. Wayland and Wayland, *A Memoir of the Life and Labors of Francis Wayland,* II, 262. Cf. also pp. 260–69.

CHAPTER 4. ASA MAHAN

1. Cf. Herbert W. Schneider, *A History of American Philosophy* (2nd ed.; New York: Columbia University Press, 1963), pp. 195–220; and Joseph L. Blau, *Men and Movements in American Philosophy* (New York: Prentice-Hall, 1952), pp. 73–109.

2. Cf. E. H. Madden, "Francis Wayland and the Limits of Moral

Responsibility," *Proceedings of the American Philosophical Society,* CVI (1962), 348–59.

3. Quoted by R. S. Fletcher in *A History of Oberlin College* (2 vols.; Oberlin, Ohio, 1943), II, 701.

4. *Ibid.,* I, 223–31.

5. Mahan, *Doctrine of the Will* (3rd ed.; Oberlin, Ohio: J. M. Fitch, 1847), p. 228.

6. *Ibid.*

7. Schneider, *A History of American Philosophy,* pp. 202–7.

8. Cf. Mahan, *Science of Moral Philosophy* (Oberlin, Ohio: J. M. Fitch, 1848, 1884).

9. Fletcher, *A History of Oberlin College,* I, 223–31.

10. *Ibid.,* p. 224.

11. *Ibid.,* p. 225.

12. Mahan, *Science of Moral Philosophy,* pp. 64–65.

13. Fletcher, *History of Oberlin College,* I, 233.

14. *Ibid.,* pp. 267–70.

15. Mahan, *Science of Moral Philosophy,* pp. 70–93.

16. Cf. Stuart M. Brown, Jr., "Duty and the Production of Good," *Philosophical Review,* Vol. LXI (1952).

17. Mahan, *Science of Moral Philosophy,* pp. 78–79. Cf. p. 58.

18. *Ibid.,* p. 81.

19. *Ibid.,* p. 83.

20. *Ibid.,* p. 84.

21. Cf. Madden, "Francis Wayland and the Limits of Moral Responsibility," pp. 349–50.

22. Wayland, *Elements of Moral Science* (revised and improved ed.; New York: Sheldon and Co., 1877), p. 39.

23. Cf. Herbert W. Schneider's review of Joseph L. Blau's edition of Wayland's *Elements of Moral Science, Journal of the History of Philosophy,* II (1964), 276–78.

24. Mahan, *Science of Moral Philosophy,* pp. 170–75.

25. *Ibid.*

26. Wayland, *The Elements of Moral Science,* 1877, pp. 118 ff.

27. *Ibid.,* pp. 121–22.

28. Mahan, *Science of Moral Philosophy,* p. 92.

29. *Ibid.*

30. *Ibid.,* pp. 89–90.

31. Fairchild disagreed with his teacher on most other points, both theoretical and practical.

32. Mahan, *Science of Moral Philosophy,* pp. 94–123.

33. Cf. Fletcher, *History of Oberlin College*, I, 230. Cf. Mahan, *Science of Moral Philosophy*, pp. 119–20.

34. Mahan, *Science of Moral Philosophy*, p. 98.

35. *Ibid.*, pp. 102–3. Cf. also pp. 104, 110–12.

36. *Ibid.*, p. 109.

37. *Ibid.*, p. 112.

38. *Ibid.*, pp. 114–16, 119–21.

39. Fletcher, *History of Oberlin College*, I, 472–88.

40. *Ibid.*, II, 701.

41. *Ibid.*

CHAPTER 5. JAMES H. FAIRCHILD

1. Cf. Robert S. Fletcher, *A History of Oberlin College* (2 vols.; Oberlin, Ohio, 1943); Herbert W. Schneider, *A History of American Philosophy* (2nd ed.; New York: Columbia University Press, 1963), pp. 195–220; and Joseph L. Blau, *Men and Movements in American Philosophy* (New York: Prentice-Hall, 1952), pp. 73–109.

2. Fletcher, *A History of Oberlin College*, II, 703.

3. Cf. Asa Mahan, *Science of Moral Philosophy* (Oberlin, Ohio: J. M. Fitch, 1884); and James H. Fairchild, *Moral Science* (revised ed.; New York: Butler, Sheldon and Co., 1892). Fairchild's book was originally published in 1869 under the title *Moral Philosophy*. The principal theme of *Moral Science* is the same as that of the earlier book. The emendations are mainly designed to take new theories into account. Some changes, like that of the title, were formal and had no essential significance.

4. Since Edwards' views on the nature of God and man and the nature of "true virtue" are not necessarily connected, Fairchild, like Finney, was not inconsistent in rejecting the former and using the latter for his own purposes. It is not necessary to excuse them by saying that they probably did not know who the author of the doctrine of disinterested benevolence was. (Cf. William G. McLoughlin's Introduction to Finney's *Lectures on Revivals of Religion* [John Harvard Library; Cambridge, Mass.: Harvard University Press, 1960], p. xlii). That Fairchild well knew he was indebted to Edwards there is no doubt. In one place he chided Jonathan Edwards, Jr., for missing the true point of his father's moral insight at the very time he thought he was defending it. Cf. Fairchild, *Moral Science*, pp. 109–10.

5. Fairchild, *Moral Science,* pp. 20–21, 25, 38, 40, 41, and 51.

6. *Ibid.,* pp. 108–9.

7. Chapter iv of *Utilitarianism* (New York: E. P. Dutton, 1910). Cf. Everett W. Hall, "The 'Proof' of Utility in Bentham and Mill," *Ethics,* Vol. LX (1949).

8. Cf. Fairchild, *Moral Science,* pp. 73–82, 128–29.

9. *Ibid.,* pp. 101–13. Note particularly pp. 104, 109–10.

10. *Ibid.,* p. 104.

11. *Ibid.,* pp. 106–7.

12. *Ibid.,* p. 107.

13. *Ibid.,* p. 108.

14. *Ibid.,* pp. 38–47, 261–64, 294–310.

15. *Ibid.,* pp. 40–41.

16. *Ibid.,* p. 261.

17. *Ibid.,* pp. 303, 294.

18. *Ibid.*

19. Cf. Mahan, *Science of Moral Philosophy,* Book I.

20. Fairchild, *Moral Science,* p. 219.

21. *Ibid.,* p. 67.

22. *Ibid.,* p. 33.

23. *Ibid.,* pp. 114–18, 124–29.

24. *Ibid.,* p. 116.

25. *Ibid.,* p. 128.

26. *Ibid.,* p. 127.

27. Cf. Fletcher, *History of Oberlin College,* II, 886–922.

28. Fairchild, *Moral Science,* pp. 134, 154, 157, 184, 206, 208, and 239.

29. *Ibid.,* p. 154.

30. *Ibid.,* pp. 239–40.

31. *Ibid.,* p. 188.

32. *Ibid.,* p. 206.

CHAPTER 6. OBERLIN REFORM

1. Robert S. Fletcher, *A History of Oberlin College* (2 vols.; Oberlin, Ohio, 1943), I, 249, 252–53.

2. *Ibid.*

3. *Ibid.,* pp. 233–35.

4. Quoted in *ibid.,* p. 233. Cf. Asa Mahan, *Science of Moral Philosophy* (Oberlin, Ohio: J. M. Fitch, 1848), pp. 64–65.

5. Fletcher, *A History of Oberlin College*, I, 267–69.

6. Quoted in *ibid.*, p. 270.

7. *Ibid.*

8. *Ibid.*, p. 266. Cf. Mahan, *Science of Moral Philosophy.*

9. Quoted by Fletcher, *History of Oberlin College*, I, 270.

10. *Ibid.*, pp. 167–78.

11. *Ibid.*, pp. 236–53.

12. *Ibid.*, p. 241.

13. Cf. William G. McLoughlin's Introduction to the John Harvard Library edition of Finney's *Lectures on Revivals of Religion* (Cambridge, Mass.: Harvard University Press, 1960).

14. Fletcher, *A History of Oberlin College*, I, 227.

15. *Ibid.*, p. 254.

16. *Ibid.*, pp. 257–64.

17. *Ibid.*, p. 264.

18. *Ibid.*, p. 265.

19. Cf. James H. Fairchild, *Moral Science* (rev. ed.; New York: Butler, Sheldon and Co., 1892), pp. 172–81, for the best statement of the Oberlin view on civil disobedience. It is ironic that the best statement of the principle should come from the Oberlinite who least practiced it.

20. This phrase, of course, was Wayland's, even though he himself came to the view quite late.

21. Fletcher, *A History of Oberlin College*, I, 386–400.

22. *Ibid.*, p. 390.

23. *Ibid.*, pp. 391–94.

24. Quoted in *ibid.*, p. 401.

25. Cf. *Oberliniana*, ed. A. L. Shumway and C. Brower (Cleveland, Ohio: Home Publishing Co., 1883), chaps. ii and iii. This book, edited by two Oberlin students in 1883, is quite rare and exceedingly interesting. It is an effort to help celebrate Oberlin's fiftieth anniversary. It is semihistorical but is important for what it exhibits rather than for what it says. It exhibits the almost total disappearance of Mahan's influence at Oberlin by 1883. The great heroes are Finney and Fairchild. It also exhibits the conformity of Oberlin in the new age of American jingoism and manifest destiny. Oberlin is now epiphenomenal. The students recall almost wistfully the excitement of Oberlin's first thirty years. The caliber of Oberlin students in 1883, if represented by the editors of this volume, was lower than in the early years.

26. Fletcher, *A History of Oberlin College*, I, 401.

27. *Ibid.,* p. 396.
28. *Ibid.,* p. 399.
29. Cf. *ibid.,* pp. 401–16, and *Oberliniana,* pp. 36–43.
30. Fletcher, *A History of Oberlin College,* I, 414–15.
31. *Ibid.,* p. 414.
32. Cf. Fairchild, *Moral Science,* pp. 184, 188, 219, 239–40.
33. Cf. Fletcher, *A History of Oberlin College,* II, 887.
34. *Ibid.,* p. 691.
35. *Ibid.,* pp. 899–902.
36. Cf. Fairchild, *Moral Science,* pp. 124–27.
37. Fletcher, *A History of Oberlin College,* II, 902.

CHAPTER 7. THE TRANSCENDENTALISTS

1. Cf. James Bradley Thayer, *A Western Journey with Mr. Emerson* (Boston: Little, Brown, and Co., 1884), pp. 123–41.
2. *Ibid.,* p. 127.
3. *Ibid.,* pp. 129–30.
4. *Ibid.,* p. 135.
5. Quoted by Edward Waldo Emerson in *Emerson in Concord* (Boston: Houghton Mifflin Co., 1888), p. 183.
6. *The Complete Works of Ralph Waldo Emerson* (Centenary ed.; 12 vols.; Boston: Houghton Mifflin Co., 1903–4), I, 60. Cf. pp. 47–60.
7. *Ibid.,* p. 50.
8. Cf. Frederic I. Carpenter, *Ralph Waldo Emerson* (New York: American Book Co., 1934), pp. xxxi ff.
9. Emerson, *Complete Works,* I, 26.
10. *Ibid.,* pp. 29–35.
11. *Ibid.,* p. 34.
12. *Ibid.,* p. 44.
13. Emerson, "Self-Reliance," *Complete Works,* II, 45.
14. *Ibid.,* "Culture," VI, 136–37.
15. *Ibid.,* "Divinity School Address," I, 141.
16. *The Writings of Henry David Thoreau* (Riverside ed.; 20 vols.; Boston: Houghton Mifflin Co., 1907), X, 144.
17. Emerson, "Self-Reliance," *Complete Works,* II, 50.
18. *Emerson's Journals,* IX, 498.
19. *Ibid.,* IX, 15.
20. *Ibid.,* VIII, 375.

21. *Ibid.,* VII, 498.

22. Cf. Emerson, "Society and Solitude," *Complete Works,* VII, 3–16. Quotation from p. 9.

23. *Ibid.,* p. 10.

24. *Ibid.,* p. 348 (E. W. Emerson's Note 1 to p. 10). This quotation is from a lecture on "Private Life," delivered by Emerson during his 1839–40 course on "The Present Age."

25. *Ibid.,* p. 15.

26. *Emerson's Journals,* IX, 425.

27. *Ibid.,* p. 153.

28. This theme permeates the whole of Emerson's "Divinity School Address" of 1838.

29. Cf. William R. Hutchison, *The Transcendentalist Ministers* (New Haven, Conn.: Yale University Press, 1959), pp. 64–82.

30. *Ibid.,* p. 4.

31. *Ibid.,* pp. 52–97.

32. *Ibid.,* p. 73.

33. Henry Steele Commager, *Theodore Parker* (Boston: Beacon Press, 1960), particularly chaps. iii, iv, and v.

34. Quoted by Hutchison, *The Transcendentalist Ministers,* p. 108.

35. *Ibid.,* pp. 113–15.

36. Blau, *Men and Movements in American Philosophy,* p. 130.

37. Commager, *Theodore Parker,* pp. 197–213.

38. *Ibid.,* pp. 214–66.

39. Particularly in his essay on "Civil Disobedience." Cf. pp. 10–32 of *Henry D. Thoreau: Selected Writings on Nature and Liberty,* ed. Oscar Cargill (New York: Liberal Arts Press, 1952).

40. *Emerson's Journals,* IX, 34.

41. The notebooks are part of the Thayer Collection at the Harvard Law School Library. Therein he identifies himself as author of several *North American Review* articles.

42. This fact emerges from the business correspondence between Emerson and Thayer contained in the Thayer Collection at the Harvard Law School Library.

43. James Bradley Thayer, "Mill's Dissertations and Discussions," *North American Review,* C (1865), 261–62.

44. Chap. iv of Mill, *Utilitarianism* (New York: E. P. Dutton and Co., 1910).

45. *Ibid.,* pp. 32–33.

46. J. S. Mill, *Letters of John Stuart Mill,* ed. Hugh S. R. Elliot

(2 vols.; London and New York: Longmans, Green and Co., 1910), II, 116.

47. Thayer, "Mill's Dissertations and Discussions," p. 263.

48. Mill, *Utilitarianism*, p. 36.

49. Thayer, "Mill's Dissertations and Discussions," p. 264.

50. Cf. Memoranda Book C.

51. Cf. G. E. Moore's discussion of the naturalistic fallacy in *Principia Ethica* (Cambridge, Eng., 1929).

52. Thayer, "Mill's Dissertations and Discussions," pp. 265–66.

53. *Ibid.*

54. Thayer, *A Western Journey with Mr. Emerson*, p. 133.

CHAPTER 8. GEORGE WILLIAM CURTIS

1. E. H. Madden, "George William Curtis: Practical Transcendentalist," *The Personalist*, XL (1959), 369–79; and Henry Steele Commager, *Theodore Parker* (Boston: Beacon Press, 1960), particularly chaps. viii–xii.

2. Edward Cary, *George William Curtis* (Boston: Houghton Mifflin Co., 1894), p. 17. In addition to Cary's biography of Curtis the following are also useful sources of information: John White Chadwick, *George William Curtis* (New York: Harper and Bros., 1893) and William Gordon Milne, *George William Curtis and the Genteel Tradition* (Bloomington, Ind.: Indiana University Press, 1956). There is also much unpublished material concerning the life and thought of Curtis at the Staten Island Institute of Arts and Sciences, the New York Historical Society, and the New York Public Library. The institute has become the most important center of Curtis manuscripts. It has excellent sources of information concerning his local activities and has acquired many of his letters which, until quite recently, were in private collections. The institute also acquired an interesting collection of letters from Curtis' correspondents including, among others, William Dean Howells, Frederick Henry Hedge, George Bradford, Henry Ward Beecher, Matthew Arnold, H. Powers, and Henry James, Sr.

In an unpublished letter to Curtis, now at the Staten Island Institute, Henry James, Sr., in a delightful but pungent way, takes Curtis to task for his "retouch" method of biography. "Cambridge, Mass., July 19, 1874. My dear Mr. Curtis: I ought before this to have acknowledged the reception of your eulogy [on Sumner], which I have read with pleasure and admiration. Whatever Sumner may have deemed the ill-luck of his office, even his inexorable shade might be satisfied, as it seems to me, with the profuse generosity men are showing to his memory. What a magic you exhibit in embalming that inflexible corpse for posterity, that you should be able to make it look so little and Debonnaire. . . ."

To his wife, "Dearest Nan," Curtis wrote in 1863: ". . . A grave old Scotch farmer from Allegheney [*sic*] county told me in the cars today, that if the government should make any more arbitrary arrests, there would be more blood shed in this state than there had been in Virginia. . . . He evidently thought we had no right to discuss slavery, because it was none of our business in the free states. Let us mind our own sins. How can we expect men to fight hard, or to support hard fighting, when they have only half a heart—and doubt whether they are not in the wrong?" (Lockport, January 14, 1863, Wednesday, Staten Island Institute of Arts and Sciences).

Curtis thought highly of Carl Schurz. Cf. letter to "My dear Burt," West New Brighton, Staten Island, N.Y., January 17, 1889, New York Historical Society Archives: "I agree with you about Schurz's speech. It's tone and temper are quite above those of any other of our public men, and its calmness and candor are very persuasive."

Curtis acknowledged his indebtedness to Emerson in numerous places in his unpublished letters. Cf. letter to Miss Peabody, West New Brighton, Staten Island, N.Y., November 1, 1882, New York Historical Society Archives: "With all the young men of my time who fell under his [Emerson's] influence I shall always cherish the most tender reverence for his memory, and the deepest gratitude for his influence in my life."

Curtis' skill as a letter writer was great. Cf. particularly his letter to his stepmother, Ashfield, July 20, 1865, previously in my possession and now at the Houghton Manuscript Library, Harvard University. This letter exhibits his playful manner and large sense of humor. If all of his published work had the grace and unaffectedness of this missive he would have been a great writer.

3. Cary, *George William Curtis*, p. 21.

4. William G. Milne, "George William Curtis and the Genteel Tradition: A Revaluation" (Harvard College Archives, 1951), p. 46.

5. Cary, *George William Curtis*, pp. 31–32.

6. Charles Robert Crowe, "George Ripley, Transcendentalist and

Utopian Socialist" (Ph.D. thesis, Brown University Library, 1955), pp. 134, 89, 102.

7. Cary, *George William Curtis*, pp. 25–26.

8. G. W. Curtis to John S. Dwight, March 3, 1844, in *Early Letters of George William Curtis to John S. Dwight,* ed. George W. Cooke (New York: Harper and Bros., 1898), p. 154. Quoted by Crowe, "George Ripley, Transcendentalist and Utopian Socialist," p. 306.

9. Chadwick, *George William Curtis,* p. 47; Cary, *George William Curtis,* pp. 109 ff.

10. Milne, "George William Curtis and the Genteel Tradition: A Revaluation," p. 35.

11. *Ibid.,* p. 42.

12. Cf. the critical sections of Milne's book.

13. For this and subsequent themes cf. particularly the following addresses in Vol. I of *Orations and Addresses,* ed. Charles Eliot Norton (3 vols.; New York: Harper and Bros., 1894): "The Duty of the American Scholar," "Patriotism," "The Present Aspect of the Slavery Question," "The American Doctrine of Liberty," "Political Infidelity," and "The Good Fight."

14. *Ibid.,* I, 42.

15. Note particularly "The Good Fight."

16. Curtis, *Orations and Addresses,* I, 15.

17. *Ibid.,* p. 99.

18. *Ibid.,* pp. 44–45.

19. *Ibid.,* pp. 125–48.

20. *Ibid.,* pp. 151–77.

21. *Ibid.,* pp. 3–35.

22. Cf. Charles Beard, *An Economic Interpretation of the Constitution of the United States* (New York: Macmillan Co., 1929), and *The Economic Basis of Politics and Related Writings,* ed. William Beard (New York: Alfred A. Knopf, 1957); Frederick Jackson Turner, *The Frontier in American History* (New York: Henry Holt and Co., 1920); and Vernon L. Parrington, *Main Currents in American Thought* (New York: Harcourt Brace and Co., 1930).

23. Cf. Louis Hartz, *The Liberal Tradition in America* (New York: Harcourt, Brace and World, 1955); Richard Hofstadter, *The American Political Tradition* (New York: Alfred A. Knopf and Random House, 1954); and Daniel Boorstin, *The Genius of Ameri-*

can Politics (Chicago: University of Chicago Press, 1953) and
America and the Image of Europe (New York: Meridian Books,
1960). Cf. also John Higham, ed., The Reconstruction of American
History (New York: Harper and Bros., 1962) and his "The Cult of
the 'American Consensus,'" Commentary, XXVII (1959), 93–100.

24. John Higham, "The Cult of the 'American Consensus,'"
p. 95.

CHAPTER 9. THE GOOD FIGHT

1. Charles Eliot Norton, ed., Orations and Addresses of George
William Curtis (3 vols.; New York: Harper and Bros., 1894), I, 2.

2. Cf. Norton's notes on each lecture. The lecture on Patriotism
was published again in the Tribune and in the Anti-Slavery Standard.

3. Cf. the accounts of this episode given by Edward Cary,
George William Curtis (Boston: Houghton Mifflin Co., 1894), pp.
126–29, and by Charles Norton in the Orations and Addresses of
George William Curtis, I, 62–63.

4. Curtis, Orations and Addresses, I, 90.

5. Curtis' letter to Mr. Forbes, North Shore, Staten Island, May
8, 1864, in the Curtis Collection at the Staten Island Institute of
Arts and Sciences: "Honesty, fidelity, sagacity, and patience will
carry us through. Do you know anybody who has more of them
than Abraham Lincoln?"

6. Cary, George William Curtis, p. 135.

7. Curtis, Orations and Addresses, I, 160.

8. Curtis' letter to Mr. Forbes. See note 5.

9. Curtis' letter to an unidentified person, North Shore, Staten
Island, March 30, 1864, New York Historical Society Archives.

10. Curtis, Orations and Addresses, I, 243–49.

11. Cf. the account given by the Rev. Edward Everett Hale in
ibid., pp. 240–42, and the one given by Cary, George William
Curtis, pp. 246–52.

12. Curtis, From the Easy Chair (New York: Harper and Bros.,
1891), p. 135.

13. Curtis, Orations and Addresses, III, 271–302.

14. Curtis, Other Essays from the Easy Chair (New York: Harper and Bros., 1893), pp. 203–7.

15. "The Works of Nathaniel Hawthorne," *North American Review*, Vol. XCIX (1864). Later reprinted in Curtis' *Literary and Social Essays* (New York: Harper and Bros., 1894).

16. Randall Stewart, *Nathaniel Hawthorne: A Biography* (New Haven, Conn.: Yale University Press, 1961).

17. *Ibid.*, p. 133.

18. *Ibid.*, p. 134.

19. *Ibid.*, p. 232.

20. *Ibid.*, p. 152.

21. *Ibid.*, p. 220.

22. Curtis, *Literary and Social Essays*, p. 73.

23. *Ibid.*, p. 75.

24. *Ibid.*, p. 76.

25. *Ibid.*, p. 77.

26. *Ibid.*, p. 82.

27. *Ibid.*, p. 83.

28. *Ibid.*, p. 84.

29. *Ibid.*

30. *Ibid.*, p. 86.

31. *Ibid.*, pp. 86–87.

32. Randall Stewart, *Nathaniel Hawthorne*, p. 49.

33. *Ibid.*, p. 72.

34. *Ibid.*, p. 246.

35. *Ibid.*

36. *Ibid.*, p. 247.

CHAPTER 10. CHAUNCEY WRIGHT

1. Max Fisch, "Evolution in American Philosophy," *Philosophical Review*, LVI (1947), 357–73; and Philip P. Wiener, *Evolution and the Founders of Pragmatism* (Cambridge, Mass.: Harvard University Press, 1949).

2. E. H. Madden, *Chauncey Wright and the Foundations of Pragmatism* (Seattle: University of Washington Press, 1963), pp. 3–30, and *Chauncey Wright* (New York: Washington Square Press, 1964), pp. 1–19.

3. A. Hunter Dupree, *Asa Gray* (Cambridge, Mass.: Harvard University Press, 1959), p. 290; and *Letters of Chauncey Wright*, ed. James Bradley Thayer (Cambridge, Mass.: John Wilson and Son, 1878), p. 42.

4. *Letters of Chauncey Wright,* p. 42.

5. Dupree, *Asa Gray,* pp. 290–91.

6. *Ibid.,* p. 291.

7. *Letters of Chauncey Wright,* p. 42, fn. 1.

8. Dupree, *Asa Gray,* p. 291.

9. *Ibid.,* pp. 291–92.

10. *Letters of Chauncey Wright,* p. 230.

11. *Ibid.*

12. *Ibid.,* pp. 233–34. For further evidence of Darwin's recognition of Wright, cf. p. 220, text and fn. 1.

13. Chauncey Wright, "The Faculties of Brutes," bMs Am 1088.5 (misc. 6), Box 11, Norton Collection, Houghton Library, Harvard University.

14. Dupree, *Asa Gray,* p. 293.

15. Wright, *Philosophical Discussions,* ed. Charles Eliot Norton (New York: Henry Holt and Co., 1877), pp. 183–86.

16. *Ibid.,* pp. 137–38.

17. *Ibid.,* pp. 130–32, 141.

18. *The Collected Papers of C. S. Peirce,* ed. C. Hartshorne, P. Weiss, and Arthur Burks (8 vols.; Cambridge, Mass.: Harvard University Press, 1931–58), Vol. VI, pars. 35–65.

19. Paul Anderson in Anderson and Max H. Fisch, *Philosophy in America* (New York: D. Appleton-Century Co., 1939), p. 419.

20. Cf. "The Doctrine of Necessity Examined" in *The Collected Papers of C. S. Peirce,* Vol. VI, Book I, chap. ii.

21. Wright, *Philosophical Discussions,* pp. 381–82.

22. *Ibid.,* pp. 200–1.

23. *Ibid.,* pp. 1–34.

24. "The Philosophy of Herbert Spencer," reprinted in *ibid.,* pp. 43–96.

25. *Ibid.,* p. 56.

26. *Ibid.,* p. 66.

27. *Ibid.,* p. 74. Cf. pp. 69–75.

28. *Ibid.,* p. 78.

29. *Ibid.,* p. 76.

30. *Collected Papers of C. S. Peirce,* Vol. V, par. 9.

31. Wright, *Philosophical Discussions,* p. 47.

32. "A Physical Theory of the Universe," reprinted in *ibid.,* pp. 1–34.

33. *Ibid.,* p. 9, text and fn.

34. *Ibid.,* pp. 17–34.

35. *Ibid.*, pp. 43–96.

36. *Ibid.*, p. 87.

37. *Letters of Chauncey Wright*, ed. James Bradley Thayer (Cambridge, Mass.: John Wilson and Son, 1878).

38. Norton Collection, Houghton Library, Harvard University, bMs Am 1088, 1088.1.

39. Thayer, *Letters of Chauncey Wright*, p. 194.

40. *Ibid.*, p. 196.

41. Cf. Lucius Garvin's discussion of this point in *A Modern Introduction to Ethics* (Boston: Houghton Mifflin Co., 1953), pp. 293–95.

42. *Letters of Chauncey Wright*, p. 195.

43. Wright treasured E. W. Gurney's epigram: "It is easy to die for an idea when we have but one." *Letters of Chauncey Wright*, p. 189.

44. Cf. John Hospers, *Human Conduct* (New York: Harcourt, Brace, and World, 1961), p. 314.

45. *Letters of Chauncey Wright*, pp. 282, 291. Cf. p. 194.

46. *Ibid.*

CHAPTER 11. PRACTICAL PROBLEMS

1. Charles Robert Crowe, "George Ripley, Transcendentalist and Utopian Socialist" (Ph.D. thesis, Brown University Library, 1955).

2. *Letters of Chauncey Wright*, ed. James Bradley Thayer (Cambridge, Mass.: John Wilson and Son, 1878), pp. 351–53.

3. *Ibid.*, p. 352.

4. *Ibid.*, pp. 351–52.

5. *Ibid.*, p. 173.

6. *Ibid.*, pp. 173 ff.

7. *Ibid.*, pp. 159–64.

8. *Ibid.*, pp. 160, 163.

9. *Ibid.*, p. 161.

10. *Ibid.*

11. *Ibid.*, p. 352.

12. Cf. Wright's "Notes on Sir Henry Maine," *Nation*, XXI (1875), 9. Cf. *Letters*, p. 283.

13. Wright, *Letters*, p. 291.

14. *Ibid.*, p. 282.

15. *Ibid.*, p. 197.

16. *Ibid.*, p. 320.

17. E. H. Madden, *Chauncey Wright and the Foundations of Pragmatism* (Seattle: University of Washington Press, 1963), pp. 3–30.

18. Cf. Susan Lesley, *Recollections of My Mother* (Boston: Houghton Mifflin Co., 1875), pp. 473 ff. Also Wright, *Letters*, pp. 34–36.

19. Lesley, *Recollections of My Mother*, pp. 470, 472–73.

20. Madden, *Chauncey Wright and the Foundations of Pragmatism*, pp. 11–12. Wright, *Letters*, pp. 49–50.

21. Madden, *Chauncey Wright and the Foundations of Pragmatism*, pp. 12–14, 20–21.

22. This point comes to light in an unpublished letter from Thayer to Charles Eliot Norton. The letter, No. 7325 in the Norton papers at Houghton Library, is dated September 16, 1877. Thayer is writing to Norton about his editorial labors on Wright's *Letters:* "There were several difficult points—especially how to deal with the one sad fact of Chauncey's life. This gave me a great deal of anxiety, but I am content with it much as it stands. . . . I have received information, which troubled me, within a week or two as to the beginning of dangerous habits as early as 1862 and I had to rewrite some things in the light of it. Nichols tells me that he and Wyman both, *at the time*, attributed Chauncey's difficulty in 1863 to the effect of too much alcohol, and this is unfortunately fortified by some other facts. But there is nothing to indicate excess then in the sense of what came in 1868 or so." Cf. Wright, *Letters*, pp. 50–51.

23. Wright, *Letters*, pp. 137–39.

CHAPTER 12. CHARLES ELIOT NORTON

1. *Letters of Charles Eliot Norton*, ed. Sara Norton and M. A. DeWolfe Howe (2 vols.; Boston: Houghton Mifflin Co., 1913). Cf. Bibliography, II, 461–65.

2. *Ibid.*, II, 3–194.

3. *Ibid.*, pp. 461–65.

4. *Letters of Charles Eliot Norton*, II, 8.

5. "The pictures of Carlyle and Ruskin are fascinating," J. F. Rhodes wrote to Sara Norton; and none is more so than Norton's picture of Carlyle reminiscing, at the time of Mill's death, about his early friendship with Mill and what had gone awry (*Letters of*

Charles Eliot Norton, I, 495 ff.). Norton's portrayal of Mill and his opinions of Mrs. Taylor and her daughter are valuable sources for Mill biographers (*ibid.*, I, 330, 400; II, 18–19).

6. *Ibid.*, I, 398.

7. *Ibid.*, I, 371. In an unpublished letter to Chauncey Wright (Siena, June 12, 1870), Norton makes a penetrating analysis of the social, economic, and political difficulties in Europe which, he thought, would lead to widespread revolution. Cf. Harvard College Library, Norton Collection, bMs Am 1088.2.

8. *Letters of Charles Eliot Norton*, I, 432.

9. *Ibid.*, I, 492, 331.

10. Harvard College Library, Norton Collection, bMs Am 1088.2.

11. *Letters of Charles Eliot Norton*, II, 18–19.

12. *Ibid.*, I, 370.

13. Harvard College Library, Norton Collection, bMs Am 1088.2.

14. Wright, *Letters*, pp. 193–98. Most of Wright's letters to Norton contain utilitarian analyses.

15. *Ibid.*, p. 195.

16. *Ibid.*

17. *Letters of Charles Eliot Norton*, I, 400.

18. *Ibid.*, II, 4–5. While Norton came to believe that in principle there is no conflict between utility and cultural value, he knew perfectly well that in fact the utilitarian is more interested in bringing about a minimum general level of physical well-being than in bringing culture to the masses. The workers in Europe and America needed decent food and solid houses more than an appreciation of Donne and Dante. Bentham and Mill successfully fought for civil liberties, repeal of the oppressive Corn Laws, revision of the British criminal code, and economic justice, not for night school classes in the World's Classics! (To be sure, they worked hard for better basic educational advantages for the poor.) Norton was wholly sympathetic with the great battle that Bentham and the Mills—the Philosophical Radicals—waged, but he also thought that in America particularly, where the working man was not so hard pressed, there was a great need to fight for higher scholarly and cultural values. And Norton was truly the great champion of the American battle. He was indeed "an apostle of culture in a democracy," and he was far more successful in his battle than one might think. He was the pioneer of the Fine Arts Department in American

colleges, and the influence of the Harvard experiment spread rapidly and widely. Moreover, his influence as an editor and a teacher was great—both quantitatively and qualitatively. Dante scholarship in America grew almost wholly from his efforts.

Yet Norton had an Achilles' heel, after all, and he was not so mighty a warrior in the great battle as he might have been. The apostle of culture in America kept urging upon his countrymen the culture of Greece, Florence, Siena, and Venice, for which many of his listeners would never have a taste, but he never recognized the real indigenous growth of American culture. After an initial enthusiasm for Whitman he neglected this poet, vastly preferring Longfellow instead. He thought Lowell and Curtis great literary lights, but he ignored Poe, Melville, and Twain. He was a close friend of William Dean Howells but never appreciated the importance of his literary realism. And Norton knew absolutely nothing about American art. The Ash-Can School of painting which flourished soon after Norton's death would have confirmed him in his view that art after 1600 was hopeless!

19. William Gordon Milne, "George William Curtis and the Genteel Tradition: A Revaluation" (Harvard College Archives, 1951), pp. 395, 473, 486, 491.

20. E.g., *Letters of Charles Eliot Norton*, II, 139–40.

21. *Ibid.*, pp. 250, 255, 355–56, 412.

22. *Ibid.*, p. 113.

23. *Ibid.*, p. 364.

24. *Ibid.*, I, 180–81.

25. For a good discussion of the controversy between Andrews Norton and the transcendentalists cf. Charles R. Crowe, "George Ripley, Transcendentalist and Utopian Socialist" (Ph.D. thesis, Brown University Library, 1955).

26. *Letters of Charles Eliot Norton*, II, 216.

27. *Ibid.*, p. 250.

28. Letter to Sara Norton, December 16, 1913, Harvard College Library, Norton Collection, bMs Am 1193 #269. There are a number of interesting letters to Miss Norton (the same manuscript number) which express various reactions to, and appraisals of, Norton's *Letters*.

29. Cambridge, December 20, 1886, Harvard College Library, Holmes Collection, bMs Am 1241.1.

30. *Letters of Charles Eliot Norton*, II, 168.

31. *Ibid.*, p. 336.

32. *Ibid.*, pp. 335–36.

33. Cf. James Ford Rhodes to Sara Norton, November 11, 1913, Harvard College Library, Norton Collection, bMs Am 1193 #272.

34. Cf. Milne, "George William Curtis and the Genteel Tradition: A Revaluation," p. 473.

35. *Letters of Charles Eliot Norton*, I, 135.

CHAPTER 13. THE CONSERVATIVE TRADITION

1. Clinton Rossiter, *Conservatism in America* (2nd ed., rev.; New York: Alfred A. Knopf and Random House, 1962), p. 159.

2. E. H. Madden, "Charles Eliot Norton on Art and Morals," *Journal of the History of Ideas*, XVIII (1957), 430–38.

3. The best biographical source is *Letters of Charles Eliot Norton*, ed. Sara Norton and M. A. DeWolfe Howe (2 vols.; Boston: Houghton Mifflin Co., 1913). Cf. also Kermit Vanderbilt's *Charles Eliot Norton* (Cambridge, Mass.: Harvard University Press, 1959).

4. William R. Hutchison, *The Transcendentalist Ministers* (New Haven, Conn.: Yale University Press, 1959), p. 4.

5. *Ibid.*, chap. iii.

6. *Letters of Charles Eliot Norton*, I, 34–58.

7. Vanderbilt, *Charles Eliot Norton*, pp. 44 ff.

8. Charles Eliot Norton, *Notes of Travel and Study in Italy* (Boston: Houghton Mifflin Co., 1859), p. 211.

9. *Ibid.*, pp. 163–64.

10. *Letters of Charles Eliot Norton*, Vol. I, chaps. v and vi.

11. Quoted in a letter to Norton, August 10, 1870, Houghton Manuscript Library, Harvard University, bMs 1088, 8291.

12. Madden, "Charles Eliot Norton on Art and Morals," pp. 430–38. Cf. *Letters of Charles Eliot Norton*, I, 180–81.

13. Of particular interest are the following letters to Wright: June 12, 1870, and September 13, 1870 (Houghton Library, Norton Collection, bMs Am 1088.2). Unfortunately the editors of the Norton *Letters* sometimes published only descriptive parts of letters and deleted the philosophical sections. Cf. Madden, "Charles Eliot Norton on Art and Morals," pp. 432–34.

14. Rossiter, *Conservatism in America*, pp. 20–66. Note particularly pp. 63–66.

15. *Ibid.*, p. 63.

16. Cf. Norton's notes in his edition of G. W. Curtis' *Orations*

and Addresses (3 vols.; New York: Harper and Bros., 1894). This item is missing from the Norton bibliography in *Letters of Charles Eliot Norton.*

17. See note 13.

18. *Ibid.* (September 13 letter).

19. Vanderbilt, *Charles Eliot Norton,* pp. 119–234.

20. *Letters of Charles Eliot Norton,* II, 215–16.

21. *Ibid.,* pp. 363–64.

22. *Ibid.,* p. 168.

23. *Ibid.,* p. 336.

24. This point carried over from his earlier conservatism—but now it is in a different context.

25. Cf. E. H. Madden, *Chauncey Wright* (New York: Washington Square Press, 1964), pp. 47–48.

26. E. H. Madden, "The Many Faces of Evil," *Philosophy and Phenomenological Research,* XXIV (1964), 481–92.

SELECTED BIBLIOGRAPHY

Anderson, Paul R., and Max H. Fisch. *Philosophy in America.* New York: D. Appleton-Century Co., 1939.

Beard, Charles. *The Economic Basis of Politics and Related Writings,* ed. William Beard. New York: Alfred A. Knopf, 1957; paperback ed., Vintage Book 42.

————. *An Economic Interpretation of the Constitution of the United States.* New York: Macmillan Co., 1929. First published in 1913.

Blau, Joseph L. "Chauncey Wright: Radical Empiricist," *New England Quarterly,* XIX (1946), 495–517.

————. *Men and Movements in American Philosophy.* New York: Prentice-Hall, 1952.

Boorstin, Daniel J. *America and the Image of Europe.* New York: Meridian Books, 1960.

————. *The Genius of American Politics.* Chicago: University of Chicago Press, 1953.

Bowen, Francis. *On the Application of Metaphysical and Ethical Science to the Evidences of Religion.* Boston: Little, Brown and Co., 1849.

Bowne, Borden Parker. "Chauncey Wright as a Philosopher," *New Englander,* XXXVII (1878), 585–603.

Brown, Rollo Walter. *Lonely Americans.* New York, 1929. Contains biographical sketch of Charles Eliot Norton.

Cabot, James Elliot. *A Memoir of Ralph Waldo Emerson.* Boston: Houghton Mifflin Co., 1887.

Carpenter, Frederic I. *Ralph Waldo Emerson.* New York: American Book Co., 1934.

Cary, Edward. *George William Curtis.* Boston: Houghton Mifflin Co., 1894.

Chadwick, John White. *George William Curtis.* New York: Harper and Bros., 1893.

Chambliss, J. J. "Natural Selection and Utilitarian Ethics in Chauncey Wright," *American Quarterly,* XII (1960), 144–59.

————. "Chauncey Wright's Enduring Naturalism," a review of E. H. Madden's *Chauncey Wright and the Foundations of Pragmatism, American Quarterly,* XVI (1964), 628–35.

Clark, J. O. A. Notes on Wayland's Lectures on Moral Philosophy (1851), in the Special Collection Room of the Brown University Library.

Commager, Henry Steele. *Theodore Parker: Yankee Crusader.* Boston: Beacon Press, 1960; paperback ed., LR-4.

Crane, Theodore R. "Francis Wayland and Brown University, 1796–1841." Ph.D. thesis, Harvard University Library, 1959.

————. "Francis Wayland and the Residential College," *Rhode Island History,* XIX (1960), 65–78, 118–28.

Crowe, Charles Robert. "George Ripley, Transcendentalist and Utopian Socialist." Ph.D. thesis, Brown University Library, 1955.

Curtis, George William (ed.). *The Correspondence of John Lothrop Motley.* 2 vols. New York: Harper and Bros., 1889.

————. *Early Letters of George William Curtis to John S. Dwight,* ed. George W. Cooke. New York: Harper and Bros., 1898.

————. *From the Easy Chair.* New York: Harper and Bros., 1891.

————. *From the Easy Chair, Third Series.* New York: Harper and Bros., 1894.

————. *The Howadji in Syria.* New York: Harper and Bros., 1856.

————. Letters and manuscripts at the Staten Island Institute of Arts and Sciences, the New York Historical Society, and the New York City Public Library.

————. *Literary and Social Essays.* New York: Harper and Bros., 1894.

————. *Nile Notes of a Howadji.* New York: Harper and Bros., 1851.

————. *Orations and Addresses,* ed. Charles Eliot Norton. 3 vols. New York: Harper and Bros., 1894.

————. *Other Essays from the Easy Chair.* New York: Harper and Bros., 1893.

————. *Potiphar Papers.* New York: G. P. Putnam and Co., 1853.

————. *Prue and I.* New York: Dix, Edwards and Co., 1856.

————. *Lotus-Eating, a Summer Book.* New York: Harper and Bros., 1852.

————. *Trumps.* New York: Harper and Bros., 1861.

————. *Works.* 6 vols. New York: Harper and Bros., 1863.

Dupree, A. Hunter. *Asa Gray.* Cambridge, Mass.: Harvard University Press, 1959.

Emerson, Edward Waldo. *Emerson in Concord.* Boston: Houghton Mifflin Co., 1888.

Emerson, Ralph Waldo. *The Complete Works of Ralph Waldo*

Emerson. Centenary ed. 12 vols. Boston: Houghton Mifflin Co., 1903–4.

Fairchild, James H. "Moral Law as Revelation," in *Christianity and Scepticism*. Boston: Congregational Publishing Society, 1872.

———. *Moral Science.* Revised ed. New York: Butler, Sheldon and Co., 1892.

———. *Oberlin: The Colony and the College, 1833–1883.* Oberlin, Ohio: E. J. Goodrich, 1883.

———. *Women's Right to the Ballot.* Oberlin, Ohio: George H. Fairchild, 1870.

Finney, Charles Grandison. *Lectures on Revivals of Religion,* ed. William G. McLoughlin. (John Harvard Library.) Cambridge, Mass.: Harvard University Press, 1960.

———. *Memoirs.* New York: A. S. Barnes and Co., 1876.

Fisch, Max H. "Evolution in American Philosophy," *Philosophical Review*, LVI (1947), 357–73.

Fiske, John. *Outlines of Cosmic Philosophy Based on the Doctrine of Evolutionism.* Boston: Houghton Mifflin Co., 1874.

Fletcher, Robert S. *A History of Oberlin College.* 2 vols. Oberlin, Ohio, 1943.

Frothingham, O. B. *Transcendentalism in New England.* New York: G. P. Putnam's Sons, 1876.

Goddard, H. C. *Studies in New England Transcendentalism.* New York: Columbia University Press, 1908.

Grave, S. A. *The Scottish Philosophy of Common Sense.* Oxford: Oxford University Press, 1960.

Hall, Everett W. "The 'Proof' of Utility in Bentham and Mill," *Ethics,* LX (1949), 1–18.

Hartz, Louis. *The Liberal Tradition in America.* New York: Harcourt, Brace and World, 1955; paperback ed., Harvest Book 53.

Hicks, John D. *The Federal Union.* Boston: Houghton Mifflin Co., 1948.

Higham, John. "The Cult of the 'American Consensus,' " *Commentary,* XXVII (1959), 93–100.

——— (ed.). *The Reconstruction of American History.* New York: Harper and Bros., 1962; paperback ed., Harper Torchbook.

Hofstadter, Richard. *The Age of Reform.* New York: Alfred A. Knopf and Random House, Inc., 1960; paperback ed., Vintage Book 95.

———. *The American Political Tradition.* New York: Alfred A. Knopf and Random House, 1954; paperback ed., Vintage Book 9.

————. *Social Darwinism in American Thought.* Revised ed. Boston: Beacon Press, 1955; paperback ed., BP-16.

Hutchison, William R. *The Transcendentalist Ministers.* New Haven, Conn.: Yale University Press, 1959.

James, William. *Collected Essays and Reviews.* New York: Longmans, Green and Co., 1920.

————. *Essays in Radical Empiricism.* New York: Longmans, Green and Co., 1912.

————. *The Will to Believe and Other Essays on Popular Philosophy.* New York: Dover Publications, 1956.

Kennedy, Gail. "The Pragmatic Naturalism of Chauncey Wright," in *Studies in the History of Ideas,* Vol. III, ed. Department of Philosophy, Columbia University. New York: Columbia University Press, 1935.

Lesley, Susan. *Recollections of My Mother.* Boston: Houghton Mifflin Co., 1875.

Madden, E. H. "The Cambridge Septem," *Harvard Alumni Bulletin,* LVII (1955), 310–15.

————. "Charles Eliot Norton on Art and Morals," *Journal of the History of Ideas,* XVIII (1957), 430–38.

————. *Chauncey Wright and the Foundations of Pragmatism.* Seattle: University of Washington Press, 1963.

————. *Chauncey Wright.* New York: Washington Square Press, 1964.

————. "Francis Wayland and the Limits of Moral Responsibility," *Proceedings of the American Philosophical Society,* CVI (1962), 348–59.

————. "G. W. Curtis: Practical Transcendentalist," *The Personalist,* XL (1959), 369–79.

————, and Marian C. Madden. "Chauncey Wright and the Logic of Psychology," *Philosophy of Science,* XIX (1952), 325–32.

Mahan, Asa. *Abstract of a Course of Lectures on Mental and Moral Philosophy.* Oberlin, Ohio: James Steele, 1840.

————. *Autobiography.* London: T. Woolmer, 1882.

————. *Doctrine of the Will.* 3rd ed. Oberlin, Ohio: J. M. Fitch, 1847.

————. *Modern Mysteries Explained and Exposed.* Boston: John P. Jewett and Co., 1855.

————. *Science of Moral Philosophy.* Oberlin, Ohio: J. M. Fitch, 1848, 1884.

————. *Spiritualism*. Cleveland, Ohio: Gray, Beardsley, Spear and Co., 1855.

McCosh, James. *The Intuitions of the Mind Inductively Investigated*. Revised ed. New York, 1882.

————. *Realistic Philosophy*. 2 vols. New York: Charles Scribner's Sons, 1887.

Mill, John Stuart. *Essential Works*, ed. Max Lerner. New York: Bantam Books, 1961.

————. *Utilitarianism*. (Everyman's Library.) New York: E. P. Dutton and Co., 1910.

Miller, Perry (ed.). *The Transcendentalists*. Cambridge, Mass.: Harvard University Press, 1950.

Milne, William Gordon. *George William Curtis and the Genteel Tradition*. Bloomington: Indiana University Press, 1956.

————. "George William Curtis and the Genteel Tradition: A Revaluation." Harvard College Archives, 1951.

Murray, James O. *Francis Wayland*. Boston: Houghton Mifflin Co., 1891.

Norton, Charles Eliot. "Abraham Lincoln," *North American Review*, C (1865), 1–21.

————. *Considerations on Some Recent Social Theories*. Boston: Little, Brown, and Co., 1853. Published anonymously.

———— (ed.). *Correspondence between Goethe and Carlyle*. London: Macmillan Co., 1887.

———— (ed.). *The Correspondence of Thomas Carlyle and Ralph Waldo Emerson, 1834–1872*. 2 vols. Boston: James R. Osgood and Co., 1883.

———— (trans.). *The Divine Comedy of Dante Alighieri*. 3 vols. Boston: Houghton Mifflin Co., 1891–92; revised ed., 1902.

————. *Historical Studies of Church Building in the Middle Ages*. New York: Harper and Bros., 1880.

————. *Letters of Charles Eliot Norton*, ed. Sara Norton and M. A. DeWolfe Howe. 2 vols. Boston: Houghton Mifflin Co., 1913.

———— (ed.). *Letters of John Ruskin to Charles Eliot Norton*. 2 vols. Boston: Houghton Mifflin Co., 1904.

————. Letters and Manuscripts, by Norton and to Norton. Norton Collection, Houghton Library, Harvard University.

————. *The Life and Character of George William Curtis*. New York: privately printed, 1902.

———— (trans.). *The New Life of Dante Alighieri.* Boston: Houghton Mifflin Co., 1892; privately printed in 1859.

————. *Notes of Travel and Study in Italy.* Boston: Houghton Mifflin Co., 1859.

———— (ed.). *Orations and Addresses of George William Curtis.* 3 vols. New York: Harper and Bros., 1894.

———— (ed.). *The Philosophical Discussions of Chauncey Wright.* New York: Henry Holt and Co., 1878.

Oberliniana, ed. A. L. Shumway and C. Brower. Cleveland, Ohio: Home Publishing Co., 1883.

Paine, Thomas. *The Age of Reason,* ed. Alburey Castell. New York: Liberal Arts Press, 1948.

Paley, William. *Works.* Philadelphia: J. J. Woodward, 1831.

Parker, Theodore. *The American Scholar.* Boston: American Unitarian Association, 1907.

————. *The Critical and Miscellaneous Writings of Theodore Parker.* 2nd ed. Boston: Little, Brown and Co., 1856.

————. *A Discourse of Matters Pertaining to Religion.* Boston: C. C. Little and J. Brown, 1842.

Parrington, Vernon L. *Main Currents in American Thought.* New York: Harcourt Brace and Co., 1930.

Peirce, C. S. *Collected Papers,* ed. Charles Hartshorne, Paul Weiss, and Arthur Burks. 8 vols. Cambridge, Mass.: Harvard University Press, 1931–58.

Perry, Ralph Barton. *The Thought and Character of William James.* 2 vols. Boston: Little, Brown and Co., 1935.

Popkin, Richard. "A Note on the 'Proof' of Utility in Bentham and Mill," *Ethics,* LX (1949), 66–68.

Porter, Noah. *The Elements of Moral Science: Theoretical and Practical.* New York: Charles Scribner's Sons, 1885.

Ripley, George. "Review of James Martineau's *Rationale of Religious Inquiry,*" *The Examiner,* XXI (1836), 225–55. Cf. William R. Hutchison, *The Transcendentalist Ministers,* chap. iii.

Rossiter, Clinton. *Conservatism in America.* 2nd ed., revised. New York: Alfred A. Knopf and Random House, 1962; paperback ed., Vintage Book 212.

Schneider, Herbert W. *A History of American Philosophy.* 2nd ed. New York: Columbia University Press, 1963.

————. "Review of Joseph L. Blau's edition of Wayland's *Elements of Moral Science,*" *Journal of the History of Philosophy,* II (1964), 276–78.

Smith, Wilson. *Professors and Public Ethics.* Ithaca, N.Y.: Cornell University Press, 1956. Cf. chap. vii on Francis Wayland.

Spencer, Herbert. *Works.* New York: D. Appleton and Co., 1910.

Stewart, Randall. *Nathaniel Hawthorne: A Biography.* New Haven, Conn.: Yale University Press, 1948; paperback ed., 1961.

Thayer, James Bradley. "Mill's Dissertations and Discussions," *North American Review,* C (1865), 261–62.

————. *A Western Journey with Mr. Emerson.* Boston: Little, Brown, and Co., 1884.

Thayer-Emerson Correspondence in the Harvard University Law School Library.

Thoreau, Henry David. *Selected Writings on Nature and Liberty,* ed. Oscar Cargill. New York: Liberal Arts Press, 1952.

————. *The Writings of Henry David Thoreau.* 20 vols. Riverside ed. Boston: Houghton Mifflin Co., 1907.

Turner, Frederick Jackson. *The Frontier in American History.* New York: Henry Holt and Co., 1920.

————. *Rise of the New West, 1819–1829.* New York: Harper and Bros., 1906.

————. *The Significance of Sections in American History.* New York: Henry Holt and Co., 1932.

Vanderbilt, Kermit. *Charles Eliot Norton.* Cambridge, Mass.: Harvard University Press, 1959.

Wayland, Francis. *The Elements of Intellectual Philosophy.* Boston: Phillips, Sampson and Co., 1857.

————. *Elements of Moral Science.* Boston, 1853.

————. *Elements of Moral Science.* Revised and improved ed. Boston: Gould and Lincoln, 1870; New York: Sheldon and Co., 1877.

————. *The Elements of Moral Science,* ed. Joseph L. Blau. (John Harvard Library.) Cambridge, Mass.: Harvard University Press, 1964.

————. *The Elements of Political Economy.* 2nd ed. New York, 1838.

————. *The Elements of Political Economy,* recast by Aaron L. Chapin. New York: Sheldon and Co., 1886.

————. *The Limitations of Human Responsibility.* 2nd ed. New York: D. Appleton and Co., 1838. The first edition was also published in Boston, by Gould, Kendall, and Lincoln, 1838. The second edition is practically identical with the first; the only difference is several additional footnotes in the second edition.

————. Manuscripts and Letters, in the Special Collection Room of the Brown University Library.

————. *Thoughts on the Present Collegiate System in the United States.* Boston: Gould, Kendall, and Lincoln, 1842.

————. *University Sermons.* 3rd ed. Boston: Gould, Kendall, and Lincoln, 1850.

————, and Richard Fuller. *Domestic Slavery Considered as a Scriptural Institution.* New York: Sheldon, Lamport, and Blakeman, 1856. First published New York: Lewis Colby, 1845.

Wayland, Francis, Jr., and H. L. Wayland. *A Memoir of the Life and Labors of Francis Wayland.* 2 vols. New York: Sheldon and Co., 1867.

White, Jacob. Notes on Wayland's Lectures on Moral Philosophy (1830–31), in the Special Collection Room of the Brown University Library.

Wiener, Philip P. *Evolution and the Founders of Pragmatism.* Cambridge, Mass.: Harvard University Press, 1949.

Wright, Chauncey. "The Faculties of Brutes." Harvard College Library, Norton Collection, bMs Am 1088.5 (misc. 6), Box 11.

————. *Letters of Chauncey Wright,* ed. James Bradley Thayer. Cambridge, Mass.: John Wilson and Son, 1878.

————. Letters to Charles Eliot Norton, Grace Norton, and Jane Norton. Harvard College Library, Norton Collection, bMs Am 1088, 1088.1.

————. *Philosophical Discussions,* ed. Charles Eliot Norton. New York: Henry Holt and Co., 1877.

————. *Philosophical Writings,* ed. E. H. Madden. New York: Liberal Arts Press, 1958.

————. "Whether the Government of This Country Ought to Interfere in the Politics of Europe . . . ," *Journal of the History of Ideas,* VI (1945), 89–90.

Wright, G. Frederick. *Charles Grandison Finney.* Boston: Houghton Mifflin Co., 1891.

INDEX

Abolitionism, 12–14, 31–37, 70, 72–82, 117–21
Academic orthodoxy: background of, 3–6, 16–17; and Francis Wayland, 16–17; and Asa Mahan, 47; and James H. Fairchild, 57
Adams, Samuel, 110, 169
Agassiz, Louis, 130

Bartol, Cyrus, 8
Beard, Charles, 113
Bentham, Jeremy, 48, 69, 101, 130, 141–42, 149–50
Birney, James G., 78
Boorstin, Daniel, 114, 116
Bowen, Francis, 5
Bradford, George, 104
Braun, Alexander, 131
Brook Farm, 104–7, 146
Brooks, Charles, 8
Brown, John, his raid on Harper's Ferry: Francis Wayland on, 41; Oberlin community response to, 81–82; James H. Fairchild on, 82
Brownson, Orestes, 8
Burke, Edmund, 166–67, 172, 174–75
Burns, Anthony: marched back to slavery, 40, 96

Cabet, Etienne, 169
Carlyle, Thomas, 12, 155, 158, 161
Chambers, Robert, 132
Channing, W. H., 8
Christian Perfection doctrine: Mahan and other Oberlinites on, 46–47
Civil disobedience: Francis Wayland on, 13, 36–43; James H. Fairchild on, 68; at Oberlin, 70–73, 79–82; Emerson on, 95; Theodore Parker, 95–96; Thoreau on, 96–98; George W. Curtis on, 117–23

Clarke, James Freeman, 8
Conflict interpretation of American history: and George W. Curtis, 113–14
Consensus interpretation of American history: and George W. Curtis, 114–16
Copeland, John A., 81
Cousin, Victor, 45
Craft, Ellen, 14, 96
Cranch, Christopher, 8
Curtis, Anna Shaw (Mrs. George William), 107
Curtis, George William: and transcendentalism, 8–10, 109–13; and abolitionism, 34–36, 117–21; and Emerson, 103–5; and Thoreau, 105; and Hawthorne, 105, 123–27; at Monday Evening Club, 105; at Brook Farm, 106; on reform, 106–8; and Theodore Parker, 107; his literary efforts, 108–9; on patriotism, 111; on political infidelity, 111–12; and conflict-consensus views of American history, 113–16; and Republican party, 119–21; on Wendell Phillips, 122–23; biographical information about, 190–91

Dana, Charles, 104
Darwinism: types of, 10; and Chauncey Wright, 10–11, 130–40; and Herbert Spencer, 137–40; and Charles Eliot Norton, 163–64, 175
Day, Jeremiah, 5
Deism: attacked by Francis Wayland, 27–29
Dewey, John, 17
Dod, Albert Baldwin, 4
Dupree, A. H., 131
Dwight, John, 8, 104

211